CRUCIBLE
JAN 2004
KOLKATA

Lured by Hope
A Biography of
Michael Madhusudan Dutt

Lured by Hope
A Biography of
Michael Madhusudan Dutt

by
GHULAM MURSHID

Translated from Bengali
by
GOPA MAJUMDAR

OXFORD
UNIVERSITY PRESS

YMCA Library Building, Jai Singh Road, New Delhi 110 001

Oxford University Press is a department of the University of Oxford. It furthers the
University's objective of excellence in research, scholarship, and education
by publishing worldwide in

Oxford   New York
Auckland   Bangkok   Buenos Aires   Cape Town   Chennai
Dar es Salaam   Delhi   Hong Kong   Istanbul   Karachi   Kolkata
Kuala Lumpur   Madrid   Melbourne   Mexico City   Mumbai   Nairobi
São Paulo   Shanghai   Taipei   Tokyo   Toronto

Oxford is a registered trademark of Oxford University Press
in the UK and in certain other countries

Published in India
By Oxford University Press, New Delhi

© Oxford University Press 2003

The moral rights of the author have been asserted
Database right Oxford University Press (maker)

First published 2003

All rights reserved. No part of this publication may be reproduced,
stored in a retrieval system, or transmitted, in any form or by any means,
without the prior permission in writing of Oxford University Press,
or as expressly permitted by law, or under terms agreed with the appropriate
reprographics rights organization. Enquiries concerning reproduction
outside the scope of the above should be sent to the Rights Department,
Oxford University Press, at the address above

You must not circulate this book in any other binding or cover
and you must impose this same condition on any acquirer

ISBN 0 19 565362 9

Typeset in Garamond (TTF) in 10.5/12
by Excellent Laser Typesetters, Pitampura, Delhi 110 034
Printed in India by Roopak Printers, Delhi 110 032
Published by Manzar Khan, Oxford University Press
YMCA Library Building, Jai Singh Road, New Delhi 110 001

To my daughter, (Amita) Gargi Bipasha
and
my son, (Antu) Panini

Contents

General Editor's Note viii
Foreword ix
Author's Acknowledgements xii
Translator's Note xiv
Chapter One   1
Chapter Two   41
Chapter Three   69
Chapter Four   110
Chapter Five   157
Chapter Six   185
Notes   212
Works of Michael Madhusudan Dutt   222
Select Bibliography   224
Index   233

General Editor's Note

This book is one in what we hope will be a series of short biographies of men and women from the late nineteenth century to the present day, who have contributed in discrete ways towards building modern India. With a non-specialist readership in mind, the biographies will provide concise, authoritative introductions to the lives and works of individuals who have had the courage to pursue their own visions and vocations—in the process, often touching the lives of many others in a positive and substantial way. These stories of outstanding lives seek to understand and appreciate achievements rather than provide a straightforward chronological retelling. We hope the biographies succeed in recapturing the topography of the past without hagiography and nostalgia.

NARAYANI GUPTA

Foreword

Michael Madhusudan Dutt (1824–73) is one of the greatest figures not just of Bengali but of modern Indian literature. While his masterpiece, the nine-book epic *Meghnadbadh Kabya*, is by every definition a classic, it is also a daringly modern work. It is modern in that it takes traditional, mythological material (the war between Ravana and Rama over Sita) and treats it in a new and unique way; it is a classic in its debt to classical epic poetry, both Indian and Western, and in its potential for being reread and reinterpreted by each generation. A literary classic is never frozen in time: Dutt's contemporaries would not have read *Meghnad* in the way we do now, and in a hundred year's time, readers will read it differently again.

In his other works too, Dutt was a path-breaker. His lyric poems about Radha and Krishna were a major advance, in feeling and form, on the medieval Bengali Vaishnava literary tradition. His *Birangana Kabya* was an unprecedented fusion of the West and the East, with its use of Ovid's *Heroides* as the model for portraying pining or deserted women from Indian mythology. As a dramatist, he laid the foundations for modern Bengali tragedy and comedy. As the first writer of Bengali sonnets, he left behind not just a few experiments but a sequence of hundred and two sonnets, unrivalled ever since. As an inimitable letter-writer in English, he threw open a new window on to nineteenth-century Calcutta.

Dutt was enthusiastically served by his 'primary biographers', Jogindranath Basu (1893) and Nagendranath Som (1921). They incorporated into their books numerous letters and documents, and recollections by Dutt's friends. Many other critical and biographical studies in Bengali followed, and in 1963 Kshetra Gupta brought out an annotated edition of Dutt's letters. But a wider appreciation of his life and works beyond Bengal had been wanting due to an unfortunate lack of books on him in English. There were, moreover, gaps in the biographical record, mistakes that had been repeatedly handed down (such as the notion that Henrietta, with whom Dutt lived after his marriage to Rebecca broke up, was French), and many textual flaws, especially in Dutt's English letters and the English poems that he wrote before taking to writing in Bengali.

In overcoming these gaps and imperfections, Ghulam Murshid has been a tireless pioneer. In the highly praised Bengali version of this biography (1995, revised 1997), he established, through exhaustive research in the SPG papers at Rhodes House in Oxford, the India Office Library and Records in London, Gray's Inn, the municipal archives in Versailles, and elsewhere, the details of Dutt's studies at Bishop's College, the exact identity of Rebecca and Henrietta, the course of his six years in Europe and his late, ill-fated career as a barrister. By amassing such a wealth of detail, Dr Murshid was able to connect Dutt's life with his works more intimately than any previous critic or biographer. Through his scholarship, we can now link Dutt's play *Sermista* with his personal life, find fully confessional self-knowledge in his celebrated ode *Atma-vilap*, identify allegorized portraits of Rebecca and Henrietta in *Birangana Kabya*, and relate the theme of sin in *Meghnad* more closely to his conversion to Christianity than had previously been acknowledged.

To make Dr Murshid's scholarship and insights available to a wider circle of readers, an English translation of his biography was essential; and in this he has been fortunate to secure the skills of Gopa Majumdar, the leading contemporary translator of Bengali prose, whose brilliant translation of Bibhutibhushan Bandyopadhyay's *Aparajito* was recently awarded a Sahitya Akademi Prize.

Ms Majumdar has wisely not attempted to translate the Bengali text of the biography in every detail, since anyone requiring that level of documentation would be able to read it anyway. Instead, she has gone for readability and vividness in English, for Dutt's personality, for the colourfulness as well as the tragedy of his life, rather than the literary analysis and meticulous footnoting that characterize the Bengali text. But nothing in the broad thrust of Dr Murshid's interpretation of Dutt's career—and in the very real personal sympathy he brings to his book—has been lost.

Combined with the new edition of Dutt's English letters that Dr Murshid has prepared—closely annotated, textually accurate, and including a number of letters from the collection of Dr R. K. Das Gupta that have not been published before—this biography marks the beginning of a new era in the appreciation of Dutt's achievement. From now on he will belong not just to Bengalis, but to India and to the world.

WILLIAM RADICE
SOAS

Author's Acknowledgements

Michael Madhusudan Dutt was the father of modern Bengali literature and undoubtedly the greatest poet and playwright of his time. He also modernized the Bengali language. Above all, he introduced humanist ideas with which he reinterpreted Hindu Puranas, including the Ramayana. Apart from his literary contributions, his colourful personality turned him into a legend during his lifetime. However, despite all this, it proved extremely difficult for others to write his biography. The first biography by Jogindranath Basu was published twenty years after the death of the poet in 1873. It soon underwent several editions. However, for reasons explained in my biography, Basu had to depend largely on hearsay. A quarter of a century later Nagendranath Som published another biography, which had more information. Even so, it was based to a great extent on fiction. Since then a number of biographies have come out, including a remarkable one by Sureshchandra Maitra in 1975. Maitra earnestly sought new materials, but had only limited success.

These biographers did not know that a huge amount of material remained unexplored at the India Office Library in London, Rhodes House in Oxford, Municipal Archives in Versailles, Gray's Inn in London and the University of Birmingham. Because I was living in England, I was in a position to unearth a great deal of material on the basis of which a new biography could be written. Thanks to Professor Rabindra Kumar DasGupta, I was also able to use the full version of some of Dutt's original letters. I also feel that the earlier biographers either resented the fact that Dutt was converted to Christianity or tried to portray him as a Hindu. They were unaware of the extent and quality of Christian influence on him. The question of religion blurred their vision to a significant degree.

I am grateful to Professor Shibnarayan Ray, who encouraged me to undertake this work. I am also grateful to Professor Sanat Saha for his suggestions for improvement and Professor Anisuzzaman for his comments. I am indebted to Dr Indrani Chatterji for attracting my attention to the Bishop's College Papers at Rhodes House, Oxford, which unfolded original material on Dutt's Christian identity. I am also grateful to Dr William Radice for allowing me to use his D. Phil. dissertation on Dutt. He also arranged for the publication of the original Bengali biography in English. I appreciate the generous encouragement I received from my teachers Professor David Kopf and Professor Ahmed Sharif.

I started working in 1986 and finished the biography in early in 1994. It was at the initiative of Mr Sagarmay Ghosh, the editor of *Desh*, that the biography was first serialized in this periodical from March 1994 to January 1995. It came out as a book in February 1995. I would always remember the support I received from Mr Ghosh.

I am forever indebted to Gopa Majumdar for her translation of my text. I should mention, however, that readers eager to learn more about Dutt and full references to his life and works will discover more in my Bengali version as well as in my forthcoming book, *Heart of a Rebel Poet: Letters of Michael Madhusudan Dutt.*

London   GHULAM MURSHID

Translator's Note

My first encounter with Michael Madhusudan Dutt's poetry was in the pages of a school book. I was then thirteen. It was an extract from *Meghnadbadh Kavya*, which included the famous line: '*Aami ki dorai, shokhi, bhikhari Raghobe?*' It was spoken by a female character in the Ramayana, but she was not one on whom Valmiki had spent much time. It was Pramila, Meghnad's wife and Ravan's daughter-in-law, and she was more or less Madhusudan's own creation. The line meant, 'My friend, do *I* have to fear that beggar, Ram?'

Had Madhusudan written that line today, no doubt devout Hindus would have demanded his head on a platter. Even at the time, only a man with a totally different vision and indomitable courage could have written it. It captured my thirteen-year old heart instantly—not so much because Ram had been referred to as a 'beggar', but because a woman had spoken those words. I knew nothing of Madhusudan's life, but if in his writing a woman had her own views *and* her own voice, then Michael Madhusudan Dutt was certainly going to be my hero.

Three years later, I left school and although I then read some of his shorter poems and learnt something about his life, the details remained somewhat hazy. Like most Bengalis, I grew up with these fixed ideas about Michael Madhusudan: (a) he had great erudition and wrote great poetry; (b) he was a pukka sahib and married a white Englishwoman; (c) he lived extravagantly and drank a lot.

Over the years, at times, my eyes fell upon the odd article, in some magazine or other, on his life and times. I learned that his life was so intriguing to many writers that some had written plays based on it. On one occasion, Madhusudan appeared as a character in a novel set in the mid-nineteenth century. But no writer—certainly not the novelist—went into further details; it just seemed convenient for everyone to preserve those ideas about Madhusudan. His problem with alcohol, in particular, was highlighted by all, for it provided both drama and entertainment.

It was only when I read Ghulam Murshid's book two years ago (having missed its earlier serialization in the magazine, *Desh*) that this legendary but indistinct figure suddenly became real and alive. For the first time, I found someone speaking of him with a clear and unbiased vision, separating hearsay from the truth, drama from reality.

What I did not know then was that, one day, I would have to translate the whole book. When the offer was made, I began my task with slow and hesitant steps. If, in due course, it gathered momentum and I could finish it successfully, it was only because of the support and encouragement I received from both the author and William Radice. William very kindly translated into English all the Bengali verse written by Madhusudan, and quoted in his book by Ghulam. Left on my own, I doubt very much that I would have found the courage to translate Madhusudan's poetry.

However, translating the Bengali verse was not the only problem. Some of the other problems that came up were much more difficult to resolve. One of them was simply related to the serialization of the entire text. When it came out as a book, the publishers did not find it necessary to have it pruned and edited. Some of it therefore remained repetitive. I did what I could do streamline and edit the narrative—but I am fully aware that perfection has not been achieved. The author has been most kind and understanding about this. I can only hope and pray that the readers will be the same.

Another problem that arose was over the spelling of Bengali words. The main difficulty lay in the absence of certain letters in the Bengali alphabet, 'v' in particular. The word 'kavya' (poetry), for instance, is spelt 'kabya' in Bengali. So what did one do? Use 'kavya', which is how it is spelt in both Sanskrit and Hindi, or retain 'kabya'? Much debate took place between Ghulam and myself, until he decided to strike a compromise by retaining the same spellings that Madhusudan himself had used, replacing 'b' with 'v', wherever necessary. For the remaining words, the standard Bengali spelling has been used throughout.

Finally, I must thank the editors of OUP, who cheerfully put up with all the delays and other complexities involved in the whole process. Had it not been for their cooperation, this fascinating account of Michael Madhusudan Dutt's life would have remained untold to all those readers who cannot have access to the original.

London   GOPA MAJUMDAR

Chapter One

'You may take my word for it, friend Raj, I shall come out like a tremendous comet and no mistake,' wrote Michael Madhusudan to his friend, Rajnarayan Basu, about himself. Today, there is truly no reason to doubt these words. What is surprising is that when (in July 1861) he made that comment about appearing as a comet, he had already reached the pinnacle of his success. Apart from the second volume of *Meghnadbadh Kabya* and *Birangana*, all his works had been published, and he was well-established as the undisputed monarch among the poets and playwrights of Bengal. Nevertheless, it is possible that in spite of his success, Michael was not content with himself. Even around this time, he was not altogether sure about having mastered the art of writing poetry. Perhaps that is why he used the future tense in his words to Raj. In the last one hundred and fifty years, various stars—big and small—have appeared in the firmament of Bengali literature. Each, in its own way, is special. But there has been only one comet—Michael Madhusudan Dutt. It is not just that, like a comet, his appearance was brief. It is also that he was different from every other writer in what he said and did, and in the circle in which he moved. He dazzled everyone with his brilliance for as long as he remained, and then was gone quickly. Even so, no Bengali reader has been able to forget either his colourful personality, or his wondrous appearance in the world of literature.

He stood apart from all his contemporaries. His arrogant behaviour, his contempt for old values, his rebellion against established traditions in life and literature, all served to set him apart from the rest. Even as a young student, he ate what was forbidden. He had no objection to drinking, which was also forbidden. He copied Europeans in his style of dressing. Unlike his friends, he did not feel overjoyed at the idea of being married, even to a girl 'as pretty as a fairy'. Instead, he became a Christian and ran away from home. Despite all social restrictions, he lived with two different English women. At a time when most men desired nothing more than the post of a deputy magistrate (the highest civilian post available to an Indian), his sole aim in life was to be a poet.

When the average Bengali would burst with pride at the possibility of simply becoming a lawyer and working in the chief civil court, Michael was the first Bengali to go to England with the express purpose of becoming a barrister. He earned a lot of money too—his income certainly exceeded that of the average man in those times. But, unlike the others, he did not buy land. He is remembered today as a great spender; even in the way he spent his money, he was remarkable. His was such an extraordinary character that, during his lifetime, some hated him, some loved him, some even pitied him—but no one could ignore or dismiss him.

※※

Madhusudan was born in a traditional but newly rich family in an ordinary village in central Bengal. He came to Calcutta when he was about eight, and was brought up there. He was educated chiefly at Hindu College. From where did he acquire the remarkable traits in his character? How much did he inherit from his forefathers? How much can be attributed to his environment? Thousands of boys went to Hindu College in its first thirty years of existence. Not one of them turned out to be quite as remarkable as Madhusudan. What could be the reason for Madhu being the way he was? The truth is that he was not influenced by any one single factor; nor did he become such a controversial character overnight.

His father was an established lawyer in Calcutta. Of his father's three elder brothers, the first, Radhamohan, was a *sherestadar* (legal clerk) in Jessore; the second, Madanmohan, was a *munsef* (junior judge) in Kumarkhali; and the third was another lawyer in Jessore.

As the next step, it would have been natural for Madhu to have become a barrister. Eventually, he did become one. But there was another side to his character which, for a very long time, kept him from going anywhere near a court. It made him roam in a world far removed from law and reason—in the world of poetry. All he ever wanted was to be a poet. How did such a strange desire stem in his heart?

One's family plays an important role in building one's character, as does the environment. Madhu was no exception in this matter. That is why, in this attempt to reconstruct his life, it is necessary to examine his family, and see how he was brought up within it. However important such a task may be, it is by no means an easy one. The family Madhu was born into was not as well known or long-established as, for instance, the Tagores of Jorasanko. There are not many written records of the lives or activities of Madhu's ancestors. In fact, his exact date of birth is not known as he was born in a small village. One hundred and seventy-five years have passed since then. Even today, it is not common practice in villages to note down the date of a significant event in a family, such as a birth, death or a wedding. There is no law in existence to make it mandatory for everyone to record these events. As a result, anyone doing research on someone's family background is really quite helpless. To reconstruct the minute details of this aspect of Madhusudan's life, therefore, is an extremely difficult—almost impossible—task.

But that is not all. There is another reason that has made it very difficult to learn more about the intricacies of Madhu's family life. This reason becomes clear if one simply looks at the headstone on his grave. What his grandsons have said about the background of their grandmother, Henrietta, is an indication of their ignorance about their own forefathers. Henrietta's full name has been shown as Amelia Henrietta Sophia. Then, in brackets, her maiden name appears as Dique. This is wrong. From her birth certificate, it is clear that her maiden name was White, not Dique. Why, then, did Madhu's grandsons make this mistake?

The truth is that when Madhu and Henrietta died, their daughter, Sermista, was not even fourteen. She died young, at the age of nineteen. She had two younger brothers, Frederick and Napoleon. At the time of Madhu's death, Frederick was eleven years and eleven months old, and Napoleon's age was six years and two months. Frederick died only two years later. The only child of Madhusudan who lived long was Napoleon. There was no one in Madhu's family who might have helped with names and dates. He had no sibling of his own, and was not in close contact with any of his many cousins. There was no one on Henrietta's side either, for she had turned her back on her family when she chose to spend her life with Madhu. When they died, therefore, there was no one to explain to their children their own family history. Even Madhu's friends were unable to help, the reason being that Madhu never spoke to them about his family. What his friends knew about him was really not much more than what his children or grandchildren had learnt. Madhusudan was known to boast about himself, but was not given to divulging important facts about his personal and family life.

Many of his friends and the people he knew wrote their autobiographies in the second half of the nineteenth century. Madhu did not do that. The only thing he ever did was send a few details of his life to a man called Kedarnath Dutt. Kedarnath was a deputy magistrate. He wrote to Madhu, telling him that he was writing a history of the Dutts. What he produced eventually was little more than a pamphlet,[†] showing how many generations of Dutts had been born since their arrival in Bengal, and where these various people were living. The historical accuracy of the document is questionable. If Kedarnath had concentrated only on Madhusudan instead of all the Dutts living in Bengal, we might have learnt some important and useful facts about him, on which his biography might have been based.

One might wonder why Madhu's grandsons chose Dique, of all names, for their grandmother. As a matter of fact, no one among Madhu's friends or family knew who Henrietta really was. It was rumoured that she had run away from Madras. Rajnarayan Basu, one of Madhu's closest friends, went so far as to suspect that they had never married.[†] They had also heard vaguely that Henrietta's father and Madhusudan had worked as teachers in the same school in Madras, and that Henrietta was French[†] (Rashbihari Mukhopadhyay had sworn that this was true, but this was not really the case). It was for these reasons that Madhu's grandsons, as well as some of his biographers, tried to find a teacher with a

---

[†] The sign refers readers to the endnotes.

French name among Madhu's colleagues. They found two names that seemed likely—Dique and Pepin.

There were, in fact, two Diques and one Pepin. All of them had worked together with Madhu in the same school. But Henrietta was not the daughter of any one of them. Thomas Bedford Pepin was married in 1843, and his daughter Margaret was born in 1848—the same year that Madhu married Rebecca. On the other hand, A. Dique and L. Dique went to Madras School, and eventually became teachers there. They were both younger than Madhu, and one was a student while Madhu was a teacher. Moreover, neither the two Diques nor Pepin were French. One of the Diques is described in the school register as East Indian. Pepin's first names—Thomas Bedford—indicate clearly that there was nothing French about him. Madhu's biographers and descendants should have considered something else—the school in Madras was a government school. In view of the relationship between the English and the French, it was hardly likely that a Frenchman would have been appointed as a teacher. Above all, they ought to have realized that if Henrietta was French, she would have spelt her name as Henriette, and her third name would have been Sophie, rather than Sophia.

It should not be difficult to imagine the complexities involved in the task of his biographers, when Madhu's own grandsons knew so little about him or their grandmother. Admittedly, his earlier biographers, from Jogindranath Basu (1893) to Sureshchandra Maitra (1975), showed a great deal of courage in undertaking their task, and achieved the impossible. Among all his biographers, Jogindranath Basu and Nagendranath Som (1921)† deserve special mention, for had they not recorded various facts about Madhu's life and work before these were lost forever, no one today could have attempted to write a complete biography of this amazing man.

Jogindranath Basu had spoken to the few family members of Madhusudan who were still alive. Mankumari Basu, a well-known poetess herself, was one of them. However, it is difficult to tell how much of what they said was true, and how much was hearsay. It is common practice to exaggerate or attribute redeeming qualities when speaking of one's family and its past glory. Equally, it is natural to want to hide scandals and skeletons in cupboards. When writing the biography of Virginia Woolf, Quentin Bell mentioned that Woolf had been the victim of sexual abuse at the age of eight.

Bell went on to demonstrate that, even when she became an adult, Woolf could never be comfortable in her thoughts about sexual relations. When writing a biography, it is essential to examine and analyse important factors such as these that Bell mentioned, in order to describe more completely the character of the person.

The question is, who but the close relations and friends of that person can provide the necessary details? In the West, it is possible to get adequate relevant information, because there, an individual may be seen, and judged, in isolation. If Bell had had to work in India, where society lays far greater emphasis on the family than the individual, he would have found it very difficult indeed to unearth that kind of information about Woolf. Everyone knows today about the suicide of Kadambari Debi, wife of Jyotirindranath Tagore. It was one of biggest mysteries of the time. The Tagores were the most famous of all the families in Calcutta, known for their erudition and talents. Yet, even today, the truth behind the mystery remains unknown.

The facts that Jogindranath gathered from Mankumari Basu and other relations were not corroborated by another more impartial source. Perhaps there was no one left to corroborate. Those who had known Madhu as a child could hardly be expected to have remained alive around 1892-3.

After Jogindranath, a quarter of a century later, Nagendranath Som tried to gather more facts; but, by then, facts had inextricably merged with hearsay, making it impossible to separate the two. Even so, any attempt at writing the history of Madhusudan's family must be based on the facts provided by these two earlier biographers. It is for this reason that, its importance notwithstanding, this particular family history is likely to remain incomplete.

Madhusudan's great grandfather, Ramkishore Dutt, lived in the Khulna (erstwhile Jessore) district. After his death, his three sons—Ramnidhi, Dayaram, and Manikram—moved to Sagardari and began living there permanently. This was the village of their maternal grandfather. It is not known why they moved. Perhaps, as fatherless children, they were too poor to live anywhere else. Even after their arrival in Sagardari, Ramnidhi could do nothing to improve his financial situation. What he did for a living is not known. But, in deference to the practice among *Kayastha*s (the caste to which Ramnidhi belonged), he did try to get his sons educated. His eldest son, Radhamohan, was taught Persian, which was the language used in courts and in legal practice. After receiving his education, Radhamohan at first did little. It seems he was simply idling away his time when, one day, at a few stern words from his father, he left home in a fit of rage, to earn a living elsewhere. It was the best thing he could have done. His knowledge of Persian helped him to find work almost immediately. Over a period of time, he was promoted to the post of *sherestadar* (legal clerk).

It was from this point that the luck of the Dutts changed. Radhamohan brought his younger brothers to Jessore and made arrangements for their education. All of them learnt Persian and began to earn well. The second son of Ramkishore, Madanmohan, became the *meer-munshi* (head clerk) in Jessore, before moving to Kumarkhali as *munsef* (junior judge). The third, Debiprasad, went a step further and became a lawyer in Jessore. The youngest, Rajnarayan (Madhusudan's father), turned out to be the most successful. The earliest biographer of Madhusudan, Jogindranath Basu, claimed that Rajnarayan's knowledge of Persian was so good that everyone called him Munshi Rajnarayan. It is believed that he was quite proud of his achievements, even a little arrogant. Since he was the youngest, he had been spoilt somewhat, and in his youth, he was said to have been quite unrestrained in his pursuit of pleasure. As we shall see later, his son inherited both qualities from Rajnarayan in full measure.

Rajnarayan also became a lawyer, but made better progress than Debiprasad. He moved to Calcutta. In those days, it was the norm to live in or around the village where one was born. Not many people had the courage or the enterprise to leave their villages and go to cities. By doing that, Radhamohan made it possible for his family to make rapid progress in life. As for Rajnarayan, having begun his life in Jessore instead of in a small village, it was that much easier for him to find the strength to move to Calcutta. According to some reports, he left home after a quarrel with his family, very much like his elder brother. But whatever the reason, he was clearly not a man afraid of facing the unknown, in an alien land. He had sufficient courage, confidence, and the desire to learn. These same traits reappeared in his son.

In short, using their education and ambition as weapons, the Dutts, in a single generation, managed to change their lives, and flourish more than most other people of those times. They used their wealth to buy land and became zamindars. At the time, society did not extend full respect to a man unless he was a zamindar. Besides, buying land with one's accumulated wealth was considered the safest and most sensible investment.

Having become wealthy almost overnight, the Dutts lost no opportunity to flaunt their wealth. They acquired large and opulent houses, complete with massive halls for pujas and other religious functions. No expense was spared to appear rich. Jogindranath cites one example which, if true, illustrates this point perfectly. On one occasion, it is said, Radhamohan performed a hundred and eight pujas to please Kali, and to seek her blessings for the welfare of his son. In the process, a hundred and eight buffaloes, a hundred and eight goats, and a hundred and eight sheep were sacrificed. The floral offerings were made with hundred and eight *jauba* flowers (hibiscus), each made of gold. Most probably it was a highly exaggerated story. However, it does indicate a tendency in the family to stun others by spending their money like water. Madhusudan, too, inherited this quality. That is why, when he spent a *mohar* (gold coin) just to have a haircut, he astounded others far more than he pleased himself.

It may not be irrelevant here to examine Rajnarayan's income. After his death, Madhu had to fight a case against other claimants to rescue some of his father's property. What he eventually managed to recover gives us an idea of Rajnarayan's total assets. The house he had lived in was sold by Madhu for seven thousand rupees. In the early 1830s, Rajnarayan must have bought it for much less. In addition to this, he had bought land near the Sunderbans. This land was sold by Madhu for twenty thousand rupees. Madhu failed to get all of his mother's jewellery, but the decree issued in this regard amounted to thirteen hundred rupees. The total value of Rajnarayan's assets at the time of his death adds up to about thirty thousand rupees. Towards the end of his life, he had little or no income. Even when times were good, his property was possibly worth only about fifty thousand. At the time, there were plenty of people in Calcutta who were far more wealthy. Only a few years before Rajnarayan bought his house, a babu in Calcutta had bought a *baiji* (a nautch girl) called Niki for a hundred thousand rupees. He used to pay her a monthly salary of one thousand rupees. Another gentleman, Ramdulal Dey, spent a hundred thousand rupees on the *shradha* ceremony when his mother died; and when he died himself, he left properties worth twelve million rupees. In 1820, another newly rich man, Ramratna Mallik, spent between seven and eight hundred thousand rupees on his son's marriage. Obviously, there was no dearth of rich men in the city. According to the Bengal Law Reports (1869), Prasannakumar Tagore, another contemporary of Rajnarayan, left a will that indicated that his annual income was two hundred and fifty thousand rupees, and it was still increasing.

How successful was Rajnarayan as a lawyer? What is generally believed is again an exaggeration of the truth. Since Rajnarayan's son achieved such fame and glory, Madhu's admirers and earlier biographers tried to thrust some of that greatness on his ancestors as well. A few biographers have said that, in his profession, Rajnarayan was a rival of Prasannakumar Tagore and Ramaprasad Roy. However, judging by what was said in some of the journals of those times, Rajnarayan certainly did not command the same respect in society that the other two did. On the contrary, the information unearthed by Brajendranath Banerjee from the journal, *Sambad Prabhakar*, indicates just the opposite:

January, 1847: The judges of the main court have recognized Prasannakumar Tagore as the best...and Ramaprasad Roy Babu as one of the well-known lawyers of Calcutta. On the other hand, they have removed Rajnarayan Dutt and a few others as unworthy of their positions.

What is not known is whether Rajnarayan held some special position in the court before this incident. What is obvious is that his reputation was tarnished on being dismissed. Prasannakumar came from the family of Tagores, famous and well established. Ramaprasad Roy, as a descendant of Rammohan Roy, also enjoyed a special position in society. Rajnarayan Dutt, on the other hand, came from a small village in Jessore; and his was the first generation in his family that had acquired education and wealth. This certainly put him at a disadvantage. Besides, in the matter of knowledge, enlightenment and social acceptance, he was far removed from the other two men. Even today, it is not hard to imagine the clear distinction between the circle Rajnarayan Dutt must have moved in, the kind of people he would have entertained in his drawing room, and the world inhabited by Prasannakumar Tagore, Ramaprasad Roy and their close associates. In those days in Bengal, whenever there were discussions on current political or social problems, or a movement for some social reform was to be launched, it was people like Prasannakumar, Ramaprasad, Ishwarchandra Sinha, Radhakanta Deb and others who were called in to play the lead roles. In these matters, Rajnarayan remained somewhere in the background.

However, he did possess certain qualities that marked him out from others. Rajnarayan Dutt was said to be a man who worshipped beauty; and if he found someone with a knowledge of music or any other form of art, he extended his full support to the person. It has been mentioned specifically that songs written and sung before and after Durga Puja (*agomoni* and *bijoya*) used to move him profoundly, and he paid the singer most generously. Madhu inherited this trait from him. Beauty moved him just as deeply, and he was as generous as his father towards those he wished to support.

The other thing that has been said about Rajnarayan is that he was self-indulgent to an unacceptable degree. Apparently, restraint and self-control were qualities he was not known to exercise. However, no satisfactory explanation has ever been provided as to what exactly he did to indicate a lack of self-control, although the implication is clearly towards sexual and moral behaviour. It must be remembered that, at the time, certain practices were common and accepted even among the educated class, particularly in places like Calcutta, Krishnanagar, and Jessore.

I have heard it said about Jessore that court officials there introduce one another to a newcomer as 'he has built a brick house for his mistress'. Building a brick house for one's mistress was considered a matter of prestige and honour.[†]

It was in Jessore that Rajnarayan began his career. Therefore, if he took a mistress, just to keep up with other professionals, there is nothing surprising about it. What is surprising is that, in spite of this established and accepted practice, Rajnarayan is accused of licentious behaviour. Could it be that he did things others had not dared? Could it also be that he had fallen prey to some disease, which was why he was not able to sire a single child after 1827–8, at which time he was a young man? There is not enough reliable information available today to answer these questions. But there can be no doubt about the luxurious lifestyle he had adopted. In this regard, Madhu was quite like his father. His desire for material pleasures was no less than his desire for fame and recognition.

It is not known when Rajnarayan was born. Possibly not before 1800. He must have been married by the time he was twenty. His first child, Madhusudan, was born probably on 25 January 1824 (this date is unconfirmed; but judging by the age mentioned when Madhu was admitted to Bishop's College, and later when he was married, this could well be his date of birth). Going by these calculations, Rajnarayan's wife, Janhabi Debi, was born not before 1807-8. Janhabi Debi's father was a zamindar in a different village in Jessore, called Katipara. It is not known whether Madhu was close to anyone in his mother's family, or whether any of them had any influence on his character. But he did inherit a few qualities from his mother.

Bengali mothers are said to be particularly affectionate. However, Janhabi Debi appears to have been blessed with this quality more than others. It was not just her own children that she treated with affection, but those of her neighbours as well. Her neighbour in Calcutta was Ramkamal Mukhopadhyay, a Brahmin. He did not have a son, but his three nephews made up for the absence. Rangalal Bandyopadhyay was one of these nephews. Later in life, he became a well-known poet. His elder brother, Ganeshchandra also published more than one volume of poetry. All three brothers addressed Janhabi Debi as 'Ma'. In those days, Brahmins seldom mixed closely with *Kayastha*s. Moreover, there were often enormous differences between the people of West and East Bengal. The most obvious difference was in their language and dialect. And, if two households were to get closer to each other, they would inevitably find differences in food, culinary practices, and social rituals. Under such circumstances, if three Brahmin boys could refer to a *Kayastha* woman as 'Ma', it is a clear indication of that woman's extraordinary ability to overcome all differences purely with her love and affection. This sincerity of feeling was something Madhu received from his mother. He did not find it easy to make friends. But those whom he did look upon as such, always enjoyed his unflinching support. He was prepared, at any time, to make any sacrifice for them.

Janhabi Debi possessed another remarkable quality. In those days, women's education was decidedly frowned upon. If a woman was educated, it was believed that she would become a widow. Most women were convinced that education would cause them irreparable damage, that it could never do them any good. In spite of this, Janhabi Debi had learnt to read and write. According to Madhu's earler biographers, she used to read aloud to Madhu from the medieval Bengali versions of the Ramayana and Mahabharata, as well as other books. Even if there is a certain amount of exaggeration in this claim, it is clear that it was she who helped the young Madhu with his studies, and encouraged him to read the Ramayana and Mahabharata. She is said to have possessed a very good memory. Apparently, she could memorize large portions of the poetry she read, and would then recite those lines for her son. It was her recitations that introduced Madhu to the world of poetry. Even as a child, not content with just reading poetry, he would memorize what he read. Much later in life when, as an adult, he began to claim that he had forgotten whatever Bengali he had learnt, there were instances when he quoted in his letters lines from old Bengali poetry. This only goes to show how deeply the poetry he had heard in his childhood had influenced him.

Janhabi Debi had two more sons by the time Madhu was four years old. They were called Prasannakumar and Mahendranarayan. Prasanna died at the age of one, Mahendra at five. Janhabi Debi had no more children after that. Consequently, Madhu, as the only child who survived, was indulged and pampered a great deal. It was not just his parents who lavished all their affection on him. As the only child of Rajnarayan Dutt, who was the youngest among his own siblings and the best educated, Madhu received a lot of love and attention—perhaps more than necessary—from everyone else in his joint family. Later in life, he developed an arrogance, a tendency to spend money without any restraint whatsoever and indulge his every whim, chiefly as a result of being spoilt by his entire family.

It is true, however, that Madhu loved his parents as much as they loved him. As a child, he was immensely proud of his father. His well-known remark—'Rajnarayan Dutt's son does not† count the money he spends'—implies not just self-importance, but also his pride in his father. Yet, when he grew up and became a young man, the same Madhu struggled hard to break through the protective cocoon his parents had built around him. His own ambitions in life were very different from those of his parents. So even at that young age, he had to rebel and fight for independence. It is entirely likely that, in this matter, he clashed not so much with his mother as with his father, who did not realize that Madhu was growing up and becoming an individual with a distinct personality of his own. Eventually, as will be revealed in due course, Madhu became a Christian and broke all ties with his family forever. There was a specific event in his life that made him do this. But the desire to break free of the control imposed by his parents had started to grow in his mind long before that event took place.

It is not clear exactly when Rajnarayan Dutt started his practice in Calcutta. Madhu's earliest biographer, Jogindranath, says Madhu was seven at the time, that is, his father began working in Calcutta as a lawyer in 1831. According to his most recent biographer, Sureshchandra Maitra, Madhu was then five or six, that is, in 1829-30. No matter when he arrived in Calcutta to work, Rajnarayan left his wife and two sons in his village, Sagardari. He became a successful lawyer almost as soon as he began to practise. Soon, he was able to buy a house on the main road in Kidderpore. It was a clear indication of his considerable income.

It is also not known when he brought his wife and child to join him. The only indication is that Madhu arrived in Calcutta after the death of his youngest brother, Mahendra. According to Jogindranath, Mahendra was four years younger than Madhu, and when he died he was five years old. If this is true, then it may be assumed that Janhabi Debi did not arrive in Calcutta before 1833-4. It was not easy at the time to break away from the traditional joint family. Perhaps Rajnarayan Dutt would not have been able to do so, had it not been for the fact that he had lost two young sons and had bought a large house in Calcutta. These reasons were important enough to warrant his family's departure for the city. Besides, he must have also thought of the little Madhu growing up and the need to give him an 'English' education.

Before his arrival in the city, Madhu went to the local school in his village; and then to another in a neighbouring village, a mile away, in order to learn Persian. He was only eight or nine years old at the time, and he had to walk the distance every day. Yet he was sent there because his father and his uncles knew very well the usefulness of learning the language. It is not known how much

Persian he actually learned. However, his tutor did teach him Persian couplets and, although Madhu was a small boy, taught him to sing *ghazals*. It is believed that, later in his life, when he joined Hindu College, Madhu used to sing *ghazals* for his friends. He was never formally taught to sing; but he had an inborn love for music, gained from his family and the atmosphere in which he grew up. Even though he did not spend a long time learning Persian, he grew to love the language and developed an interest in Muslim culture. The days of his learning Persian certainly made an impression, however slight, that came through in his writing years later. He often expressed the desire to write about matters related to Muslims, which might well have been the result of studying Persian as a child.

Madhu must have returned to Sagardari many times, even after he began living permanently in Calcutta, particularly during the time of Durga Puja. Even so, it was apparently from that time that his ties with his homeland began to weaken. A decade later, he broke away from his family altogether. In spite of that, he could never forget his roots. An analysis of his literary works and various events of his life would bear testimony to his deep attachment to the land he left behind.

What touched him most profoundly was the natural beauty of rural Bengal. Many of his works have repeated mention of this enduring love. When he wrote *The Captive Ladie* and other works in English, he was in Madras, far removed from his home, family and friends. Yet nature, as he had seen her in his childhood, returned again and again in everything he wrote. Much later, when he was in Versailles, his memories of Sagardari reappeared, brimming with life and vigour, in the sonnets that he wrote. In Calcutta, even when he was writing tales of valour and courage, his imagination soaring well above the confines of the earth, he spoke of greenery, rivers and wide open spaces, sometimes a little unnecessarily. In *Tilottama-sambhab Kabya*, for instance, the paradise he describes is really the village seen in his childhood:

> Soaring silk-cotton, *sal*, palm-trees
> Piercing the sky; coconuts whose breasts
> Nourish the thirsty with juice like mother's milk!
> Betel-nut; *chalita*; *jaam* whose fruit
> Are like glossy bees; lofty tamarind;
> Jackfruit with their grains of gold
> As in Kubera's palace!

The very mention of areca, rose-apple (*jaam*), tamarind, and jackfruit would tell anyone that this particular paradise was situated not very far from Sagardari and central Bengal. The truth is that his mind wandered about near the river Kapotaksha until the day he died. The small villages that lined its banks, a broken temple here, or a lonely banyan there—each of these images left an indelible mark on his mind.

After 1843, Madhu lost close contact with his village. The rest of his life was spent in various cities—Calcutta, Madras, London, and Versailles. After he grew up, however, two other aspects of nature influenced him as well—the sea and mountains. The first time he thought of the sea was when he began dreaming of travelling all the way to England. Later, when living in Madras, he got the chance to form close ties with the sea. It is clear that he loved both the sea and the mountains for their grandeur, although he never lived near a high mountain. In fact, it is not known whether he ever saw a high mountain at all.

※※※

At the time of Madhu's birth, the society in Calcutta was already undergoing a major upheaval. Influenced by Western thought and philosophy, many people were bidding farewell to the old, and welcoming the new. Hindu College was established in 1817 in order to prepare future generations for the new age, by giving them a Western education. The following year, the first Bengali newspaper was published, and a book written to propagate female education. Some had even begun to think of reforming religious practices. In 1803, Rammohan Roy, for example, wrote *Tuhfatul Muhhayedeen* in Arabic, and a book on monotheism in Persian. He formed a society in 1828 to take that idea forward. A massive debate broke out regarding the practice of suttee. Some Hindus, however, remained untouched by this new wave. After spending the whole day working for the British (*phirangis*), they would bathe in the Ganges before returning home. This helped them regain their purity as Hindus, and appeased their conscience.

In every area, new ideas were clashing with old traditions. In the midst of it all, commerce flourished, and some businessmen made a lot of money. With their newly acquired wealth, they bought land, became zamindars and came to be known as *babus* or newly-rich aristocrats.

In his childhood, Madhu was untouched by any of this. The pace of life in his village was slow and easy, all its values medieval. The wave of modernity had not yet crossed the borders of the city to disturb the peace and quiet of that village. But, suddenly, he was plucked out of his familiar, tranquil surroundings and brought to the wholly unfamiliar city to live there permanently. The problems he had to confront at first as a result of this move are not known. However, he gradually learnt to cope with them. Going to a new school, coming to grips with its new syllabus and teaching methods, building up a relationship with new teachers, dealing with the curiosity and, sometimes, envy of his classmates before they became his friends—all these factors must have played on his mind. Back at home, torn from the unfailing love and affection of the joint family he had lived in, he felt lonely and had to find new playmates among the children in his neighbourhood.

Without doubt, his move to Calcutta marked the beginning of a new chapter in his life. His parents were the only people to remind him of and bind him still, in some ways, to the old life he had left behind. Another chapter in his life started when he became a Christian, and yet another when he moved to Madras. Then he returned to Calcutta. The chapter in Madras closed forever, and he started afresh. This was followed by years spent in England and France. Although Madhu did not live long, his life can be divided into seven distinct phases.

It has already been mentioned that Madhu did well at school in his village. He was genuinely interested in all that he was taught, and had a natural flair for languages. It was, therefore, easy enough far him to catch up with the boys in Calcutta who knew English. Making friends and communicating with others must have proved far more difficult. Needless to say, to a touchy and sensitive child like him, grappling with the unfamiliar ways of the city must have brought many an anxious moment. To start with, when he first arrived, he did not know any English, and spoke Bengali with an accent that betrayed his past, and the fact that he had grown up in a village in Jessore. His accent, together with his rustic clothes, must have led to him being ridiculed by some of the boys in his class. It is likely that, at such a time, Madhu—like his favourite poet, Shelley—wiped his eyes secretly in his class, and drew pictures of his village in his exercise-book. If, in his conversations with his fellow students, he made frequent references to his father being a wealthy lawyer, it was quite possibly just an attempt at protecting himself from being teased. Eventually, what he at first used simply as a weapon for self-defence, became a habit. It was this feeling of inferiority that developed into a tendency to show off. In later years, when he offered financial assistance to his friends, bought them expensive gifts and invited them to sumptuous meals, it was partly due to this mixed feeling of inferiority and self-importance.

There is no definite information regarding which school Madhu was first put into when he arrived in Calcutta. Some believe that he joined an English school in Kidderpore. At the time, children between eight and twelve were eligible for admission in the junior branch of Hindu College. Madhu certainly fell into this age-group. Why, then, did he not join Hindu College straightaway? There does not appear to be a satisfactory explanation anywhere.

However, what is important is not the name of his school, but the kind of education he received there. The number of English schools was limited then, as were opportunities to receive a private education. According to Ramkamal Sen, a good private tutor in those days had to be paid a monthly salary of something between four and sixteen rupees. What most students learned in the name of English were simply the English words for a few objects, and a few verbs. Those whose learning went a bit further sometimes mastered the alphabet. But Madhu's grasp of the language was thorough and fluent, much better than that of many of his classmates. So it seems clear that Rajnarayan sent his son to a good school, possibly one that had British or Anglo-Indian teachers. In this matter, it is necessary to remember Rajnarayan's realistic and practical approach to life. He did not have to learn English to practise law. In fact, there is no evidence that he knew the language at all. But, as a successful and self-made man, he had realized that Persian was losing its importance; if anyone wanted to gain as much success as he had, a knowledge of English would now be necessary. Not long after Madhu was put into school in Calcutta, English was made the official language of India on Lord Macaulay's recommendation. The school that Madhu went to had to be the best in town. Some say that he learned not just English there, but also Latin, Greek, and Hebrew. He was already a bright student when he arrived. Now, in his new school, he began to show how quickly he could grasp new languages.

Madhu joined Hindu College in 1837. At the time, it had thirteen classes. Eight of the lower classes formed the junior branch; the upper five fell within the senior section. The class Madhu joined was the fifth, if counted in the ascending order, and ninth when counted in the reverse order. In those days, it was customary to count in the descending order when determining the class in which a child was. Be that as it may, it was in Hindu College that he received a true education. He was introduced to world literature, and later became a poet himself, thanks chiefly to what he was taught in Hindu College.

Madhu joined this institution six years after Derozio's[1] death. In fact, Derozio had died even before the child Madhusudan's arrival in Calcutta. By the time Madhu joined Hindu College, certain things had changed. The enthusiasm with which Derozio had encouraged his students to read Hume, Kant, Reid, Stewart, and Tom Paine had subsided a little. But the great tradition that he had established in teaching methods and in building a special relationship between students and teachers still continued as before. Some of his old students were still in the college.

Derozio did not just teach literature; nor did he create a revolution among the students of the college simply by talking of literature. He created ripples in the minds of these young men by teaching moral philosophy, which was a part of their syllabus. It must be emphasized that he never confined himself to the prescribed texts, but taught his pupils to think independently, opening to them a door to the big wide world. His personality had

[1] Henry Vivian Louis Derozio (1809–31) was an Anglo-Portuguese teacher at Hindu College. He was appointed a teacher at the age of sixteen and worked there for only five years, but left a lasting impression on his students and on the history of the college—indeed, he also left a permanent impression on the socio-cultural history of nineteenth-century Bengal. He died at the age of twenty-two in December 1831.

Strangely enough, the house where Madhu lived in Kidderpore also had a connection with Derozio. Before Madhu moved into it, Kashiprasad Ghosh used to live there. Kashiprasad was one of Derozio's students and the first Bengali poet to write in English. Derozio's poetry had influenced him greatly, particularly his ardent patriotism. Although Derozio was only twenty-two when he died, he left an extraordinary impact both on Hindu College and on the literary circles in Calcutta.

two sides to it. On the one hand, he was a Romantic poet, his chief asset being his imagination. On the other hand, he was a firm believer in reason and logic. His followers, influenced by his rational thinking, gave up most of the traditional values. Twelve years after Derozio was forced to leave Hindu College, James Kerr became its principal. Kerr was a man Madhu disliked intensely. This is what Kerr said about Derozio:

Derozio's followers developed a tendency to examine everything in the light of rationalism. God, the future, relations within the family, things that we look upon more with emotion than cold reason, began to be questioned by Derozio's followers, once they had adopted his own beliefs.†

The rise of scepticism among the students caused great anxiety not only to their guardians, but the entire middle-class society in Calcutta. As a result, Derozio had to leave the college long before it was time for him to do so.

When Madhu joined Hindu College, more than one journal was being published by Derozio's students. In these, there was always an open invitation to question established beliefs. The same group of students also formed societies where Hinduism was attacked frequently. Although Madhu did not actually take part in these protests, he could not help hearing about them.

His main contact with Derozio was through poetry. Some called Derozio the 'Anglo-Indian Byron'. But Madhu was influenced by other Romantic poets as well, such as Scott, Moore, Burns. The patriotism for which he is now so well known came not only from Derozio, but also another Romantic poet, Thomas Campbell. The vigour and liveliness that ran through Campbell's poetry left its mark on the young Madhu in his early days.

Derozio's influence on Madhu worked in another way, quite apart from literature. Many of Derozio's followers had broken away from their families and risked social ostracism, to stand by their beliefs and what they saw as the truth. Needless to say, such an act called for indomitable courage. Some of these men were Krishnamohan Bandyopadhyay,[2] Rashik Krishna

---

[2] Krishnamohan Bandyopadhyay (1813–85) was one of the students of Henry V. L. Derozio. He was profoundly influenced by Derozio and lost his faith in Hinduism, especially in the social customs associated with Hinduism. He was one of the early converts to Christianity from among high-caste Hindus. He later became a priest. Apart from his missionary work, he was

Mallik,[3] Dakshinaranjan Mukhopadhyay,[4] and Maheshchandra Ghosh.[5] Their concern for religious and social reform was so intense that they took several bold decisions which not many would have dreamed of. Unlike them, Madhu did not oppose his family and society in order to fight superstition or social injustice. In his case, what he regarded as 'truth' was his poetry and his individuality. When these were threatened, and his family stood in his way, Madhu did not hesitate to give up his personal comfort and turn away from those who were his own.

A few years after Derozio's departure from Hindu College—in 1835 or 1836—the man who joined the college to teach English literature had once been in the army. His name was Captain David Lester Richardson (1801–65), and he came to be known as DLR. In 1819, he joined the Bengal Army as a cadet and soon proved his mettle. Some say that he eventually became a major. However, his real weapon was not his gun, but his pen. He was a poet in his heart and soul. When he left the army and was assigned civic duties, he served for a while under Governor-General Bentinck, before moving to the education department. In 1827 he returned to England, where he published a journal called the *London Weekly Review*. Two and a half years later, he came back to Calcutta.

---

known for his scholarship. He published a number of books, of which a Bengali encyclopaedia called *Bidyakalpadrum* was the best known. One of his sons-in-law was Jnanendramohun Tagore, the first Bengali barrister and the son of Prasannakumar Tagore.

[3] Rasik Krishna Mallik (1810–58) was well known for his honesty and truthfulness as well as for his opposition to traditional Hinduism. He lost his job at a school for criticizing Hinduism, and was driven away from his parental home.

[4] Dakshinaranjan Mukhopadhyay (1814–78) was a favourite student of Derozio and later came to be known as an ardent social reformer. Even before the Widow Remarriage Act was passed in 1856, he married a widow. He was also one of the few who started criticizing the East India Company's exploitation of India, as early as the 1840s.

[5] Maheshchandra Ghosh (1813–37) was another follower of Derozio. A staunch critic of Hinduism, he converted to Christianity soon after Krishnamohan Bandyopadhyay in 1832. He went on to study Christianity in Bishop's College. However, it appears from the Bishop's College records that he drowned in 1837 while he was still a student of that college.

At first, he became the editor of the *Bengal Annual*, and then the *Calcutta Literary Gazette*. In addition to that, he published his own poetry and essays. His first book of poems, *Miscellaneous Poems*, was published in London. Apart from that, his *Sonnets and Other Poems* also came out in London, in 1825. In 1836, *Literary Leaves* was published. Until 1855, he produced other collections of poems, as well as reviews of poetry. However, what is important is not so much the number of his books, but the quality of his work and the standards he set in literary reviews. On the basis of those alone, he may be judged as the best among British-Indian litterateurs of the time. Macaulay was one of his admirers. It was on Macaulay's recommendation that he joined Hindu College as a teacher of literature, replacing Dr Tytler when the latter retired.

Within a short time, it became obvious that Richardson's ability to teach was as great as his ability to write. Derozio and David Hare had already established a tradition of paying individual attention to students, and treating them with compassion. Richardson took that tradition further forward. In their memoirs, many of his students talked about his teaching and mentioned how good he was with them. Rajnarayan Basu, for instance, is quite extravagant in his praise:

Captain sahib had a remarkable grasp of English literature. I have never seen or heard anyone else read from Shakespeare—and explain the text—so well.... I cannot describe the love and reverence I feel whenever I think of him.... It is not as if his character was totally faultless, yet I have these feelings for him.[†]

Even Macaulay said of him that he, Macaulay, might forget everything about India, but he would never forget the lines from Shakespeare that he had heard Richardson recite.[†] If Richardson had not lived overseas, thousands of miles from home, he might have found recognition in England, too. It is likely that Richardson himself was aware of this, and hence tried, from Calcutta, to maintain contact with the English Romantic poets. Leigh Hunt was one of them. A few letters from Richardson were retrieved from Hunt's papers[†] in later years.

Richardson, like Derozio, proved to be an extraordinary teacher. However, there was little else they had in common. Derozio taught logic, philosophy, and literature. He believed very strongly in the need to be aware of philosophical and social issues, as well as literary matters. But Richardson had no interest in philosophy. 'Derozio laid emphasis on reading Locke, Hume and Paine. In DLR's time, they were replaced by Byron, Keats, Shelley and other Romantic poets,' says Dhirendranath Ghosh.[†] DLR was not concerned about social upheavals or politics; and he remained unquestionably loyal to the government. Derozio was not afraid to criticize the government. DLR, on the other hand, thought such views amounted to treason. A particular incident may be mentioned in this context.

On 8 February 1843, a meeting was held in the hall of Sanskrit College. At that meeting, Dakshinaranjan Mukhopadhyay, one of Derozio's old students, stood up to read an article on the courts and the police in Bengal. As soon as the subject of the article became clear, DLR stopped Mukhopadhyay from reading it any further. But the *Hurkaru* newspaper published it the following month. This little incident reveals DLR's attitude. When it came to dealing with social issues, his advice to his students ran along rather conservative lines.

The differences in their characters affected the students of Derozio and DLR in different ways. Derozio's followers chiefly became social reformers. Those that DLR influenced became writers. Madhu was truly fortunate to have found someone like DLR to teach him literature right from the beginning. That was the reason why his interest in and his knowledge of literature became so profound. Both showed a direct influence of Richardson. In the letters Madhu wrote, there are occasional references to history, but none to philosophy, or a single philosopher. The social awareness that students in the 1830s possessed, and their desire to bring about reforms, were virtually non-existent in Madhu. It is an indirect indication of how deeply Richardson influenced him.

In 1840, on Macaulay's request, Richardson published an anthology of British poetry, called *Selections from the British Poets* from the time of Chaucer to the present day. It ran into more than a thousand pages. Not only did it help his students in building and developing their taste in literature, but it also introduced them to English poets, ranging from Chaucer to the young Tennyson (who was then thirty-one); Derozio to Richardson, even Kashiprasad Ghosh, the contemporary Indian poet who wrote in English. Five complete plays of Shakespeare were included, and selected portions of a sixth. A large section of Milton's poetry was included, too.

Perhaps it was through this collection that Madhu came to know Milton's works so well. Translations of the works of other European poets formed a whole section, which featured Homer, Virgil, Dante, Tasso, Goethe and others. The poetry was accompanied by a short biography of each poet, and an article on his style and other characteristics. It was the addition of these two features that made the book so special. Madhu was so impressed by it that he is said to have told his friends, 'If only *I* could write such an Introduction!'

Richardson began working as the principal of Hindu College from 1839, two years after Madhu joined it. It did not take long for Madhu—a bright student and a young poet—to attract the attention of his principal. It is likely that DLR inspired him to write poetry. The earliest poems written by Madhu that have been located are dated 1841. These show quite clearly that Madhu had started to write poetry long before that date. In his early days, Madhu wrote several sonnets. It was undoubtedly an unusual thing for a young poet to do, particularly one whose mother tongue was not English. But that might be another indication of Richardson's influence, since he was always partial to sonnets. DLR soon grew quite fond of his young student.

Madhu, too, realized that his principal treated him with special affection. For him, it was an important realization because, in later life, like the North Star, it showed him his way forward. For his part, he held DLR in such high esteem that, on one occasion, when DLR was away on leave, Madhu decided he would stop going to college. One reason for taking such a decision (although he did, in the end, change his mind) was that he did not like James Kerr, DLR's replacement. How far Kerr himself was responsible for Madhu's dislike, we do not know. He might have done things to incur Madhu's displeasure, but whatever it was, Madhu is very likely to have overreacted, only because of his strong loyalty to DLR.

It may be pertinent here to take a look at the syllabus that was taught at Hindu College. Both the junior and senior branches had moral philosophy. The junior branch was taught Abercrombie's *Intellectual Powers,* Waitley's *Easy Lessons in Reasoning,* Russell's *Modern Europe,* and Tytler's *Universal History.* Essays by Goldsmith and Addison were also taught, as well as mathematics and Bengali. In the senior division, the students read the Text Book Society's *English Reader,* Murray's *English Grammar,* Crombie's

Etymology and Syntax, and Marshman's *History of Bengal*. When DLR's anthology of poetry was published, it was added to the syllabus of both divisions. In the final two years, known as the 'college' division, Milton, Shakespeare, Pope, and Gray were taught, as well as Bacon. During their history lessons, the students were taught from Hume's *History of England*, Gibbon's *The Decline and Fall of the Roman Empire*, Meatford's *History of Greece* and many other books, including some on Indian history.

It is not difficult to see that it was this syllabus that introduced Madhu not only to the best that English literature had to offer, but also to European classical literature, with which he became quite familiar. He was not interested in philosophy, but history was another subject he learnt thoroughly. Later, when he went to Madras to teach, and to edit a journal, his knowledge of history helped him a great deal.

Bengali was also taught at the college and, at the time, there were two Bengali teachers—Ramchandra Mitra and Ramtanu Lahiri. Both were well known—the former for his publications and the latter for his contributions to social reform. Moreover, from his later correspondence, it seems Madhu personally liked and had a great deal of respect for both of them. However, the students of Hindu College, including Madhu, did not appear to pay much attention to learning Bengali, their own language. In 1841, Ramkamal Sen was the examiner for Bengali. He was very disappointed with the results. He wrote:

In short, they appear to understand English better than their own language, to which they attach little or no interest in comparison with English.†

Another subject that Madhu and his fellow students learned little about was science. In fact, it was wholly absent from their syllabus. It is true that Bengalis at the time had not started studying it in any detail. But schools in England were already teaching science. There were excellent facilities in some places for carrying out scientific experiments. Shelley was deeply influenced by his study of science, and was known to have started a fire more than once while conducting experiments. It is difficult to tell why the British in India did not find it necessary to include science in the school syllabus. Perhaps they did not want to create scientists and their chief intention was to create clerks. Whatever the reason, the fact remains that Madhu did not learn science. But he was fully aware that science was crucial in the development and progress of mankind. That is why, when he wrote a poem describing how the students of Hindu College would one day bring glory to their motherland, he laid emphasis on the role of science:

> Oh! how my heart exulteth while I see
> These future flow'rs, to deck my country's brow,
> Thus kindly nurtured in the nursery!—
> Perchance, unmark'd some here are budding now,
> Whose temples shall laureate-wreaths be crown'd
> Twined by the Sisters Nine: whose angel-tongues
> Shall charm the world with their enchanting songs.
> And time shall waft the echo of each sound
> To distant ages:—some, perchance, here are,
> Who, with a Newton's glance, shall nobly trace
> The course mysterious of each wandering star;
> And, like a God, unveil the hidden face
> Of many a planet to man's wandering eye,
> And give their names to immortality.

Apart from a good education, what Madhu acquired in Hindu College was a small but loyal group of friends. It was not easy for him to make friends, for he was reserved, shy, and an introvert. He liked going out with this small and select group, and mixed freely with them. Even so, he did not confide in them about his own personal problems, or his innermost thoughts. Some of these friends remained in touch with him all his life, and eventually became well known among the intellectuals of Bengal.

The oldest friend who can be traced was Bhudeb Mukhopadhyay. Bhudeb went to Sanskrit College and three other smaller schools before he joined Hindu College, with the chief purpose of learning English. Madhu made the first move to get to know him. Both were good-looking, both bright students, and both the only son of their parents. A close friendship developed between them quite soon, although in the matter of social consciousness, the two were entirely different. Bhudeb was most conservative in his outlook, while Madhu was a radical. It is actually surprising how such an enduring friendship could develop between them. Perhaps Bhudeb's good looks were a reason.

In 1841, Bhudeb ran into financial difficulties and it began to seem as if he would have to leave college. At the time, the monthly tuition fee in Hindu College was five rupees, which was a lot of money. As soon as Madhu heard about his friend's difficulties, he offered to pay the fees from his own pocket money. This is a clear indication of their closeness, and how much Madhu cared for his friend. However, a few years later, when Madhu became a Christian and added 'Michael' to his name, Bhudeb could not forgive him. According to Bhudeb, turning into a Christian harmed Madhu to such a degree that even physically, he appeared dull and lacklustre.

After this event, the two friends drifted apart a little, but Madhu could not forget this friend he had known since his adolescence. Even many years later, when he returned from England as a barrister, very much a pukka sahib, he visited Bhudeb in a village outside Calcutta, dressed in traditional Bengali clothes, and had lunch with him, sitting on the floor. Besides, he dedicated one of his works, *Hektor-badh* (The Slaying of Hektor), to Bhudeb. It was written at a time when Madhu was weak and ailing, and was never completed.

Apart from Bhudeb, the man who remained a lifelong friend, and to whom Madhu was the closest, was Gourdas Basak. They met in 1840. It is not known where Gourdas studied before joining Hindu College. He stood by Madhu, through thick and thin, until the final years of Madhu's life. Madhu wrote innumerable letters to him from his house in Kidderpore, or from Madras, and then from Versailles. Of these, seventy letters have been traced. In these letters, the language Madhu has used to express his love for Gour is similar to that used by one lover for another. Eight of his first fifty poems were either dedicated to Gour, or written about him. In one of them, Madhu made this promise:

> Tho' short, oh! too short is the time we've, My Gour!
> To meet on this side of the tomb, killing thought!
> Yet Friendship and Love shall be e'er ours, My Gour!
> Where'er may Fate land me, thou shan't be forgot!

It seems from these lines that his love for Gour ran into something deeper than friendship. The truth is that his feelings for Gourdas were totally different from his feelings for Bhudeb, both in nature and degree.

In 1840, Madhu made two more friends—Bankubihari Dutta and Shyamacharan Law. Bhudeb, Gour, Bankubihari, Shyamacharan, and Madhu were all good students. In 1841, all of them won scholarships, but more importantly, all were promoted from the fifth class straight to the second in the senior section of the college. Like Gour, Bankubihari became a close friend. He has spoken of the times when he spent a few days in Madhu's house. Madhu's parents, particularly his mother, also treated Bankubihari with great affection. Another close friend of Madhu was Bholanath Chandra, who later became well known as an author and social reformer.

Among the other students who later came into Madhu's life was Rajnarayan Basu. In 1840, he came from David Hare's school to Hindu College, and joined the fourth class. Madhu was then a couple of years junior to him; but in 1842, when he was promoted to the second class, he became Rajnarayan's classmate. It took them some time to get to know each other, possibly because the older students did not look very kindly upon the five younger ones who were allowed to skip three years and join a higher class. Moreover, Rajnarayan had also won a scholarship, and had considerable knowledge of literature. It would not be surprising if for these reasons he felt a little envious of Madhu and decided initially to ignore him. They met one day in the house of Ramtanu Lahiri, one of the teachers in their college. It was there that Rajnarayan was impressed by Madhu's ability to freely recite lines from Milton and Shakespeare. He did feel pangs of envy, but could not help feeling, at the same time, a new respect for Madhu.

It appears that in the matter of reading, there was a healthy competition between Madhu and his friends. From some of Madhu's letters written to Gour, it is clear that Gour, too, was fond of reading books and journals outside their prescribed syllabus. Madhu came to be known as a 'bookworm', which shows how much he used to read, even at that young age. However, the reason why Madhu read so much was different from that which applied to some of his friends. The others simply wanted to do well in exams. Madhu was genuinely interested in learning more, although he did very well in exams, too. It was because of this love for learning that Madhu later turned into not so much a Romantic poet as a scholar poet. It was due to this cast of mind that he developed a great admiration and liking for Milton's poetry.

Mathematics was a subject he did not much care about. But if he put his mind to it, he could perform better than the others. On one occasion, he is said to have solved a problem that no one else could, and remarked, 'See? If Shakespeare had so wished, he could have been a Newton; but Newton could never have been a Shakespeare.'

Rangalal Bandyopadhyay was another man to whom Madhu referred as 'my childhood playmate from Kidderpore'. In actual fact, Rangalal came to live permanently in Calcutta as Madhu's neighbour in 1843, after Rangalal's mother died. Around the same time, Madhu became a Christian and moved out of Kidderpore. So it is not likely that the two were very close. It could be that Rangalal had paid brief visits to Madhu's neighbour, Ramkamal Mukhopadhyay's (Rangalal's uncle) house before 1843, and played with Madhu when both were younger. It is true that Rangalal and his two brothers addressed Madhu's mother as 'Ma'. But that came about possibly after 1843, when Madhu left home and Janhabi Debi effectively lost her only child. The three boys next door had recently lost their mother, so a natural bond of sympathy grew between her and the boys.

※※※

There were certain Romantic poets that Madhu worshipped, but none so much as Byron. He developed this love for Byron partly through the influence of DLR. Madhu's love for Byron was so great that he not only read his poems, and his biography by Thomas Moore (published in 1838), but started imitating everything that Byron had done. He even imitated Byron's letters. However, by the time Madhu himself emerged as a poet, he was considerably older than these British poets, who had started to write at a much younger age. Byron and Shelley's works had been published in their early adolescence. Perhaps Madhu's development as a poet was delayed by the fact that he spent his childhood in a village, and had to make a fresh start in Calcutta. Whatever the case, it cannot be denied that it was in Hindu College that the foundations of his life as a poet were laid. The person who made the deepest impact was, of course, Richardson; but most of the other teachers, the subjects they taught and their own views and interests—all these contributed to Madhu's development.

In fact, his college did not just teach him about poetry and literature. It helped to shape his mind, his whole outlook.

Madhu was always opposed to old and traditional practices, in virtually every sphere of life. Although—unlike some of his senior contemporaries—Madhu was not a social reformer, in his own way he was a rebel. One reason for this was that he was highly indulged by his family, and allowed to get away with everything he did. But that was not the only reason.

Let us reflect on a story related by Gourdas in his reminiscences. Once they had become friends, Madhu visited him in his house a few times. Then he invited Gour to his own, together with another boy called Bholanath Chandra. The two boys dressed with care, and turned up at Madhu's house, as requested. The sight that met their eyes made them take a step backwards. They found Rajnarayan Dutt smoking a hookah. When he finished, he passed its long pipe to his son. Madhu took it from his father, quite unperturbed, and began smoking with great relish. It is difficult to say how heavily such a scene would have been frowned on in the 1840s. Certainly, it was not customary for young men to smoke in the presence of someone older. When Gourdas eventually found his tongue and asked Madhu to explain, Madhu told him that his father, unlike other guardians, did not care about such trivial matters.

Some believe that, even at that young age, Madhu used to have a drink before going to bed. One of his friends, Bankubihari, maintained that this was true. But one cannot be sure whether such was indeed the case, or whether his friends and previous biographers simply made that assumption in view of his legendary drinking in later years.† However, it is true that drinking, in those days, was not as uncommon as it is thought to be. Nor was it considered a deplorable vice. Many educated Bengalis drank, some because it was seen as being fashionable; and others because they thought they could break their ties with old conventions by drinking. It was seen as a sign of being progressive.

Madhu's friend, Rajnarayan Basu, was a heavy drinker. In his autobiography, Rajnarayan gave an elaborate description of how he started drinking every night with his father. Later, when he became addicted to drinking, he found others, especially his classmates, to drink with. He became such a heavy drinker that he fell ill and had to leave Hindu College early. In 1846, when he became a Brahmo, he ate biscuits and drank alcohol as a symbolic gesture to indicate that he was forsaking old values and customs.

Eating biscuits was considered most improper by Hindus as they were made by either Muslims or Christians.

Other well-known figures in Bengal also drank regularly, including Rammohan Roy who started the Brahmo movement, and Debendranath Tagore, who propagated Brahmoism with considerable spiritual zeal. In 1851, he decided to stop drinking as a result of Akshaykumar Dutt's influence on him. In his play, *Is This Called Civilization?*, Madhu drew a very good picture of how the westernized young men of those days viewed drinking. Rajnarayan Basu offered this explanation:

At that time, the students of Hindu College used to think drinking was a sign of being civilized, there was nothing wrong with it. They drank, but they did not go to whores. A generation ago, men did not drink, but frequently visited brothels. They smoked *ganja* and *charas*, flew kites, laying bets on who could fly them better; wore their hair long, and draped themselves in fine *dhoti*s from Dhaka. The young men of our college did not indulge in any of these passions.†

Rajnarayan and Madhu were not particularly close while they were in college. Their friendship developed much later. Had they been more intimate as fellow students, perhaps Rajnarayan would have found Madhu a companion in Gol Deeghi, where he went to drink. But no matter what he felt about drinking, Madhu, like the other students of his college, had no time for prostitutes.

It is not known whether Madhu's family were devotees of Kali, the goddess of power; but, like the worshippers of Kali, they were fond of eating meat. In a letter to Gour, Madhu offered to take him on a boat ride, and said he would bring biscuits and mutton patties. It was perhaps an attempt to tempt his friend. Gourdas came from a strictly vegetarian Vaishnav family. But the growing popularity of meat affected him as well. He had his first taste of meat in Madhu's house, and admitted to enjoying it very much. Other friends also ate meat with Madhu, either in his house, or when Madhu took them out to a restaurant. In fact, several students of Hindu College, including Rajnarayan Basu, had no objection to eating beef either. In his autobiography, Rajnarayan has said that sometimes they became so impatient that, instead of leaving through the college gate, he and his friends would climb over the wall to go out of the building, so that they could go and buy kababs. It is not known whether Madhu, too, ate beef that early in his life. But it is clear that he kept an open mind not only about biscuits and alcohol, but other food items as well.

It is not difficult to judge Madhu's attitude towards his elders from the fact that he did not mind smoking a hookah with his father. He was not disrespectful towards them, but it is quite clear that, unlike many others, he did not consider all the established rules of social behaviour as important. A few years later, when a marriage was arranged for him, he decided to leave home and make a life for himself, wholly disregarding his father's command and his mother's tears. The seed of rebellion was sown in his mind long before this event actually took place. He broke the norm in virtually everything that he did. Bhudeb Mukhopadhyay wrote in his reminiscences about Madhu's new haircut, which copied the style sported by Englishmen. But what has turned into a legend is the story of his spending a gold mohar simply on a haircut. Even in his attire Madhu was different. He did begin by wearing dhotis, but later started wearing an *achkan*, or a jacket and trousers. Judging by the reminiscences of some of his contemporaries, no student in Hindu College had ever worn Western clothes before Madhu.

It may be pertinent here to examine Madhu's views on women, which—again—were very different to those held traditionally. At a time when women were seen as little more than inanimate objects, only to be used and enjoyed by men, Madhu looked upon them in a different light. His views and attitude became clear in the essay he wrote on women's education for an essay competition in 1842, for which he won a gold medal. The silver medal went to his friend, Bhudeb. Madhu did not forget to make the most important point, that unless a mother was educated herself, she could not educate her children; but what he added further was this:

Extensive dissemination of knowledge amongst women is the surest way that leads a nation to civilization and refinement, for it is a woman who first gives ideas to the future philosopher and the would-be poet. The happiness of a man who has an enlightened partner is quite complete.... In India, I may say in all the Oriental countries, women are looked upon as created merely to contribute to the gratification of the animal appetites of men. This brutal misconception of the design of the Almighty is the source of much misery to the fair sex, because it not only makes them appear as of inferior mental endowments, but no better than a sort of speaking brutes. The people of this country do not know the pleasure of domestic life, and indeed they cannot know, until civilization shows them the way to attain it.

The education of women, to Madhu, was a prerequisite for domestic happiness and a sure sign of progress. Only an educated woman could be a true partner for a man, and his soul-mate. Madhu was known to quote a Persian poet to prove that a woman with an enlightened mind was more precious than all the jewels of Bukhara and Samarkand. According to his friends, and even his mother, it was Madhu's belief that no Bengali woman could ever match either the beauty or other virtues that English women possessed. Since they were uneducated, there would always be something gravely lacking in the relationship between Bengali women and their husbands. As things turned out, Madhu proved in his later years that he believed in this idea wholeheartedly; it was not just something he chose to write in an essay.

Gourdas has said that falling in love at first sight was an idea that appealed greatly to Madhu. Needless to say, the thought of marrying the woman of his own choice, and not one chosen by someone else, came to him only through his close studies of Western literature, and the lives of some of the English writers. Normally, at the time, most young men were happy to marry whoever their guardians chose. Besides, unless there was a specific problem, virtually every girl was married before she turned twelve. The question of courtship simply did not arise. Yet, Madhu dreamed of courting the girl with whom he might one day fall in love.

The particular branch of English literature that captured Madhu's heart was Romantic poetry. He read every famous and lesser-known Romantic poet, from Wordsworth to Campbell; but Byron remained his favourite. Unlike his classmates, he was not satisfied with just the poems included in Richardson's compilation. He wanted to read other works by the same poets and learn about their lives. In fact, he went a step ahead and began, consciously, to imitate those that he admired. Once he became more familiar with classical literature, Madhu's passion for Romantic poetry waned. But his love for Byron's works lasted longer than that for any other Romantic poet.

One reason why Madhu's parents pampered him so much was that he had emerged as one of the brightest students in his class. They had lots of dreams regarding his future, and were naturally very proud of him. If they were sad that they had no other child, the fact that Madhu was so brilliant made up for such an absence. Rajnarayan Dutt and Janhabi Debi must have both wanted to find a suitable, pretty young girl for him, so that their son would be happy, well settled in life, and could bring them further pride and glory.

Neither could have imagined that Madhu would do just the opposite, by turning away from his home and his family, leaving them forever.

It is not known exactly when Madhu started to write poetry, but it was presumably before he turned seventeen. Seven of his earliest poems are dated 1841. Judging by the language, rhythm, and style of these early poems, Madhu had already had some practice in writing poetry. As an example, we may look at this oft-quoted poem, written in 1841:

> I sigh for Albion's distant shore,
> Its valleys green, its mountains high;
> Tho' friends, relations, I have none
> In that far clime, yet oh! I sigh
> To cross the vast Atlantic wave
> For glory, or a nameless grave!
>
> ~ ~ ~
>
> My father, mother, sister, all
> Do love me and I love them, too
> Yet oft the tear-drops rush and fall
> From my sad eyes like winter's dew.
> And, oh! I sigh for Albion's stand
> As if she were my native land.

The Albion for which he sighed or shed tears had no high mountains; there was no need to cross a turbulent Atlantic in order to get there from India; nor was a sister weeping for him at home. Yet, the poem does not lack emotion, or true poetic qualities. Clearly, the poet was not a complete novice; he must have started writing at least two years prior to the date on this poem.

An analysis of the poetry written in his teens highlights some special features: a deep longing, and tumultuous emotions. At the time, Madhu had not met any 'blue-eyed maid' or fallen in love. The only person he could express his love to was Gourdas. Yet, with an 'aching heart' he dreamed of the 'blue-eyed maid' and laid his heart bare at the feet of that unreal dream.

Shelley, at the age of sixteen, had found his cousin, Harriet, and fallen in love with her. She did not return his love, but raised no objection to Shelley addressing his poems to her. Poor Madhu found no one, even from a distance, to whom he might have addressed, or dedicated his poems. In the absence of such a person, he dedicated many of his poems to Gour.

As time went by, the youthful passion in Madhu's poetry gave way to a new maturity. Around 1843, he wrote a poem like *King Porus*. It was his longest poem to date, running into six stanzas. The first and the last were structured in a similar fashion; the remaining four were all different. It was published in the *Literary Gleaner* magazine. It marks the beginning of Madhu's interest in narrative poetry. The short lyrical poems that he started to write under Richardson's influence had very little 'substance' in them, most of them being full of sighing and longing. Once an element of story-telling entered his poetry, the frothy emotions disappeared and it took on a more definite shape.

King Porus contained another aspect of Madhu's vision. It was his patriotism. The West attracted him greatly; in 1841 he wrote of Albion 'as if she is my native land'. But, two years later, in *King Porus*, his language changed:

But where, oh! Where is Porus now?
Where the noble hearts that bled
For Freedom—with the heroic glow
In patriot-bosoms nourish'd—
—Hearts, eagle-like that recked not Death,
But shrank before foul Thraldom's breath?
And where art thou—fair Freedom!—thou
Once goddess of Ind's sunny clime!
When glory's halo 'round her brow
Shone radiant, and she rose sublime.
Like her own towering Himalaya
To kiss the blue cloud thron'd on high!

When this poem was written, India's struggle for independence had not started, nor had nationalism spread its roots. Even so, his love and pride for his motherland are quite obvious. This feeling lasted until the day he died.

Towards the end of 1841, Madhu produced a handwritten magazine. It proved to be an important and useful tool for self-expression. Like other writers, Madhu had the desire to be read by a wider range of people and win acclaim. It is not known whether he had read the biography of Shelley as well as that of Byron; but it is known that before his poems were published in journals, Shelley borrowed some money from his grandfather and had a collection of poems written by his sister and himself, printed for distribution among his friends. Madhu did a similar thing. He had a few poems privately printed, before he could find a publisher. One assumes he showed them to his friends. In view of the strong need to be recognized by a large number of people, the handwritten magazine played an important role. It remained in existence for only three or four months, but even in that short time, Madhu earned the envy of senior students, and praise from his principal. Richardson read every issue of this magazine, and encouraged the young Madhu by advising him on how to improve his technique.

It may be that Richardson also told him that he had the potential for becoming a great poet, for it was from this time that Madhu began to dream, with growing conviction, of attaining that goal. He mentioned this to Gourdas, and even told him that he would love it if Gour could one day write his biography. There is no doubt that Richardson's encouragement strengthened his self-confidence. In that respect, it must be admitted that, short-lived though it was, the handwritten magazine made a significant contribution towards the making of a poet.

From 1842, Madhu's poems began to be published in such journals as the *Literary Gleaner, Calcutta Literary Gazette, Bengal Herald, Oriental Magazine,* and *Comet.* The *Literary Gleaner* was the first to print his poems. Once he had gained a larger readership, Madhu no longer needed the handwritten magazine, and so it ceased to exist from early 1842.

Only a few months after seeing his poems printed in magazines in Calcutta, Madhu's confidence grew so much that on 4 October 1842, he sent some poems to the *Blackwood's Magazine* in England. What he said in his letter to the editor is not known. However, a few days later, he sent some more poems to *Bentley's Miscellany*, also in England. The letter that accompanied those poems has been traced. It said:

Sir,

It is not without much fear that I send you the accompanying productions of my juvenile Muse, as contribution to your Periodical. The magnanimity with which you always encourage the aspirants to 'Literary Fame' induces me to commit myself to you. 'Fame', Sir, is not my object at present; for I am really conscious I do not deserve it;—all that I require is Encouragement. I have a strong conviction that a Public like the British—discerning, generous and magnanimous—will not damp the spirit of a poor foreigner. I am a Hindu—a native of Bengal—and study English at the Hindu College in Calcutta. I am now in my eighteenth year,—'a child'—to use the language of a poet of your land, Cowley, 'in learning, but not in age'.

The poems he selected to send to *Bentley* had initially been dedicated to Gourdas. However, it occurred to Madhu now that the name of his friend would mean nothing to the people in England. So he dedicated the whole lot to Wordsworth. Alas, that did not work, and *Bentley* did not print his poems. Madhu was doubtless severely disappointed, and convinced that they had failed to recognize true talent.

The very fact that he thought a magazine in England would publish what he had written shows how confident he was about the standard of his poetry. It cannot be denied that Madhu did think very highly of himself, and considered himself superior to others. But it was not just arrogance that made him write to those English magazines. It was simply that he was totally immersed in the joy of creation. That was what gave him such confidence.

Eventually, of course, Madhu was not satisfied with just sending his poetry to journals in England. He became convinced that in order to achieve greatness as a poet he had to go there himself. It is not easy to say exactly when or where this idea began to grow. The poem in which he pines for Albion indicates that he was already thinking of going overseas. In 1842, he again expressed the wish to go to England. In fact, this desire was so strong that he said his own motherland, to him, felt like a prison:

> Oft like a sad imprisoned bird I sigh
> To leave this land; though mine own land it be;
> Its green robed meads,—gay flowers and cloudless sky
> Though passing fair, have but few charms for me.

The natural beauty of his own country had made an everlasting impression on his mind. However, he was so attracted by Albion's land that it was only visiting that distant country that he cherished:

> For I have dreamed of climes more bright and free
> Where virtue dwells and heaven-born liberty
> Makes even the lowest happy;—where the eye
> Doth sicken not to see man bend the knee
> To sordid interest;—climes where science thrives
> And genius does receive her guerdon meet;
> Where man in all his truest glory lives,
> And Nature's face is exquisitely sweet;
> For those fair climes I heave the impatient sigh,
> There let me live and there let me die.

In England, the Romantic poets were in close contact with one another. They discussed their work and, as a result, one would influence the other. The contact between Byron, Shelley, Keats, Moor, and Hunt is particularly noteworthy. In Madhu's case, there was no one with whom he could discuss his poetry, or gain anything by such a discussion. Could that be the reason why he began dreaming of going to England? Certainly, he was afraid that in his own country true recognition might not come his way. Richardson himself did not get his due because he spent most of his life away from England. It is likely that he expressed his regret before his students. That must have fuelled Madhu's desire to visit England—the land that awarded true merit to poets.

At the time, very few Bengalis had been to Britain. In the eighteenth century, a handful of men and women had gone as servants and ayahs, but nobody from the educated upper classes had dared to undertake the journey. The first educated man from Bengal to visit England was Mirza Abu Talib Khan (1752-1806). He was sent to Europe by the Nawab of Murshidabad in 1799. He visited different countries in Europe and lived in England for three years. On his return to Bengal he wrote a book describing his experiences in those countries. The book was published in 1803 and later translated into a number of European languages including English, French, and German. However, among educated Bengalis, it was Rammohan Roy who was the first to set foot on British soil in 1830, followed by Dwarakanath Tagore in 1842, and then in 1846. Rammohan was labelled a traitor who had abandoned his own people and religion; and although Dwarakanath was wealthy enough to buy several people off, traditional Hindus strongly disapproved of him.

Going to England, of course, was an expensive business. It was also considered a sin by Bengali Hindu society. Therefore, those who did have the money feared social ostracism. In fact, even towards the end of the nineteenth century, many orthodox Hindus were still refusing permission to re-enter society to those who had been overseas and crossed 'kalapani' (literally, 'the black waters'). In 1894, a society was formed in Calcutta to protect such people. Many had to go through a ritual and a process of 'penance' before their families accepted them back. In short, Madhu had no example of a fellow Bengali who had gone to Britain. Why, then, did that idea take such a firm hold on his mind? It is yet another reflection of his rebellious spirit.

But then, at the time—or perhaps all his life—Madhu was prepared to make any number of sacrifices for the sake of his poetry. Sometimes, his friends referred to him as 'Pope'. It was because the poet, Alexander Pope, had said somewhere that in order to serve poetry, one must be prepared to forsake everything, even one's family. Madhu believed in this philosophy with all his heart.

Would his parents allow him to go to England? Madhu must have asked himself this question several times. He might even have raised the subject with his mother, though he knew very well that, indulgent though they were, his parents would never allow him to travel all the way to England. So he mentioned his desire only to Gourdas, who must have pointed out at once that Madhu would have to face parental opposition. In reply to that, Madhu wrote to him in November 1842, declaring that he was prepared to do what Pope had said, and leave his family. He did not know then that soon, there would be enormous problems over the question of his marriage. So, certainly at that particular moment, his dream of going to England was related only to his wish to be recognized as a great poet.

In 1842, he went to Tamluk and wrote to Gourdas from there: 'I am grieved to think that I will not meet ye to-morrow; but, Gour, there's one consolation for me. I am come nearer that sea which will perhaps see me at a period (which I hope is not far off) ploughing its bosom for "England's glorious shore". The sea from this place is not very far: what number of ships have I seen going to England!' It is clear from this letter that the thought of going to England had become almost an obsession.

The fact was that despite the affection his parents showered on him, Madhu had started to drift away from them, perhaps unconsciously. His hopes, aspirations, even his values were different from the average man's. It does not seem likely that his parents were fully aware of these 'extraordinary' qualities in him; nor did they appreciate the fact that he was now a young man, an individual in his own right. However, in August 1842, something happened to create a conflict between father and son. The details of what happened are not known, but Rajnarayan ordered Madhu to leave Calcutta immediately and go back to their village, Sagardari. Presumably, Rajnarayan's intention was partly to discipline his son, and partly to keep him away from his friends for a few days. On 7 August, Madhu wrote to Gour:

True too, true my dearest Gour! The storm has at last hurled upon me! I am ordered to depart from own [sic] this very night for our country-house. But Oh! where shall I go? Had I had the power of opening my heart, I could then show you the state of my feelings! Language cannot point them! To leave the friends I love—particularly ONE,—(imagine who that 'one' could be) my poor heart can't but break! Well, may I exclaim in the language of the poet,—'Oh! insupportable, Oh! heavy grief!'—I wish I could see you;—but Oh! that cannot be!—I am not allowed! dear, dear, Gour! dearest friend! do not forget me!

If I do not start tonight, I shall see you tomorrow at the College. As I am to embark at Balliaghata, I shall once step into the College when I go there. Your Byron shall be sent tomorrow with the fatal letter to Mr Kerr. Farewell! I don't know when I shall return from my country-house. When you go to the Mechanic's give my compliments to Harris. 'FAREWELL FOREVER'.

This letter shows how distraught he was at the thought of leaving Calcutta. It also shows that Madhu had not yet found the courage to disobey his father. However, as it happened, he was spared on that occasion and did not, after all, have to go to Sagardari. Perhaps his mother intervened, or may be Rajnarayan realized that his exams were about to begin. It was in October that Madhu told Gour finally that instead of Sagardari, he was going to Tamluk.

Rajnarayan Dutt was the lawyer of the 'royal' family in Tamluk. He had to visit Tamluk during the Durga Puja holidays, in connection with a court case. He decided to take Madhu with him, in the hope that, away from his busy life in Calcutta, he would get to know his son better. He had not fully grasped just how different his son was from other young men of his age. But he did realize that there was a problem with Madhu's personality. A few days away from home, he thought, would be good for both of them. He had no doubt that his son would, one day, become a brilliant lawyer, or—failing that—a deputy magistrate.

He had no idea—his own flesh and blood though he was—that when he would get to see his son more closely, Madhu would be a complete stranger to him. His thoughts, his ideas, beliefs and ambitions were so different from Rajnarayan's that he could hardly recognize him. Apart from anything else, he noted that Madhu did not appear in the least interested in Durga Puja, or any other religious ritual. No aspect of their traditional life seemed to hold any appeal for him. He lived in a world of his own.

Rajnarayan was not just surprised by this discovery. He was considerably alarmed, and began wondering at once what could be done to rectify matters. Eventually, on his return to Calcutta, he decided to take that single step which, he thought, would cure his son, once and for all.

Chapter Two

After spending a little more than a fortnight in Tamluk, Rajnarayan Dutt returned to Calcutta with his son. He got busy with his work as soon as he returned, but did not forget the problem he had noticed in Madhu. In his opinion, there was only one solution to it. At that time, if a young man appeared to be going through a mental crisis that affected his behaviour, marriage was considered to be the panacea for all symptoms. Therefore, professional matchmakers began visiting Rajnarayan Dutt's house, with details of prospective brides. Only four weeks after his return from Tamluk, Madhu was told that a date had been fixed for his wedding. It was to take place in three months.

Rajnarayan was a well-known lawyer. He was wealthy, and so were his brothers. The Dutt family was certainly well established. As for the bridegroom, no one could be better qualified than Madhu. He was the only child of his parents, good looking, well mannered, and known quite widely for his academic brilliance. He would, one day, certainly become, if nothing else, a deputy magistrate, the highest government post a native could hold. The perfect match for a beautiful girl. When one was found, the girl's family accepted Rajnarayan's proposal with alacrity. Madhu said in a letter to Gour that she belonged to a zamindar family. According to Gour's description, she was 'as pretty as a fairy'. But we do not know anything more about her.

Could it be that Madhu thought he was not old enough to get married, or the time was not appropriate? Such a thing seems very likely. But he did not have the courage to say so, in so many words. Three of his closest friends—Bhudeb, Gour, and Rajnarayan Basu—were already married and had no problem in accepting their wives. At the time, it was indeed the norm to give one's consent to whatever marriage one's parents arranged.

The conflict in Madhu's mind arose from the fact that he held rather romantic views about love and marriage. Where did he acquire such views? In his innumerable letters to Gour, he talked of his ambitions, hopes, and dreams. But nowhere did he say anything about women, or how he felt about them. He spoke about his dream-girl only in his poetry. But even there, the only thing he said was that this girl was 'blue-eyed'. It is not difficult to see the influence of Western literature on him. The English poets he admired had all chosen their own wives, and been through a period of courtship. None of them had had an arranged marriage. The stories of their lives, particularly that of Byron, must have made a strong impact on Madhu's thinking.

Anyone even remotely familiar with Byron's life would know about his many affairs, both with women and men. Whether Madhu condoned or supported Byron's sexual exploits is not known, but he must have realized that if a poet's works had true merit, his life-style or social censure could not take that merit away. He would remain, for all times, a great and famous poet.

In his personal life so far, Madhu was, if anything, conservative in the matter of sex or liaisons with women. As time went by, a number of accusations were flung at him, but no one ever charged him of sexual misdemeanours. Although visiting brothels was a common practice in those days, even among the educated upper middle class, Madhu was wholly against the idea. In fact, he opposed the whole concept of sex without love.

When he went to Tamluk with his father, he apparently had a brief experience of 'love'. Naturally, he did not fall in love with a little girl of eight, or ten. It is likely that he met a widow, or perhaps a married woman, and felt attracted to her for a brief period. For an eighteen year old, it must have been an exciting experience. However, even this brief encounter made Madhu feel guilty. He wrote to Gour: 'I had here a little love-affair;—thus, you see, from an anchorite and monk, I am becoming a decided Rake.' Two things become clear from this comment. One, he was known as a 'monk' in the matter of women; and two, even when he did come close to a woman, however briefly, he was tormented by guilt.

To Madhu, the concept of love was still something to be held as absolutely pure, to be idolized. When he heard that his family had gone ahead and chosen the girl with whom he was expected to spend his entire life, he felt greatly alarmed. His close contact with Western literature and Western values had made him believe in the freedom of the individual. Besides, the idea of falling in love and *then* marrying the woman of his dreams had taken a firm hold on his mind. Now, he was faced with an insurmountable problem. His father wanted him to marry a very young girl, perhaps seven years old or, at the most, ten or twelve. The very thought terrified him. But he was not yet strong enough, or brave enough, to face his father squarely and refuse to get married. After all, he had no income of his own; he was totally dependent on Rajnarayan. So he did the only thing he could do. He wrote to Gour (on 27 November 1842), pouring his heart out:

> I wish (Oh! I really wish) that somebody would hang me! At the expiration of three months from hence I am to be married; dreadful—It harrows up my blood and makes my hair stand like quills on the fretful porcupine! My betrothed is the daughter of a rich zamindar;—poor girl! What a deal of misery is in store for her in the ever inexplorable womb of Futurity! You know my desire for leaving the country is too firmly rooted to be removed. The sun may forget to rise, but I cannot remove it from my heart. Depend upon it—in the course of a year or two more, I must, either be in England or cease 'to be' at all—*one of these must be done*! You are my friend, Gour! I disclose these secrets to you, without the slightest fear of their ever seeing the light: *You are a gentleman*. Hitherto I kept these secrets even from you. But now I cannot. I want sympathy—and to whom am I to look for it?

Both his language and the tone in this letter are clear indicators of just how distressed he was at the thought of marrying a girl others had chosen for him. Such a reaction, at the time, was totally extraordinary and quite unheard of. Forty years after this incident, another young man from a well-known and erudite family, who had already been to England, agreed to marry an eleven-year-old uneducated village girl selected by his family. His name was Rabindranath Tagore. Was Rabindranath happy with the idea? We do not know. What we do know is that he raised no objection. Moreover, he printed a personalized letter of invitation to ask his close friends to attend the wedding. In the nineteenth century, certainly in the 1840s, no man apart from Madhu is known to have behaved in a different way.

This incident eventually changed the entire course of his life. Until now, he was the much-pampered son of wealthy parents; his life was well protected and carefree. Never had he had to face the harsh realities of life. Now, in the face of this huge problem, Madhu could think of only one solution. What he did, put an end to the old familiar world in which he had grown up. Nothing was the same, ever again.

Initially, he thought Gour would help him. But close friends though they were, in certain matters their views were completely different. The question of marriage was one of them. Gour himself was already married. He could see nothing wrong with the idea that Madhu get married, too. He did not understand Madhu's agony, and so failed to offer him any support. Besides, he was as loyal to Madhu's parents as he was to his friend. Rajnarayan Dutt and Janhabi Debi tried to reason with their son through Gour. We do not know how many letters Madhu wrote to him in the next three months. Only two have been found. Both are devoid of any mention of friendship or love. It shows that Madhu could no longer trust his best friend. By then, he had started visiting other people to devise a scheme to avoid marriage.

It is safe to assume that Madhu did not speak to his father directly and express his feelings. He might have spoken to his mother, saying that he wanted to finish his education before thinking of marriage. But, despite all her love and concern for her son, Janhabi Debi could see absolutely no reason why a young man should refuse to marry a beautiful girl.

If his parents had realized how or why he was so distressed, they would certainly have thought twice before insisting that he get married. After all, they wanted their son to be happy; and certainly they had no wish to lose him forever. Apart from anything else, Rajnarayan Dutt was well aware of the need for a descendant who would carry forward the family name and take care of their wealth and property. In later years, his desire for another child grew so strong that it made his behaviour seem insane. When Madhu was facing this crisis, did he openly threaten to leave home? That seems unlikely. Had he done so, his mother would surely have treated the matter more seriously; and Gour—who knew that Madhu was considering such a step—would not have warned him that he, Gour, would reveal this plan to Madhu's parents.

As far as one can see, it was all a question of bad timing. If Rajnarayan Dutt had arranged this marriage two years before, Madhu would probably not have objected so violently because he would have been young enough to be malleable. Two years later, he would have been close to finishing his education and would, therefore, have been in a better position to earn his own living. Hence he might have found the courage to oppose his father. However, in November 1842, he was neither a boy nor a mature adult. Even if he left home, where could he go? How would he support himself?

Just as he was beginning to despair, an idea occurred to him. It may have been suggested by someone else. He thought that if he went to the missionaries and became a Christian, he could kill not just two but several birds with one stone. If nothing else, all talk of his marriage would cease instantly.

Secondly, if he became a Christian, the British authorities and the entire Christian community would help and support him. He had noticed that if a member of a well-established and well-known family became a Christian, the missionaries treated that as a glorious example of their achievement. Only a few months before Madhu was faced with this crisis, a young man in Kidderpore (possibly called Nabinkrishna Mitra, though the church records do not show his name) became a Christian, which led to an upheaval in the Hindu community, as well as amidst the English and the missionaries.

There were other men who had become Christians, notably two of Derozio's followers, Krishnamohan Bandyopadhyay and Maheshchandra Ghosh. Some of Madhu's classmates also sang praises of Christianity. Rajnarayan Basu went a step further and spoke highly of Islam. Madhu himself was not really interested in religion, although he did participate in family events. His knowledge of European cultures must have made him aware of the malpractices allowed by orthodox Hindus, and so he began to question the validity of all that he had been taught. Besides, all the poets that he admired, including DLR, were Christians. This may have led him to think that, as a religion, Christianity was far superior. At least, he had read quite extensively about the progress made by the Anglo-Saxons. Compared to Indians, they were miles ahead. The tolerance and rationalism of Christian Europe really attracted him.

There may have been another reason to think of conversion. Perhaps Madhu was tempted by the thought of creating an uproar in society. Most important of all, when he approached the missionaries, he could stipulate that he would convert only if they were prepared to send him to Britain. If he could go there, he would not have to get married; he could settle scores with his parents since they were going to force him into marriage; and, above all, he would get a golden opportunity to fulfil his dream of becoming a poet. So conversion to Christianity appeared to be the best possible solution. But he knew that if the news of his intention leaked out, his whole plan would be ruined. He knew he would have to talk to the missionaries secretly.

Did he consider in any detail how adversely such a conversion would affect his life? It is difficult to tell, but it seems very likely that he did not think of all the consequences. Certainly, the thought of losing his comfortable home and loving family forever did not occur to him; nor did he realize that studying in Hindu College with his friends would also come to an end. Had he thought about these things calmly, perhaps he would not have taken such an extreme step, just to avoid getting married.

How could he become a Christian? Who should he contact first? Madhu decided to go to Krishnamohan Bandyopadhyay. He was an ex-student of Hindu College, so the two had something in common, although it is not known whether they had met before. Krishnamohan was then working as a priest in Christ Church. Madhu introduced himself simply as one who wanted to find out more about the religion of the Christians. After two or three visits, Krishnamohan realized that Madhu's interest in going to England far exceeded his interest in converting to Christianity. He knew such a demand would not be easily met. So he advised Madhu not to confuse one issue with the other. Disappointed, Madhu stopped his regular visits to Krishnamohan's house.

However, one day, Krishnamohan happened to mention Madhu's case to someone in the Anglican church. It was Archdeacon Mr Thomas Dealtry. Dealtry said he wanted to meet Madhu, although he was told about Madhu's stipulation. At the time, he occupied the second highest position in the Anglican church in Calcutta. It is likely that Dealtry offered some reassurance regarding a visit to England. Madhu took a letter of introduction from Krishnamohan and went to meet him. The Archdeacon was most encouraging. He even introduced Madhu to the Deputy Governor of Bengal, Mr Bird. Madhu was convinced that he would definitely be sent to England. He was both young and naive, and saw no reason to suspect what he was told.

Another person Madhu might have met was the priest who had conducted the conversion of Krishnamohan. It was Alexander Duff. He worked for the Church of Scotland, and was the best known among all the missionaries in Calcutta. He had started several schools for teaching English. Duff himself learnt to speak Bengali and was able to communicate easily with the locals. He played a role in the education of women, too. The students of Hindu College knew him and liked him. However, it seems that Duff told Madhu frankly that he would not be able to send him to Britain. Even so, Madhu remained in touch with the Church of Scotland later in his life.

Over the next two and a half months, Madhu continued to live at home, but maintained his secret contact with the missionaries. He could not expect anyone from either his family or friends to offer him any sympathy; so he told no one of his plan.

While he was visiting the missionaries, the date of his wedding was drawing closer. On 5 January 1843, in the Town Hall, a function was held to distribute prizes to the students of Hindu College. It was attended by various luminaries, including Mr Bird. Madhu was given a gold medal for his essay on female education. His friend, Bhudeb, won the silver medal. However, it turned out that Madhu had not done all that well in the annual exams which had been held the previous year, in September. He failed to get the senior scholarship.

Nevertheless, his father was so proud of his son that he kept the gold medal with him and showed it to everyone. When Madhu's friends wanted to see it, Madhu wrote to Gour, 'My medal is with my father'. Only two letters have been found from the ones that Madhu wrote to Gour during this period. Both are very brief. There is no indication of his mental turmoil, no hint of his secret plan. On the contrary, he invited some of his friends to a meal, and wrote a long poem, possibly *King Porus*. This seems to imply that, by this time, Madhu had overcome his initial trauma.

January went by quickly. Madhu's favourite teacher, DLR, was away on leave; James Kerr, who Madhu loathed, was in charge. Madhu did not feel like going to college, but did, if only to meet his friends. It still did not occur to him that, if he became a Christian, he could no longer study with them, or that some of them would cease to be his friends altogether.

The date for his actual conversion was fixed for 9 February 1843. About a week before that day, Madhu had his legendary haircut, in the style of Europeans, which cost him a gold mohur. His friends did not like it, but Madhu—for once—did not argue with them. He knew he would soon be a Christian, and possibly in England. No one there would criticize him for either his haircut or his western clothes.

One day, Madhu suddenly disappeared without telling a soul where he was going. When he was finally traced, he was in Fort William. The missionaries were very proud of the fact that the son of a well-known lawyer and a brilliant student of Hindu College had come to them. Usually, both in India and Britain, they were accused of luring poor, low-caste Hindus with promises of food and money to get them to convert. For this reason, every time they managed to find someone from a higher caste, they wanted wide publicity of their work. Madhu was one such 'catch'. However, there were certain risks involved in converting a high-caste Hindu. It was bound to enrage local communities. Sometimes, a freshly converted Christian was forced by his family to go through a process of 'penance' before being converted back to Hinduism. In Madhu's case, there was an additional problem. Krishnamohan Bandyopadhyay reminded the missionaries that Rajnarayan Dutt was fully capable of sending a band of armed men, carrying heavy bamboo rods and spears, to snatch Madhu away from them. It was Krishnamohan's idea to hide Madhu in the fort.

When Rajnarayan heard what had happened, he thought of every possible method that might be used to rescue Madhu. Yes, he also thought of his armed men. After all, unlike his son, he did not live in a dream-world. He knew very well what the consequences of Madhu's action would be. So he tried very hard to get in touch with his son. At first, he asked one of his neighbours, Satyacharan Ghoshal, to see Madhu and deliver a message from his family. Ghoshal was wealthy and had connections in high places. The message simply said that if Madhu returned home, Rajnarayan would send him to England and cancel his wedding. No pressure would be applied on him. His mother was almost crazy with anxiety, or something to that effect.

However, the authorities at Fort William denied Ghoshal entry when he arrived. Even then Rajnarayan Dutt did not give up. Eventually, a few people were allowed to meet Madhu. They were his cousin Pyarimohan; Ramchandra Mitra, a teacher from Hindu College; and Gour. Each tried to reason with him, and explain the consequences. It is said that Rajnarayan even sent his son East India Company bonds worth a thousand rupees to show that he was serious about sending him to Britain. Why, even after this, Madhu refused to go back home is a mystery. Was it just because he was under a lot of pressure from the missionaries? His conversion had certainly become a matter of prestige for them. However, it was not because of external pressure alone that Madhu did not change his mind.

On 9 February, in the evening, the ceremony for his conversion was conducted in the Old Church. Armed guards were appointed at the gate. Archdeacon Dealtry washed away Madhu's past sins with water from Jordan. Madhusudan became Michael. He had written a hymn† for the occasion, which was sung with due solemnity:

Long sunk in superstition's night,
By sin and Satan driven—
I saw not,—cared not for the light
That leads the blind to Heaven.

~ ~ ~

I sat in darkness, Reason's eye
Was shut,—was closed in me;—
I hastened to Eternity
O'er Error's dreadful sea.

~ ~ ~

But now, at length thy grace, O Lord!
Bids all around me shine;
I drink thy sweet,—thy precious word,—
I kneel before thy shrine!—

~ ~ ~

I've broken Affection's tenderest ties
For my blest Saviour's sake;—
All, all I love beneath the skies,
Lord! I for Thee forsake!

After the hymn, everyone prayed that Madhu should never stray from the path of virtue. In his hymn, Madhu presented Christianity as a religion superior to Hinduism.

In the history of conversion to Christianity in Bengal, Michael Madhusudan Dutt is a very special name. He was certainly different from the average Hindu who sought conversion. The missionaries were fully aware of this. Archdeacon Dealtry took him to his own house as his personal guest. There is no doubt that Dealtry played a key role in the matter of Madhu becoming a Christian. However, Madhu himself did not hold him responsible. A few days after his conversion, Gour wrote to Madhu, blaming Dealtry for the whole thing. In reply, Madhu wrote to him:

...I am extremely gratified at the friendly feelings you evince towards me. But I cannot help pitying you for some mistakes you seem to labour under (I mean, unfortunately labour under). Why should the hour that brought Mr Dealtry here be stigmatized as *inauspicious*? Do you think that he persuaded me to embrace Christianity? You are miserably, pitifully mistaken.

It is clear from this letter that Madhu was prepared to take full responsibility himself for becoming a Christian. Dealtry was not to be blamed, though Madhu says nothing about whether or not he was 'lured' by the prospect of going to England.

But, undoubtedly, the immediate reason behind Madhu's conversion was the pressing need to put a stop to the plans for his wedding, and to arrange for a visit to England. That is why all his previous biographers have acknowledged this event as a very significant one; but none have examined whether Madhu was sincerely affected by the concept of Christianity. If anything, his biographers and critics have always tried to prove that the Christian religion did not influence Madhu's personal beliefs. In the hymn that he wrote, there is mention of sin and superstition in his own society. He talks of having emerged into the light of reason, from deep darkness; and, in order to do that, he forsakes all that he holds dear. There is no reason to believe that every word in that hymn was written just to impress the missionaries, or that none of it was sincerely meant.

Thirty years after his own conversion, Madhu wrote a poem to mark a child's baptism. There, again, he referred to conversion to Christianity as an event that denoted 'purity' of the soul. It would be wrong to say that Madhu became religious as soon as he turned into a Christian. But within a short time, he did form a genuine attachment to Christianity. He believed in Christian values and, within two or three years, even expressed the wish to become a missionary himself.

Six years after his conversion, Madhu wrote a long poem called *Visions of the Past*. In it, he showed how the first man and woman were tempted by Satan to leave a world of peace and benediction, to be thrown into a world of darkness. Although a heavenly light did help them to step out of this dark world, they could not return straightaway to the joys of heaven. In order to go back there, they were required to go through a process of repentance and penance. Needless to say, the idea of these two contrasting worlds came from Christian traditions, not Hindu beliefs.

It was because he was exposed to western education and culture that Madhu became aware of superstitions and malpractices in the Hindu religion. The voice of reason was, as yet, almost totally unheard among Hindus. It was not just something Madhu might have learnt and observed from a distance, but he became a victim of this 'lack of reason' himself, over the question of his marriage. A case like Madhu's is not very common, it is true. But there is at least one other well-known instance, where another equally sensitive and conscientious young man had suffered when his father forced him to marry, against his will, for the second time. That man was Shibnath Shastri. Having married the second woman, he could not abandon her; nor could he allow himself to start a new married life with her. Eventually, he tried to marry her to another man, who might give her the happiness she deserved. In Madhu's case, things did not get that far. He ran away from home before such a disaster could take place. Nevertheless, it established, beyond any possible doubt, that the society he lived in did not believe in acting reasonably. That is why, it seems that what he wrote in that hymn were sentiments genuinely felt; there was nothing fake about them.

Had Madhu so wished, he could have gone back to his old comfortable life, without being forced into marriage, and with the prospect of travelling to Britain to look forward to. But he did not do so. Why? What made him remain a devoted Christian for so long, despite all the hardships he had to suffer? The answer to this question was not known until now. But from the letters and other writings of George Withers and Alfred Street, who taught at the time at Bishop's College, an explanation emerges. According to these men, Madhu did not just believe in some of the Christian values, but he was really and truly drawn towards Christianity. The depth of his feelings became clearer when he joined Bishop's College a year later. At the time when his father wanted him to change, Madhu could not forget the many 'superstitions' of the Hindus and thought that Christianity was superior to Hinduism. Besides, he could not give up his individuality. He must have believed that it was his new religion that would help him retain his freedom as an individual. It might be pertinent here to remember that, ten years later, Madhu gave a lecture in which, once again, he tried to establish Christianity's superiority over Hinduism.

How did Madhu fare after he left home? Did he really make the right decision? It is not possible to answer that question with a simple 'yes' or 'no'. What is obvious is that his life, which had been running smoothly, suddenly came off the track and everything was thrown out of gear. Whatever arrangements he made were always temporary in nature. What would have happened to him had he not left home and become a Christian? It is now impossible to tell.

How did Madhu's parents react when they failed to stop his conversion? The first thoughts that went through Rajnarayan's mind must have been: 'Who is now going to inherit my property? How will I stay in touch with my son? Will I not be socially ostracized?' But, most important of all, he must have wondered, 'If I don't have a son, who will perform the last rites when I die?' Both parents were heartbroken at the thought of losing their son. Yes, he was alive; but, given the circumstances, he might as well be dead. Madhu's earlier biographers have not dwelt upon his parents' anguish, possibly out of sympathy for Madhu. What must be remembered here is that, hurt though he was, Rajnarayan Dutt took some steps without delay to ensure his son's welfare. In due course, he spent a lot of money (certainly by the standards of those days) so that Madhu could complete his education. It could not have been easy to maintain contact with a son who was a Christian, since no doubt the traditional Hindus frowned heavily on him. Being a lawyer, Rajnarayan was particularly vulnerable, as his success in procuring work depended on the goodwill of his fellow men.

The enormous complexities that rose between Madhu and his parents after his conversion settled down in a few weeks. Gradually, their relationship became better defined. In mid-April 1843, Madhu wrote a letter to Gour, saying, 'I am not about to come and live with or rather near to my father.' In another letter he mentioned receiving a lot of financial help from home. But his dearest wish of going to England soon was not fulfilled. He wrote to Gour: 'I won't go to England till December next. I am not going to England with Mr Dealtry; my father won't allow that.' It seems from this letter that Rajnarayan had reassured Madhu that he *would*, one day, send him to Britain. Mr Dealtry was scheduled to leave soon. Madhu wanted to go with him, but Rajnarayan put his foot down. Perhaps he thought that if Madhu could feel that his own father was prepared to send him there, he would not mind leaving the missionaries. If he had gone with Dealtry, not only would Rajnarayan have failed to tempt him away from them, but Madhu might have grown even closer to the Christian missionaries. So Madhu was told that he would leave the country later in the year, possibly in December. However, when the time came, Madhu's father gave him neither permission to go to England, nor any money. The reason behind this refusal is not clear. Did Rajnarayan think that if Madhu could be kept away from other Christians and comforted with the possibility of seeing his dream fulfilled, he would agree to perform a 'penance' and rejoin his family as a Hindu? Perhaps. At least, it is natural that Madhu's father should have thought on those lines.

Rajnarayan Dutt wanted his son to go through a ritual that would symbolize a 'penance', so that he might be allowed to start living at home. Madhu refused. In view of strong social opposition, Rajnarayan could not let his son return home; nor could Madhu find anywhere to stay that was reasonably close to his parents. All he could do was visit his parents, particularly his mother, from time to time.

As for his education, things began to go seriously wrong on that front as well. When Madhu tried to go back to Hindu College, he discovered that its doors were closed to him. As it happened, only high-caste Hindus were allowed to study there. It took another ten years for this particular regulation to be relaxed. Madhu had probably thought that once the initial shock and horror died down, he would be allowed to rejoin his college as a special case, since he was an old student. His father spoke to all the influential people he knew. Madhu himself saw Richardson many times. Richardson was sympathetic, but did not permit him to join the college immediately. He asked Madhu to wait, although his own tenure was over and it was soon time for Richardson to return to England. He became busy with preparations for his departure. According to Madhu, he saw DLR during this time (March–April) about fifty times. He even bought four books from him which cost Madhu twenty-six rupees. But the question of his returning to college remained unresolved, even when DLR left for England on 15 April 1843, by a ship called *Hindustan*.

On 19 April, James Kerr took over as principal of the college. Later, on 19 June, the government officially confirmed the appointment. Not only did Kerr refuse to allow Madhu to go back to the college, he also ordered the other students not to see Madhu without his permission. In at least two of his letters written to Gour, Madhu refers to the business of seeking the principal's permission. Presumably, Kerr was fully aware of the adverse effect it might create on the other students and their guardians if they came to know that their wards were mixing with a boy who had turned his back on his own religion. Twelve years before, under similar circumstances, Derozio had been forced to resign from Hindu College. This time, Kerr decided to take precautionary measures. However, Madhu's father could not give up hope. He paid the college fee regularly from February to July. The college authorities accepted it, but after July they took a final decision in the matter—no student who had converted to a different religion would be allowed to study in the college, since that might encourage others to follow suit. The doors of Hindu College were shut forever to Madhu. All hope was snuffed out.

Now the full implications of his conversion began to sink in. Madhu could neither go back home, nor join his college. The problem of accommodation was most acute. Although Dealtry had initially welcomed him in his own house, Madhu could not stay there for more than a few days. He then moved to the Old Church on Mission Row, where his conversion had taken place. It was while staying there that Madhu began to feel, for the first time, that he had been abandoned by all his friends. Bhudeb saw him once, but that was all. No other friend went to see him, or even wrote to him, with the only exception of Gour. He went to see

Madhu, although clearly it was not easy for him. Sometimes, when he appeared to be making excuses for not going to visit Madhu, the latter implored him:

'He is a friend indeed, who helps you in need' says the Proverb. Well I'm 'in need' and if you are my 'Friend indeed' show it now. Do you think I want to borrow money from you? Do you think I want to tease your interest with friends to procure me anything?—No. No. No. Nothing of the sort—Don't startle. Alas! I am *Alone*! and am 'in need' that is I want company. Well! Will you come and pass this day with me? *I am almost sure you won't,* but still as you profess to be my *friend* I think it something like duty to me to inform you that I am dreadfully 'in need'.

Thus beseeched, Gour had to come. Judging by some of Madhu's letters, on some rare occasions Gour succeeded in persuading some of the other friends to accompany him. There is evidence to suggest that Madhu went out with them to attend some function. Yet Madhu's thirst for company was not quenched. He continued to feel lonely.

Perhaps the guardians of the other friends had forbidden them to see him. In fact, even with Gour, things were sometimes awkward. Gour could not forget that Madhusudan had now become Michael. He began to address his friend in a new fashion. In one letter, he said, 'My dear Christian friend, Michael Madhusudan Dutt.' Hurt, Madhu said in his reply, 'You write on the back of your letter "To Christian M. M. Dutt from GDB". *I do not like it.*' Madhu must have wondered why people judged everything on the basis of religion. Simple and naive as he was, he could not change his feelings for those who were dear to him, nor redefine them. If he had become a Christian, that was his personal affair. Why should that affect his friendship with others? Madhu just could not understand the strange attitude of traditional Hindu society.

However, losing his friends was not the only problem Madhu had to cope with. After spending a few months in the Old Church, Madhu had to look for new accommodation again. At the time, finding suitable accommodation for an Indian Christian was extremely difficult. No Bengali Hindu family would allow him to stay in their house. At the same time, Madhu could well feel the difficulties in staying among the British, although he was now a Christian. Eventually, help came from a kind priest from the Scottish church, Mr Thomas Smith. Madhu had become an

Anglican Christian. Competition between the various branches of Christianity was fierce; the existence of some of the churches in Calcutta depended on how many conversions they could effect. Even so, Mr Smith from the Scottish church offered to keep Madhu in his own house. It is probable that his fellow priest, Alexander Duff, had something to do with it. He could not conduct the conversion himself, but now tried to bring Madhu within his own precincts by offering him shelter.

Madhu's studies were now badly disrupted. Not only did his formal education come to a standstill, but the upheaval in his life kept him from doing any useful reading. Having moved to Smith's house, he now tried to get hold of his old books and began reading again. His host noticed this and offered him further help. Although he was a priest, Mr Smith had a deep interest in literature. During Madhu's stay in his house, in May 1844, a journal called the *Calcutta Review* began publication. Smith became its fourth editor (Duff was the second). He had a specialist's knowledge of Shakespeare. Smith began teaching Madhu what he knew. Later in his life, Madhu found these lessons immensely useful. The truth is that it was from this time that Madhu's literary tastes began to change. It is not as if he had not read Shakespeare before. In Hindu College, DLR was well known for his ability to teach Shakespeare. But, at that time, Madhu was much more interested in the Romantics. He read Shakespeare and Milton, but did not feel drawn towards their writing. Perhaps, at that stage, he did not have the ability to appreciate these authors. Now, Mr Smith opened the door to a whole new world.

Something else seemed to have changed for Madhu during his stay with Mr Smith. There was a time when he was totally indifferent to religion. But now, having lost contact with his family and friends, it became necessary to find his own place in his new world. Smith's company and his influence created an interest in Christianity. Madhu was, in fact, going through an identity crisis. He seems to have clung to Christianity to find comfort and reassurance. This interest ran so deep that, in 1844, he began to think of becoming a missionary.

Madhu stayed in Mr Smith's house for nearly a year. Although he learned a lot of literature from Mr Smith which later shaped his own vision, his immediate problems regarding his formal education and accommodation remained unresolved. It also became clear, certainly by early 1844, that he would not be going to England. By this time, after many arguments, Madhu had made it plain to his family that he was not going to revert to Hinduism. On the contrary, he began talking openly about joining Bishop's College to get an education, and then to become a missionary. Krishnamohan Bandyopadhyay was already one (1838). Maheshchandra Ghosh had also joined Bishop's College with the same objective, but unfortunately he died in a few years. Another man, Gopalchandra Mitra, became a deacon in 1843. At the time, the most junior post among the missionaries was that of a catechist, who was paid eighty rupees. A deacon's salary was one hundred and fifty rupees, and a priest was paid two hundred rupees. To an educated Bengali, such a job must have seemed tempting. At any rate, Madhu found nothing wrong with the idea. So he went and discussed the matter with the authorities in Bishop's College. Perhaps Mr Smith helped him in this matter. The authorities agreed to admit him.

Every student in Bishop's College, at that time, received a scholarship. None of them had to pay anything towards board and lodging, or tuition fees. Madhu wanted to try for a scholarship, too. But his father raised strong objections to this, because he could not accept the idea of his son becoming a missionary. It was bad enough that he was a Christian. This matter becomes clear from a letter written by the principal of the college, George Withers,[†] on 20 November 1844:

The 4th, Moodhu Sudun Dutt, is a lay student, the first we have ever admitted. He wished to come as a Theological student, but his father who is still a heathen, was very averse to it, and preferred rather, which he can well do, to pay for his maintenance and tuition.

The difference between a fee-paying student and one on a scholarship becomes more clear from another letter written by Alfred Street, who was a teacher in Bishop's College:

He (Dutt) came here with the professed determination to become a missionary. His father, a native of some substance, in order to prevent at least this, offered to maintain him as a lay student. And has done so.

If a student could pay the fees, there was no need to make any promises in advance about becoming a missionary. Perhaps Rajnarayan had hoped that, in time, Madhu would have a change of heart and return to the religion of his forefathers. So he allowed

Madhu to join Bishop's College. Madhu resumed his academic career on 9 November 1844, after a gap of exactly a year and nine months. The college was divided into three sections. Most new students started in the third. So did Madhu, but within a few weeks he was promoted to the second.

Joining Bishop's College solved two of his immediate problems: he found somewhere to live, and could continue his education, for which there were excellent facilities in Bishop's College. He was given a single room in the college hostel. Rajnarayan had to pay a hundred rupees every month—sixty-four to cover hostel and tuition fees, and thirty-six towards Madhu's pocket money.† It would not be unreasonable to assume that Madhu received extra money from his mother as well.

Admission to Bishop's College helped Madhu to resume his formal education, but it did not revive his poetical activities, which had been seriously set back by his conversion. In 1841–2 he wrote quite a few poems. But soon after his annual exams in 1842, when his father decided to have him married, Madhu was swept away by such a torrent of problems that he could find neither a favourable atmosphere nor enough inspiration to write. Three months after his conversion, when contact was re-established with his family, Madhu began to think of writing again. He wrote to Gour (in the only letter that has survived from this period): 'I have written very little poetry ever since my baptism. I am plotting something though. They will appear, where do you think, Boy? In no less a place than London itself.'

None of the havoc in his life affected his tendency to dream, or to show off. This single letter is enough to highlight this aspect of Madhu's character. In September 1843, the *Literary Gleaner* published *King Porus*, which Madhu had started writing in January that year, and finished after his conversion. A comparatively settled life at Bishop's College did not inspire him to write any poetry. Or, at least, no poetry written during his time in Bishop's College has been traced.

There were enormous differences between the two colleges. Although Hindu College was exclusively for Hindus, it was purely secular in character and there was never any attempt at teaching anything about Hinduism. All that was taught was moral philosophy. Besides, as long as Derozio lived, many students were encouraged to think critically of their religion. Even though no one has said anything about Madhu getting involved in any activity that might be seen as anti-Hinduism, it is obvious that he had scant regard for many established Hindu practices. Bishop's College, on the other hand, was a truly religious institution. It was started with the express purpose of spreading Christianity outside Britain. The religiousness that grew in Madhu's mind after his conversion—whether as a result of an identity crisis, or because of the influence of the missionaries on him—found a strong base to grow further in Bishop's College.

The man who played a leading role in setting up this institution just outside Calcutta was the Bishop of Calcutta, Mr Middleton. At his request, the Governor General, the Marquis of Hastings, gave a large plot of land near the Botanical Gardens. Later, Charles Metcalf, the next Governor General, donated more land. Middleton himself donated five hundred pounds and five hundred books. Help came from various other sources, including the Oxford and Cambridge University Press, each of which gave copies of all the books they had printed. From the very beginning, therefore, the library of the college was well stocked with valuable books.

The college began functioning from December 1820 as a centre for training Christian missionaries. Very few students came to study here. It was an expensive place. Those that did come were from various parts of the country. Some came from distant Sri Lanka, or southern India. For only twenty students, there were three full-time professors, and four other Indian teachers. In addition to religious education, classical languages and literature were taught at Bishop's College with equal care. More important than anything else, in the atmosphere of the college, a feeling of religiousness and solemnity was always maintained.

The stringency of the policies maintained by the college becomes clear from a letter written by Alfred Street. It is dated 1 February 1847. We learn from this that, towards the end of the previous year, Madhu and his classmate, Charles Egbert Kennet (who came from Madras) went to meet the Roman Catholic Bishop of Calcutta, Dr P. J. Carew. Kennet's mother was a Catholic, as was Kennet himself in his childhood. But when he grew up, he joined his father in his Anglican beliefs and became an Anglican. Nevertheless, he had friends in Calcutta who were Catholic. It was for this reason that he and Madhu went to visit Dr Carew. When he was introduced, Madhu is said to have kissed the Bishop's ring as a mark of respect. The news spread, and Bishop's College asked both students to submit a written explanation of their behaviour. Archdeacon Dealtry was informed. He asked the authorities to keep an eye on them. Eventually, both were given a warning, and told not to visit a Roman Catholic Bishop unless it was absolutely necessary. It was some months before the matter was forgotten. It is clear from Street's language how seriously it was viewed not just by the college, but by the entire establishment of Anglicans in Calcutta.

Some of Madhu's earlier biographers have claimed that he learnt Latin, Greek, and Hebrew in the school that he went to before joining Hindu College, although no one so far has been able to indicate how well he knew these languages. Now, a letter from the principal of Bishop's College (Rev. G. U. Withers) has come to light which speaks of this matter. It was written to Ernest Hawkins, on 20 November 1844:

The fourth student (M. Dutt) is much better acquainted with English, and has moreover a creditable knowledge of Latin, and of the elements of Greek.

Bishop's College offered him a second chance to learn both languages. Withers had written a book on Hebrew grammar, but there is no evidence that Hebrew was taught in his college. In due course, Madhu mastered Latin and Greek before he left the college.

Within two months of restarting his academic career, Madhu became totally immersed in his studies. On 27 January 1845, he wrote to Gour, explaining how busy he was:

It is a matter of regret to me that I haven't been able to answer your two *very* kind letters ere this; but if you were to know how my time is engaged here, I am sure you would excuse me. However, at any time that is convenient to you, I should be extremely happy to see you as well as the friends you intend to bring with you. By the bye, you ought to address me in the following manner: 'M. Dutt Esqr, or Baboo' (if you please) Bishop's College; and nothing more. I must beg pardon for this short letter, but upon my word, I can't afford a minute more; so good-night.

Bishop's College was teaching him a new way of appreciating literature, laying more emphasis on classical literature. In Hindu College, contemporary writing was taught as well as the works of classical authors. Madhu's passion for the Romantic poets, in particular, was well known. After he joined Bishop's College, that passion gradually waned, and was replaced by a very deep and enduring love of classical literature. Byron was the only poet he continued to mention later in his life. Others no longer aroused his emotions.

In Bishop's College, Greek and Latin literature was taught with special care. It was here that he was introduced to a playwright like Euripedes. But the greatest emphasis was laid on literature related to Christianity. The Bible written in Greek was taught in great detail. Some Bengali students read Sanskrit and Bengali.[†] It is not clear whether English literature formed a part of the syllabus[†] in Bishop's College, but there is no doubt that the seeds of the literature that Madhu himself produced in later life were sown during his years at Bishop's College. Had he not studied here, it is questionable whether he would have finally emerged as a poet with so much erudition; and had he not become a Christian, it is doubtful whether he could have used stories from Hindu mythology and given them a humanistic expression, instead of confining himself to stereotypes. Many of his other creations, including *Visions of the Past*, were born as a direct result of his brief but significant stay in Bishop's College.

Having learnt Latin and Greek, Madhu could not be content with reading classical literature in its English translation. He tried to read everything in the original. Later, when he went to Madras, he learnt Tamil in order to read the Ramayana written in that language. In 1861, after his return to Calcutta, he started reading Tasso's works in Italian. All this showed the lasting influence of having studied in Bishop's College.

Seen in this light, becoming a Christian and joining Bishop's College, both turned out to be blessings in disguise for Madhu's development as a gifted writer. It may be worth noting what Street said about him just before he left the college, to Rev. Fagan, on 23 July 1847:

He is very intelligent, a good Greek and Latin scholar and thorough master of English, as you may suppose when I mention that before coming here he affected fame as an English poet. A piece with boyish vanity not without its correspondent conceits now, yet, he is obedient, honourable, moral, and I believe religious. He came here with the airs and notions of liberal Young Bengal—though not its bad practices—but the power of education on Church system, or, if you will, of Instruction seasoned by the fear of God, has been shown in the constrained [sic] and taming of human freedom.

Street himself was a missionary. It is reasonable to assume that he wished to believe that the religious education he imparted had had the desired effect. However, even if there is an element of exaggeration in what he has said, it is clear from Street's comments that during his years at Bishop's College, Madhu's character underwent a perceptible change.

If he had remained at Hindu College, Madhu's student life would have come to an end in 1845–6. Some of his contemporaries left the college before this date; others left in 1846. Gour was busy with his exams in July 1846, as some of Madhu's letters to him suggest. Eventually, Gour and a few others from Madhu's class became magistrates. Bhudeb Mukhopadhyay and Rajnarayan Basu chose to become teachers.

Madhu fell behind by about a year and a half. When he left Bishop's College towards the end of 1847, he was a student of their senior division, but he had not yet passed the final exams. That does not, of course, mean that he was not a good student. According to a letter written by Rev. Withers in January 1846, in the exams held in December 1845, Madhu obtained the second highest marks in religious studies and classical literature. There is no doubt that he was always busy with his studies. Six of his letters written to Gour between 1845 and 1847 have been recovered. All are very short and all mention how busy he was. In one, he says, 'I cannot, of course, call on you now, as it is term-time with us.' But there is a further hint to indicate that he was busy even when his college was closed: 'I am really sorry to say that for various reasons I have suffered our last vacation to pass without giving you a call.'

Another factor that stands out in these letters is the absence of great emotion and declarations of love that were so common in his previous letters to Gour. By this time, Madhu had outgrown his passionate outbursts, and Gour had simply become a friend who he knew would stand by him at all times. 'I am sure I am a great *villain* not to mind more those who really *love* me...' Madhu wrote in January 1846. The truth was that, with the exception of Gour, all his other friends had drifted away. Yet, it was essential for Madhu to have one or two close friends. Who became his friends in Bishop's College? From the letters written by his teachers, it appears that Madhu had at least three friends who were close to him: George Mann, Charles Egbert Kennet, and Robert Walker.

In spite of the friendship of these young men, life in Bishop's College was not easy for Madhu. Mercifully, by this time he had learnt to fend for himself and was no longer the pampered child he once was. Had that not been the case, it is doubtful whether he could have coped with the further upheavals that were in store.

Not much is known about the details of Madhu's activities in his final year in Bishop's College. In the middle of 1847, he wrote to Gour, two weeks before his final exams: 'Since I last heard from you, I have been almost half-dead with all manner of troubles.' Neither he nor anyone else has ever explained the nature of these 'troubles' that rendered him half-dead. Most probably, they were related to his studies, and happenings in his family. By the end of 1846, Rajnarayan Dutt stopped paying his fees, as a result of which he had to leave the college. Presumably, Madhu's father took this step before November that year. On 22 November 1846, Street wrote to the Society for the Propagation of the Gospel (SPG): 'One of our students, Dutt, is leaving us since his father is no longer paying his fees, and he does not have the means to pay for himself.'

Madhu had to leave Bishop's College without taking the final exams that were held in mid-December. Had he passed those, there would have been no obstacle in his way to becoming a missionary. His untimely departure before these exams is a clear indication of the gravity of the situation. Mentally and financially, Madhu must have hit rock bottom.

Rajnarayan Dutt paid the college fees for nearly three years. From this fact, one might deduce that, during that time, relations between father and son were good. That, however, was not the case. There were arguments and misunderstandings on more than one occasion. Rajnarayan could still not accept the idea that his son would never revert to Hinduism. In addition to that, there was the question of who would inherit his property after his death. Rajnarayan was not prepared to leave everything to a son who was a Christian. Tired of these arguments, Madhu tried, more than once, to leave the college and start working as a missionary. So far, his biographers have speculated a great deal on this issue, but no one has provided any facts. The real story emerges from the records kept in the Bishop's College Papers.

The first time Madhu tried to give up his studies and get a job was towards the end of 1845. The principal, Rev. Withers, recorded the event. According to him, Madhu's closest friend, George Mann, died after a period of illness that lasted only four days. Soon after his death, Madhu wanted to leave the college and go to Mauritius as a missionary. In February 1846, Withers wrote on Madhu's behalf to the Bishop in Madras, George John Trevor Spencer. Spencer replied saying that Mauritius did not fall within his jurisdiction. Withers then wrote to the SPG in London, requesting them to open a mission in Mauritius. Neither the SPG nor any other organization agreed to do this. Madhu, therefore, had to abandon his idea of going to Mauritius.

When he failed to go to Mauritius, he explored the possibility of becoming a missionary in southern India under the jurisdiction of the Bishop of Madras. However, he was not happy when the Bishop offered him only the post of a junior catechist at a salary much lower than that of a regular priest. The Bishop was also disappointed with him. This is implied in the letter Street wrote to Rev. Fagan, on 23 July 1847:

Some eighteen months ago, the lad feeling, as he fancied more decided than ever on being Missionary, became sensible that it was not right to continue to receive his father's support, on the supposition on the latter's part that he, the son, had given up his first wish.

However, what Street then went on to say suggests that Madhu had another motive for turning into a missionary; it was not just his devotion to Christianity. It seems this other motive had purely to do with the rift between his father and himself.

He accordingly asked whether he would be provided for as a foundationer if his father executed his threat of casting him off and disinheriting him. I told him I made no doubt of it provided he gave himself to the Society's work. But he proceeded to ask *what* provision. I said the same as for other native students, food and employment when you are fit for it, though I cannot say what [the] salary will be. This self-delusion then came out to view. He could not submit to dress as the other native students, nor consent to a lower rate salary than others had had, should such rate be fixed. I should have premised by the way that he came here, with habits thoroughly Europeanized (i.e., as regards dress, eating and drinking) from the Hindoo College I did not omit to urge on him, though I felt it be vain, the duty of simply confessing the determination with the professed, and to trust in it to provide for him better than father, or household, or money, or lands.

Street quoted another instance to prove that simply the desire to spread the word of Christianity did not fill Madhu's heart. Although he could not help in the matter of starting a new mission in Mauritius, the Lord Bishop of Madras offered Madhu a job in early 1846. Madhu was told that if he was prepared to go to south India to help with converting the local people there, he would be given a regular job. But Madhu showed no interest in taking up this offer. Even so,

The Lord Bishop of Madras also sent for him and spoke to him, but concluded, as I could not help doing, that it was a case of a coat and allowances in one scale against the Missionary calling on the other.

One thing that this letter shows is that Madhu was already thinking of travelling to some distant land to make a new life. Later, he would leave Calcutta and set off for Madras, then England and France and, in the final chapter of his life, the unknown Panchakot.

An analysis of Street's letters reveals a number of facts, chiefly the friction between Madhu and his father. Madhu's conscience seemed to be troubling him about his continued dependence on Rajnarayan. If he did not change his mind about becoming a missionary, was it right to take further help from his father? Rajnarayan Dutt, on the other hand, did not fail to renew his threat to cut him off totally if he did not do what was expected of him. Nevertheless, Madhu did not hesitate to stand by his own convictions. There was no question of backtracking and going back home, once more a Hindu. On the contrary, his devotion to Christianity, coupled with his desire to be independent, became so strong that he was no longer afraid to declare openly his intention of becoming a missionary. There was only one thing he could not give up—his love of worldly pleasures and creature comforts. Besides, he still thought of himself as not just different from, but better than others. It was impossible for him to accept that, despite his qualifications, he would be paid the same as other Indian missionaries, and less than British ones.

For these reasons, he could not get a job in 1846, and had to stay on in Bishop's College. Fortunately, a temporary truce was declared at the same time between his father and himself, although it is not known how far his mother's tears were responsible for such an event. Madhu went back to his studies, and for several months, life was more or less normal. Then, in May 1847, he wrote to Gour, declaring himself to be in trouble once more. It was related to fresh problems with his father. Neither father nor son recorded the reason behind this 'trouble', but it is not difficult to guess. It is my belief that the conflict arose as there was a clash of expectations. Rajnarayan Dutt had waited for two and a half years. Still, Madhu showed no sign of doing a 'penance' and going back home. Now, Rajnarayan's patience ran out. He took two steps to try to bring his son back from the Christians. The first of these was to stop his college fees.

It is likely that there was another bigger reason behind Rajnarayan's action, for which Madhu cannot be held responsible at all. It had to do with Rajnarayan's career. Up until then, he had been doing very well as a lawyer in the civil court. But in late 1847, he was accused of some professional incompetence and/or irregularity. That is why, in December 1847, the judges in an appeal case 'dismissed' Rajnarayan Dutt. It is not known whether this dismissal was temporary or permanent in nature. Was Rajnarayan holding some special post? We do not know. An ordinary lawyer is usually not 'dismissed'. If he is involved in some serious misconduct, then the court can, of course, debar him and deprive him of his right to practise. Unless more facts are unearthed, it is difficult to say whether Rajnarayan had indeed done something seriously wrong. Whatever the grounds, his income, as a result of his dismissal, must have been reduced. Perhaps that is why he stopped paying Madhu's fees, convinced by now that he was not going to return home. As far as Madhu was concerned, at this stage there was no fear of being forced into marriage if he did choose to rejoin his family. Had he done so, he could have continued with his education without having to worry about a job. But he still refused to comply. This is a clear indication that if he remained a Christian and continued his association with the missionaries, it was not simply to avoid his father, but because he was genuinely drawn towards Christianity and thought as a religion it was better and superior than Hinduism.

The second step Rajnarayan took had less to do with Madhu, and more to do with Rajnarayan's concern for his own welfare in the other world, as well as the state of his assets in this one. In Madhu's absence, someone—preferably a direct descendant—was required to inherit his wealth, and perform the last rites when he died. With this end in view, he decided to marry again. It is not very clear exactly when he married his second wife, Shibsundari. She died soon after their marriage, possibly without ever setting foot in his house in Calcutta. At first Rajnarayan suffered pangs of guilt when he married for the second time. But when Shibsundari died (Rajnarayan described her as Janhabi Debi's 'handmaiden'), he lost little time before marrying for the third time. His third wife was called Prasannamoyee. It is said that when Madhu visited his mother, she asked Prasannamoyee to look after him and offer him refreshments.

According to Madhu's biographer, Jogindranath Basu, Rajnarayan's third marriage took place before Madhu could leave for Madras. In the last letter that Madhu wrote to Gour from Bishop's College in May 1847, he mentioned being in trouble, but there was no mention of his father's marriages. This made his biographers assume that Rajnarayan remarried only after May 1847. But there is no real evidence to prove that such an assumption is correct.

What *is* known for sure is that no matter when he took a second wife, he did so without his first wife's knowledge or consent. He went to Sagardari to marry Shibsundari. He wrote to Janhabi Debi after the event expressing his regret and guilt, and begging to be forgiven. This was, in fact, an unusual thing to do, for in those days a second marriage was not at all uncommon. If anything, in view of Madhu's conversion to Christianity and departure from home, Rajnarayan could have been seen as totally justified in marrying a second time. Even adopting a son would have been perfectly acceptable. Had he got himself a mistress, with his wife's knowledge, society would not have frowned on him. In spite of that, he asked Janhabi Debi to forgive him. That shows a degree of commitment towards his wife. For her part, it is likely that Janhabi Debi felt hurt not so much because her husband had found another woman, but because he had given her the status of a wife. Nevertheless, she accepted the inevitable. Madhu's biographers have blamed Rajnarayan heavily for causing this upheaval. He has been accused of marrying girls much younger than him. This particular accusation seems a little unfair, since in those days, it was not possible to find older yet unmarried women, even if one set out to look for them.

How Madhu reacted to his father's marriages, we do not know. His immediate concern must simply have been that his father would no longer support him. This was a threat that hung over him throughout his stay in Bishop's College. When his worst fears were confirmed, Madhu may have felt sad, but it could hardly have come as a surprise. He had to look immediately for means of supporting himself. Desperate, he began looking for a job. He even went to meet Henry Hardinge, the Deputy Governor, and the Chief Secretary, to ask for a job. Both told him to wait, and seemed reluctant to help.

Only a year earlier, Madhu had refused to accept the job of a missionary because of the disparity in the wages paid to Indian and British missionaries. But now he was left with no choice. He agreed to take the job of a missionary, regardless of the pay. In the letter mentioned before, Street went on to say:

The Principal, who has seen a copy of my letter touching him and the other student, thinks I hardly did him [Madhu] justice in omitting to state that he volunteered for Mauritius, or to serve for any salary anywhere and that the salary question had not been raised. I own that I forgot this at that time.

There may be a slight exaggeration in what his teachers wrote about Madhu's enthusiasm to become a missionary. But that does not hide the underlying truth of the situation.

Madhu was now forced to sell his books and other possessions just to survive. Could he have gone home, like Shelley, to have a showdown with his father at this stage? Madhu was then twenty-four. For a long time now, he had been taking care of himself and was no longer the spoilt young boy he was in Hindu College. He was stronger and far more assertive. So it should not be surprising if indeed he went back to ask for money and there were further arguments. It must have been extremely distressing for Madhu, since he had once worshipped his father and thought him to be the ideal parent. Besides, he would have seen his mother's tears and the look of pain in her eyes, caused by his father's two marriages. Madhu's anger against Rajnarayan could only have grown at such a sight.

Eventually, it all became too much to bear. It was impossible to continue to live in Calcutta. Madhu just had to get away. Before this, only on one occasion had he been uprooted from his familiar surroundings—when he ran away from home to become a Christian. Then, over the next four years and nine months, the situation had stabilized. But now, another storm rose and hit him unexpectedly. Under its impact, the roof over his head was blown away and, in less than five years, he was homeless once more.

Chapter Three

'When I left Calcutta, I was half mad with vexation and anxiety. Don't for a moment think that *you alone* did not receive a valedictory visit from me. I never communicated my intentions to more than two or three persons.' Thus wrote Madhu to Gourdas on 14 February 1849.

Madhu did indeed keep his plans for going to Madras a secret from his family and friends. This was a special feature of his character. Seldom did he confide in anyone, or discuss anything, before plunging into action.

Although he had a number of extraordinary qualities, even his admirers could never have called him judicious. His impulsive behaviour, throughout his life, led to complications. It was because of this impulsiveness that he had started to plan to go to England and had not hesitated to convert to Christianity in order to avoid an arranged marriage. He was able, no doubt, to avoid his wedding, but must have soon realized that not everything would go as he had planned. It was perhaps because of an impulsive and emotional reaction to the death of his friend, George Mann, that he thought of going to Mauritius to preach Christianity there and thus fulfil Mann's ambtion. His decision to go to Madras and seek his fortune there was just another example of his impulsiveness.

Why did he choose Madras, of all places? There has been a lot of speculation on this issue, but so far no one has been able to provide a satisfactory answer. Some of his earlier biographers seemed to think that the suggestion was made by the south Indian and Sri Lankan students in Bishop's College. Sureshchandra Maitra thought that Madhu went to Madras with the others from south India, all travelling by the same ship. That is not correct. The truth is that the idea of going to Madras came not from any of the other south Indian students, but from his close friend, Charles Egbert Kennet (1826–84),[†] who returned to Madras either in late October, or early November 1847, possibly without taking his final exams. Then he began his career as a catechist. He was slightly older than Madhu, but the two became close friends in college quite soon. As has been mentioned before, it was with Kennet that Madhu went to meet the Catholic Bishop in Calcutta, thereby inviting a great deal of trouble.

When his father withdrew his support, Madhu had few people to turn to. He needed money urgently. Even though he had seen high officials and had asked them for a job, he had not got one. They had given him their support at the time of his conversion, but were now reluctant, even unwilling, to help him in the desperate situation that he was in. Madhu also talked to Street and offered to become a missionary, but the latter was not convinced about his sincerity and declined to help. Charles Kennet, being his closest friend, heard about what had happened and suggested he go to Madras. Madhu had met the Bishop of Madras the year before, and had been offered a job. He had not accepted it then; but now, it is entirely likely that he thought it might be a good idea to approach the Bishop again.

Madras was very far away, and was considered to be a foreign land. But it was not a place with which Madhu was wholly unfamiliar. He had travelled there the year before to meet the Bishop. Besides, he had learnt a great deal from Charles. Charles's father was the manager of the treasury in Madras. He was also the secretary of a well-known charitable organization for twenty-seven years. Charles must have reassured Madhu that his father would help him, even if no one else did.

It is interesting to note that Madhu did not inform Gour of his intention. The first letter he wrote to him (quoted above) was written thirteen months after his arrival in Madras. It is clear that, dearly though he loved his friend, he was no longer prepared to trust him. It may have had to do with the fact that when, in November 1842, Madhu was determined to go to England, Gour had threatened to tell his parents. In the end, he did *not* betray

Madhu's confidence, but Madhu must have decided that it was too risky to tell Gour of any drastic step he was contemplating.

<hr />

A non-stop journey to Madras by sea, in those days, usually took four or five days. A cabin cost at least a hundred rupees. Some companies charged a hundred and sixty rupees; one of them charged two hundred and twenty rupees. There was a time when Madhu did not lack money at all. He was brought up to believe that money would always be plentiful, there was no need to think before spending it. But now, those days were gone. Madhu failed to raise enough money to pay for a cabin on a ship that went directly to Madras. Presumably, he got no help from his mother because he could not bring himself to tell her that he was leaving Calcutta. With whatever little money he could scrape up from elsewhere, he bought a ticket on a smaller ship—to be precise, a coaster—called the *Lady Sale*. It went to Madras via Ganjam, Kalingapattam, Vishakhapatnam, and Karinga. It took him twenty days to reach Madras. He left Calcutta on 29 December 1847, and arrived in Madras[†] on 18 January 1848, a week before his twenty-fourth birthday.

Five years before that date, Madhu had gone to Tamluk and was delighted to be close to the sea. It was a reminder that, one day, he would be sailing to the land of his dreams, to 'England's glorious shore'. But now, although he was out in the open sea, he had torn himself away from his family and friends to make a journey that would take him simply to another city in India, a city smaller and lesser known than the thriving Calcutta. This city, at the time, was popularly called 'benighted' Madras. Sorrow and anxiety must have cast deep, dark shadows on whatever joy the sight of the sea might have brought him.

On the ship, Madhu was one of the few Indian passengers. Apart from him, there were four native servants and a few sepoys. Everyone else was either British or Anglo-Indian—Captain Doveton, Mr and Mrs Pressgrave, Misses Langley and Macfarlane. Madhu, as the only 'dark' passenger, must have stood out like sore thumb; but that did not humble his spirit, or the desire to prove that he was no less important than the others. In the list of passengers, there are names with only the prefix 'Mr' or 'Mrs'. There is no other description. The only exception is the name of Mr M. M. Dutt,† which is followed by the words 'of Bishop's College'. It is as if he wanted to announce loudly that a passenger on the cheap quarter-deck though he was, he was nevertheless an important man. This trait of showing off remained with Madhu all his life. Whenever he felt he might be slighted or overlooked, he tried to inflate his ego, be it in Madras, London, or Versailles.

When he landed on a shore far less glorious than England's, what did he feel? Could he have arrived with a lot of ambitions? That does not seem likely, for he could not have had a clear idea of what kind of work he might possibly get. He had to struggle very hard to support himself in Madras. In the letter he wrote to Gour thirteen months later, he said, 'Since my arrival here I have had much to do in the way of procuring a standing place for myself,—no easy matter, I assure you—especially for a friendless stranger.'

Madhu knew that the Bishop of Madras was no longer favourably disposed towards him. Even so, he may have approached him for help. Mr Thomas Dealtry was one of the few people who knew about Madhu's departure to Madras. Dealtry is likely to have asked the Bishop to assist Madhu. However, there is no evidence to suggest that any assistance came from the Bishop.

The only people who did offer support were the Kennets. Charles Egbert Kennet's father, also called Charles Kennet, was the secretary of the Orphan Asylum. Father and son almost certainly discussed Madhu's case with a view to finding him a job. Eventually, Madhu found the job of an usher (assistant teacher) in the boys' school that the Asylum ran. He was lucky, as the only teacher of the school—Richard Nailor—had just left. It was a small job, and the salary most unenviable. But Madhu found the atmosphere in his place of work quite favourable. In other respects, though, he wasn't as lucky. He had the misfortune of contracting chicken-pox almost as soon as he started working. Judging from the fact that he survived instead of dying penniless, it is clear that there were people (particularly the Kennets) to take care of him.

As things turned out, it did not take Madhu long to make friends outside the church. At the time, there was only a handful of Indians in Madras who knew good English. That immediately distinguished Madhu. Compared to Calcutta, Madras was like a small town. According to the census report of 1862, the total population of Madras was three hundred and fifty thousand, of which sixteen thousand were Anglo-Indian and British. English was hardly taught at any of the local schools. Bruce Norton, who was previously a teacher and, several years later, the Advocate-General of Madras and a member of the governing body of Madras High School, wrote to the authorities in England in 1854, lamenting that Madras had only one English-medium school, whereas Bengal had more than forty.† As a matter of fact, the first college where English was the main medium of instruction was established in Madras thirty-five years after Hindu College came into being in Calcutta. Under these circumstances, it could not have been very difficult for Madhu—whose English was impeccable—to find the job of an usher. Indeed, it is surprising that he did not get a better job.

The full name of the organization that employed him was Madras Male and Female Orphan Asylum and Boys' Free Day School. While the Military Orphan Asylum was established in 1787 in order to help the orphans of military officials, the Female and Male Orphan Asylums were established in 1816 and 1823 respectively in order to help the orphans of European and Anglo-Indian civilians. A school established in 1807 to educate such orphans was taken over by the Orphan Asylum and renamed Male and Female Orphan Asylum's Free Day School. It was at this school that Madhu was employed.

Madhu's salary was about forty-six rupees. The term 'assistant teacher' may well suggest that there were a lot of teachers in the school, and Madhu joined as one of their assistants. That, however, was not the case. Until 1850, only one teacher was employed to teach the Bible, languages, literature, history and some other subjects. Madhu's predecessor was Jessie Ray Nailor (also known as Richard Nailor). He was the only teacher in the school. When he left, Madhu replaced him, but only as an assistant teacher since he did not have the necessary experience to qualify as a full-fledged teacher. The annual reports of the school, published between 1845 and 1854, say nothing about the exact date of Madhu's appointment, or his salary; nor is there any indication whether, in 1848-9, there was any teacher other than Madhu.

Another noteworthy factor is that although it was called the 'boys' school', it included girl students from the female orphan Asylum. It was not until 1851 that separate arrangements could be made for the girls' education.

Between 1848 and 1851, the number of students remained close to fifty. The boys were divided into four classes, the girls into three. Classes took place in two sessions, one between eight and one o'clock; the other from two until five. The boys were taught vocational work in addition to their academic pursuits. It ranged from carpentry to shoe-making. It appears that the boys spent more time on learning these crafts than studying. Between 1848 and 1852, the Asylum earned five hundred rupees or more every year by selling the products made by its students. The girls were taught to sew. A few teachers were employed to teach in both workshops.

The number of occupants in the male Asylum was between seventy and seventy-five; the female Asylum had between seventy-five and eighty occupants. Every year, a few orphans found new homes, or help and support from elsewhere, and left the Asylum. Some of the girls got married. In 1847–8, in the female Asylum, six members got married. In 1848–9, three members got married one of them called Rebecca.

She lived in the female Asylum, and attended the boys' school. In 1847–8, the total number of students in this school was fifty-one. Although the boys and girls were taught different crafts, they followed more or less the same academic syllabus. Great emphasis was laid on teaching the Bible. In addition to that, English literature and British history were taught in the first class; in the second and the third were taught English grammar, the history of Asia and Europe, and geography. It was in these classes that Madhu found Rebecca as a student.

Needless to say, Madhu had to teach each of the prescribed subjects. For four years, he taught the Bible and its history, although in later years he declared that he had no interest in or respect for the religious rituals followed by Christians. At Bishop's College he had learnt the Bible thoroughly and most certainly had acquired the ability to teach it. Moreover, he was also assisted by Rev. Robert Posnett, the priest of the local Blacktown Church. When Posnett left and Rev. John Richardson became the chaplain, he helped Madhu as well.

Soon after he began his new job—in February 1848—the annual exams were held in his school. Three priests arrived to conduct these. They were Revs. Tailor, Brotherton, and Rogers. They were joined by George Giles White, who was previously a teacher of the

Asylum school and, at that time, a teacher in Madras School. A friendship grew between Madhu and White, which later influenced Madhu's life greatly. The examiners were all satisfied with the performance of the students. They said in their report that some of the senior students showed 'a high standard' in their performance. This standard continued to be maintained over the next few years. In the examiners' report[†] in 1850, it was said:

> ...under the judicious superintendence and instruction of the Master and Mistress, the progress made by pupils in various parts of their education and the (*Directors*) confidently trust that the objects contemplated in the nurture and education of these orphans have been realized.

The chaplain, Rev. W. P. Powell, mentioned Madhu's name in particular. While praising the efforts of two of the best students, he said: '...the first as right to be expected, evinced powers of thought, and habits of thinking, which reflected very great credit on their master, Mr Dutt.'

Madhu himself had always been a bright student, and had been taught by good teachers. That is why, even if he did feel a little unsure of himself initially, he was soon able to master the techniques of good teaching. It is clear from the comments made by the examiners that, within a very short time, he became a successful teacher and earned a lot of praise.

However, it does not seem likely that he was happy with a job that brought him only forty-six rupees a month. The post of an assistant teacher was neither important, nor well paid. At one stage, he had refused the job of a catechist, although the salary he was offered then was eighty rupees. It must have caused Madhu a great deal of pain to have to manage now on a much lower salary. Thoughts of family and friends must have disturbed him, too. For the first time in his life, he was truly alone and struggling with the harsh realities of life. It took him some time to settle down and find a proper home. But, eventually, that did happen and Madhu even found himself a wife. The following year, an apparently happy Madhu wrote to Gour: 'However, thank God, my trials are, in a certain measure, at an end, and I now begin to look about me very much like a commander of a barque, just having dropped his anchors in a comparatively safe place, after a fearful gale!'

Apart from finding a job in Madras and earning praise from his employers, Madhu's biggest achievement was falling in love with, and marrying, a white woman. It was the girl called Rebecca, a student in his school. His long-cherished dream of finding a 'blue-eyed maid' was finally fulfilled. Here she was, in the flesh, although it is not known whether she had blue eyes. Marrying her was an extremely unusual event. Until then, many Englishmen, like DLR, had been known to either marry or have relations with Indian women. However, there is no record of an Indian man marrying an English woman. Since such an event was unheard of, quite a few people were keen to stop it. In the same letter, Madhu wrote to Gour: 'I had great trouble in getting her. Her friends, as you may imagine, were very much against the match. However, "All's well that ends well!"'

His wedding took place on 31 July 1848. The witnesses present at the wedding were Jessie Ray Nailor, Jessie's wife Suzannah H. Nailor, and Edward Price. Nailor was only a year older than Madhu. The two remained good friends throughout Madhu's stay in Madras. In fact, a few years later, Madhu was joined by Nailor as a colleague in Madras School. The priest who conducted the ceremony was the chaplain of Blacktown, Robert Posnett.[†] He was one of the directors of the Asylum. The wedding of Madhu and Rebecca[†] became more or less a family affair for the Asylum. The only people missing were the real family members of both the bride and the groom.

How did Rebecca and Madhu fall in love? It is impossible now to say anything for sure. Madhu was dark, unknown in Madras, almost penniless. Yet Rebecca was attracted to him, presumably because she was young, lonely, without any family or close friends to turn to; and Madhu was smart, talented, charming. It was his colourful personality that must have attracted her more than anything else. She also learnt about his passion for poetry, and his romantic outlook. Madhu must have appeared to her as one who would be able to give her the love and security she craved. That is why the colour of Madhu's skin, or his financial situation, did nothing to put her off. Besides, both Charles Kennet and Madhu had told her that although he was a poor usher at the orphan Asylum in actual fact he was the only child of 'an advocate at the Calcutta Supreme Court', Rajnarayan Dutt.

At the time of his wedding, Madhu was required to give details of his father. His tendency to boast made him describe him as an advocate. That was far from the case. In 1848, there were only nineteen advocates in Calcutta. All of them were English, all were barristers. There were fifty-three attorneys,† and even those were either English or Anglo-Indian. Ordinary Indians were pleaders, and there were about four hundred of them at the time. Rajnarayan was one of them. Another point worth noting is that Madhu referred to the chief civil court as the 'Supreme Court'. That, too, may strike some people as an exaggeration. What can be said in Madhu's defence is that, at the time, there was no High Court in Calcutta. In its absence, the *Sadar Diwani Adalat* (chief civil court) and *Sadar Nizamat Adalat* (chief criminal court) were referred to in English as the 'Supreme Court'.

In the matter of providing details of her father, Rebecca's description was just as distorted, but her motives were different. In the marriage register, she put down her father's name as Dugald McTavish. That was not her father's name at all. In the church register, the age of Rebecca Thompson McTavish was shown as seventeen, which meant that she was born in 1831. The church records of 1831 reveal the real names of her parents. Rebecca was born in Nagpur, and baptized on 21 December 1831. Her father's name has been recorded as Robert Thompson, who was a gunner in the Horse Artillery Brigade. Her mother was called Catherine Thompson, and was described as 'Indo-Briton'. This proves that although Madhu told Gour quite proudly that his wife was 'of English parentage', she was not wholly English.

Madhu wrote to Gour in the same letter that Rebecca's father was an indigo-planter. According to the church register, Dugald McTavish was an indigo-superintendent, employed by the Arbuthnott Company. Neither was he the owner of a plantation, nor was he dead. But Madhu clearly did not wish to reveal these discrepancies to his friend.

If Rebecca had signed the register as Rebecca McTavish, one might have accused her of trying to hide her real identity. But she did not do that. She signed her name as Rebecca Thompson McTavish, merely adding 'McTavish' to her real father's surname. Why should she have done that?

From what little is known of Robert Thompson, he married Catherine Dyson in Bangalore in 1825. Banns were put up before their wedding, as in the case of Rebecca and Madhu. Robert and

Catherine had other children apart from Rebecca. The last one of these, Sarah, was born in January 1836. Robert died on 12 April 1844. It is not known what happened to Catherine and Sarah Thompson. However, it is likely that Dugald McTavish offered all of them his support after Robert's death, and became a foster father to Rebecca and Sarah. It was his surname that Rebecca added to her own name at the time of her wedding.

Later in her life, she continued this practice of using the names of her benefactors. Charles was added to the name of her first son, after Charles Kennet and Charles Egbert Kennet, who were so kind to Madhu. J. W. Saalfelt was a family friend and well-wisher. Rebecca added 'Saalfelt' to the name of her second daughter. Her third child was given the name of 'McTavish'.

There is no evidence in the church records to show that Dugald McTavish and Catherine were married. Dugald was born in Scotland in 1783. His younger brother, Colin, also came to India as an assistant surgeon in the army and spent most of his time in and around Bombay. Both brothers married in Britain and went back home when they retired. That is why neither the church records in Bombay nor Madras show details of any birth, death or marriage involving the McTavish brothers. The only mention is in Rebecca's marriage certificate. Although she used his name, she could not have been Dugald's daughter for she lived in an Asylum meant for orphans. Nobody from her family was present at her wedding, which points to the fact that Rebecca was truly an orphan. In his letter to Gour, Madhu mentioned that her friends were opposed to their marriage, but he said nothing about her family. If their marriage took place despite strong opposition from Rebecca's friends, it was only because what Rebecca herself felt in this matter was of paramount importance. The views of others did not matter.

Having met Rebecca, it did not take Madhu long to fall in love with her. In fact, Rebecca's presence in his life made the love in his heart, as well as the poetry in his soul come surging forth. There was no one in the city who knew him well, no one to treat him with tenderness. It was an ideal situation for a man to lose himself completely over a pair of compassionate and admiring eyes. It is clear from Madhu's poetry how deeply he loved Rebecca. Soon after their wedding, when Madhu's heart was still overwhelmed with love and new-found happiness, four of his poems were published in the *Madras Circulator*, in August–September

1848. All were love poems. Madhu wrote these under the pseudonym, Timothy Penpoem. It is not known why he chose the name Timothy. Shelley's father was called Timothy, but Shelley was not a poet to whom Madhu was partial. However, there were certain strange similarities between Shelley's life and his own. The name Timothy is another reminder of those similarities.

The publication of these poems naturally brought greater joy and strengthened his self-confidence. About three and a half months after their marriage, Rebecca became pregnant, which must have added to his happiness. He was thus able to rise above all hardships and deprivations, and devote himself to writing more poetry.

Nevertheless, the harsh realities of life did not fail to rear their heads. Madhu admitted to Gour that things were not easy, although Rebecca's demands could not have been very high. She was an orphan, and before she became one, she had lived with a father who was only a gunner. There was little chance of her harbouring great expectations. Besides, she knew Madhu had no money when she married him. Even so, as a married man Madhu had added responsibilities, which put an extra strain on his finances. By this time, he had moved out of Blacktown and was living in a place called Rayapuram, closer to the sea. The rent he was paying there was higher. Presumably, he began writing in various magazines in late 1848, or perhaps took an extra job, just to make ends meet.

In spite of his difficulties, Madhu wrote *The Captive Ladie* for the *Madras Circulator*. Its full title was *The Captive Ladie (An Indian Tale) in Two Cantos*. He started writing it in early November 1848, and finished it on 25 November. In the introduction, Madhu mentioned that it had been written during a period of grim struggle with want and poverty. He wrote to Gour on 14 February 1849, '...though beset by all manner of troubles, I have managed to prepare a volume for the press. This will by my first regular effort as an author.'

In its opening lines, Madhu pays a tribute to his wife. When it was first published in the *Madras Circulator*, it was dedicated to Richard Nailor, who had helped him greatly in gaining Rebecca's hand in marriage. His feelings for Rebecca are expressed freely in the first few lines:

I'll weave the sunny dreams, those eyes inspire
   In wreathes to consecrate to thee alone,—
Love's offering, gentle one!—to Beauty's Queenly throne.

His beloved had wiped out all his loneliness, his life was now full to the brim. There was no sorrow any more:

> The heart which once has sigh'd in solitude
>   And yearn'd t'unlock the fount where softly lie
> Its gentlest feelings,—well may shun the mood
>   Of grief—so cold—when thou, dear one! art nigh,
> To sun it with smile, Love's lustrous radiancy?

It was not beauty and love alone that he found in plenty in Rebecca; he found an extraordinary source of hope and inspiration:

> ...like that star which, on the wilderness
>   Of vastly ocean, woes the anxious eye
> Of lonely mariner, and woes to bless,—
>   For there be Hope writ on her brow on high,
> He recks not darkling waves,—fears the lightless sky!

It was possible to forget all adversities with her by his side:

> Tho' ours the home of want,—I never repine,
> Art thou not there—

When he wrote to Gour, Madhu described *The Captive Ladie* thus:

...The volume will consist of a tale in two cantos. ...It contains about twelve hundred lines of good, bad and indifferent octo-syllabic verse and (truth, 'pon my honour!) was written in less than three weeks.' It could be that he had laid a bet with someone to finish the whole thing by a certain date. Certainly, in his later life, he was known to lay bets on how long it might take him to finish his work.

He did not give Gour any details of the story on which *The Captive Ladie* was based. However, he explained it in his preface:

The following tale is founded on a circumstance pretty generally known in India and, if I mistake not, noticed by some European writers. A little before the famous Indian expeditions of Mahommed of Ghizni, the king of Kanoje celebrated the 'Rajshooio Jugum' or as I have translated it in the text, the 'Feast of Victory'. Almost all the contemporary princes, being unable to resist his power, attended it, with the exception of the king of Delhi who, being the lineal descendant of the great Pandu Princes—the heroes of the farfamed Mohabarut of Vyasa—refused to sanction by his presence the assumption of a dignity—for the celebration of this Festival was a universal assertion of the claims to being considered as the lord-paramount over the whole country—which by right of descent belonged to his family alone. The king of Kanoje, highly incensed at this refusal, had an image of gold made to represent the absent chief. On the last day of the Feast, the king of Delhi, having entered the palace in disguise with a few chosen followers, carried off this image, together, as some say, with one of the princesses Royal whose hand he had once solicited but in vain, owing to his obstinate maintenance of the rights of his ancient house. The fair princess, however, was taken and sent to a solitary castle to be out of the way of her pugnacious lover, who eventually effected her escape in the disguise of a Bhat or Indian Troubadour. The king of Kanoje never forgave this insult, and when Mahommed invaded the kingdom of Delhi, sternly refused to aid his son-in-law in expelling a foe, who soon after crushed him also. I have slightly deviated from the above story in representing my heroine as sent to confinement before the celebration of the 'Feast of Victory'.

By his own admission, Madhu changed the event as recorded by historians. He was not eager to preserve historical authenticity. His main aim was to focus on the human angle, on the love story. He gave no indication as to why he chose this particular story. But what may be worth considering are the events leading to his own marriage—the son of a rich and famous lawyer in Calcutta wants to marry a young orphan girl, but her friends, who are all from a far less privileged class than the rich lawyer's son, wish to stand in the way. This idea may have subconsciously worked on Madhu's mind before he selected the story of *The Captive Ladie*.

Since it was written in a hurry, a few imperfections remained in it, of which Madhu was aware. He said in his introduction, 'It was originally composed in great haste for the columns of a local journal—The *Madras Circulator and General Chronicle*—in the midst of scenes where it required a more than ordinary effort to abstract one's thoughts from the ugly realities of life. Want and poverty with the "battalions" of "sorrow" which they bring leave but little inspiration for their victim.'

Despite its shortcomings, the editor of the journal was enchanted by *The Captive Ladie*. His enthusiasm strengthened Madhu's belief that his long-cherished dream of attaining fame and glory as a poet was about to be realized. The only stumbling block that stood in his way was lack of funds. He admitted to Gour that the cost of printing in Madras was very high.[†] The poem in two cantos ran about ninety pages. The cost of printing it might well have been between a hundred and fifty and two hundred rupees.

Madhu wrote to Gour in the same letter, 'I am publishing my book by subscription.... Can't you get me a few subscribers? I am sure, if you try, you will succeed. Two rupees per copy is the charge. Surely you will get, at least, forty even from amongst our old school fellows.'

It was not Madhu's intention to make money from this venture. All he wanted to do was recover his costs. A student of Bishop's College, who was visiting Madras, was soon going to return to Calcutta. Madhu wanted to seize this opportunity to send a large number of copies through him.

It would be wrong to assume from this that Madhu renewed his contact with his old friend Gour just to get subscribers for his book. If he did that, one might call him selfish. But he was not like that. The truth is that it was Gour who had tracked him down and written to him first. He had also learnt about Madhu's marriage. How he had received this information is not known. It could be that once he had calmed down, Rajnarayan Dutt tried to find out the whereabouts of his son. It is very likely that he made enquiries at Bishop's College. Or it could be that Madhu himself had informed his mother about having moved to Madras.

Madhu had expected *The Captive Ladie* to be out by early March. Sadly, that did not happen. It saw the light of day only by early April. By that time, the student of Bishop's College had already returned to Calcutta. Madhu had to pay for the despatch of his book by the ship called *Lady Sale*, the same ship which had brought him to Madras.

Madhu's friends in Calcutta came forward quickly to help him. Gour found him eighteen subscribers within three weeks. Others in Bishop's College found twenty-five. Old friends such as Bhudev Mukhopadhyay, Bankubihari Dutt, and Swarup Bandyopadhyay wrote to Madhu on receiving this book, perhaps with names of additional subscribers. Gour told Madhu that it might have been possible to sell the book more easily if there was a 'prospectus' to go with it, explaining what the book was about. However, he asked for fifty copies, even without the prospectus. A few free copies had to be given away, either as gifts to important people, or as review copies to journals. Among the people who received the book as a gift were J. E. D. Bethune (President, Education Council), Digambar Mitra, and Ramchandra Mitra. What is surprising is that there is no evidence that a copy was sent to DLR, who was back in Calcutta at the time, having replaced James Kerr for a year as the principal of Hindu College. But then, even if DLR did get the book through someone else in Hindu College, it is likely that he said nothing complimentary about it, for he was not fond of narrative poetry. If he had uttered even one word of praise, Madhu was sure to have boasted about it to his friends.

Back in Madras, the printer began harassing Madhu for outstanding payments almost as soon as the book was published. He was paid in part, but that did not satisfy him. Madhu wrote at least on two occasions to Gour, asking him to send the money raised by selling his book. On 6 July 1849 he said, 'My printer is impatient...I make you my plenipotentiary to sell the books at any rate you like; only let me have money to pay my printer.'

The Captive Ladie was printed at the Madras Advertiser Press. It was owned by one Abel Penn Simkins. Although initially he put a lot of pressure on Madhu to recover his money, in later years he became quite close to Madhu and offered him his support.

The publication of *The Captive Ladie* forced Madhu to face a few mundane realities of life; but although he had to find enough money to pay his printer, the experience did not teach him to be canny. His only aim in life remained simply to be recognized as a great poet. In that respect, Madras offered him a lot of encouragement. When *The Captive Ladie* was published in a journal, it evoked a most favourable response among the readers and critics. Besides, when the Advocate-General, George Norton (to whom it was dedicated) told him that he felt honoured to receive a literary work that held such extraordinary promise and evidence of the poet's remarkable talents, Madhu was left with no doubt about the excellent quality of his work. In fact, he was convinced that the whole of Madras was prepared to admire him as a poet. He wrote to Gour on 6 July: 'You know that when I came here I had no friends; but now, many a barbarous villain, born and bred here, would be glad to be in my shoes.'

Such a valuation of his work and himself might have been a shade exaggerated, but it is true that *The Captive Ladie* did receive considerable praise in literary circles. In the *Athenaeum*[†] magazine in Madras, a letter was published from a reader who called himself 'Laelius'. The letter was full of praise for *The Captive Ladie*, particularly for its introduction:

There is a melancholy tenderness in that introductory address, which at once charms from its poetic feeling, and elevates from its ardent manliness. In the whole range of recent Poetry we shall rarely meet a sweeter strain of sentiment....

Later, Laelius pointed out some weaknesses in the main work:

The Poem, itself too much—and too fatally perhaps for its popularity—recalls the ov'r burdened sentimentality of the Byron school, and may probably be the effusion of youthful or unpractised musing. It sins, therefore, in exuberance of epithet, and in wanderings of fancy.... More care and fondness is displayed in dressing up the thoughts than in expressing the thoughts themselves.

However, he then followed that up with

But it would be to deny Keats and Shelley, and even to Byron himself, one-half of their poetic merit, to refuse all admiration of beauties, which, however graceful in themselves, often encumber rather than adorn the sentiments to which they are allied.

The points raised by the writer of this letter are all valid. He took the trouble to explain that the poet was not personally known to him: 'In offering a few critical remarks, which some may think of too favourable a character, I must premise that they proceed from a total stranger to the author of this poem—the Preface and Introductory verses to which but too plainly proclaim an obscure and unbefriended man.' In spite of this declaration, it seems likely that the letter was written by someone who knew Madhu well (Richard Nailor, perhaps?). An ordinary reader would certainly have found it difficult to procure a copy as soon as the book was published, read it and write a lengthy letter, all in the space of two weeks. However, if this surmise is wrong and the letter was indeed written by a total stranger, Madhu must have felt delighted to see his work being compared to that of the Romantics. May be he thought that fame and glory would be his, even without landing on England's shore.

No matter what readers and critics said in Madras, Madhu waited impatiently to hear how his poem was received in Calcutta. He asked Gour, more than once, to let him know what their friends had said, or whether any reviews had been printed. Perhaps it was his intention to send *The Captive Ladie* to an English publisher, if Calcutta showered as much praise on him as Madras had done.

There was no response, either from friends or critics, for several weeks. The only person who wrote of his appreciation and admiration for Madhu's skills was his old and devoted friend, Gourdas. He wrote, 'It gives me great pleasure to say that when I finished reading your poem, my beliefs about your talent grew stronger. I can now say with firmer conviction that you will play an important role in Indo-British literature.' However, it is not known what reassurance these words brought Madhu, for Gourdas was not exactly well known for his understanding of literature. Madhu continued to ask him for the views of other friends. At one point, he even considered placing an advertisement for *The Captive Ladie* in the *Hindu Intelligencer*, but changed his mind. In the weeks that followed, he kept telling himself that there was no reason why his work should not be appreciated. Then, on 19 May 1849, a bomb exploded in the pages of the *Bengal Hurkaru*.

It was the first review of *The Captive Ladie*, but it was really more of a personal attack on Madhu than anything else. Fun was made of his name, and the writer went so far as to reveal his own racist attitude by referring to 'heathendom':

There is nothing poetical in the curt and dumpy name of Dutt.... Unpoetical as it sounds *now*, it designates a family whom the gods seem to have made poetical or, at all events, endowed with the wish to be, or the belief that they are so. In Calcutta we have at least three of the name who write English verse...and now we find they have another, if not more, at Madras—yes! at benighted Madras of all places in heathendom!

Then the writer lashed out at what Madhu had said in his introduction, about having written the poem in a hurry and, more importantly, while battling with want and poverty: 'Possibly had our poet looked the ugly realities of life manfully in the face instead of trying to abstract his thoughts from them, he might not have been dependent on Want, Poverty & Co. for his inspiration.' Then he went on to offer Madhu some advice, to the effect that had he 'worked' when he was supposed to (that is, paid attention to his education), he would not have had to face poverty: 'We are not of those that think a poet must necessarily be poor and miserable; but we believe that a youth who pens a stanza when he should engross has only himself to blame if his pen neither brings him fame nor food.'

Strangely enough, when it came to discussing the actual poem, this critic did not say a great deal, except 'The style—which is Scott-Moore-Byronical—and quality of the poem may be judged from the following passage with which it commences and which we think is not bad.'

> The star of the Eve is on the sky,
> But pale it shines and tremblingly,
> As if the solitude around
> So vast—so wild—without a bound,
> Hath in its softly throbbing breast
> Awaken'd some maiden fear—unrest;
> But soon—soon will its radiant peers
> Peep forth from out their deep-blue spheres
> And soon the Ladie Moon will rise
> To bathe in silver Earth and Skies
> The soft-pale silver of her pensive eyes.

After this, the critic goes on to quote another twenty-six lines, proving thereby that the beauty of Madhu's poetry and his sensitive imagination had not failed to move him, no matter what he thought of Madhu as a person. He did not, however, stop here. *Visions of the Past*, which Madhu had added after *Captive Ladie* in the same book, came in for some harsh criticism: 'We like not the *Visions* so well as the *Tale*. The "fragment" is in blank verse, neither very powerful nor very musical.' Even so, he quoted nineteen lines from it.

The critique ended most rudely, with these comments:

These verses of M. M. S. Dutt are very fair amateur poetry; but if the power of making has deluded the author into a reliance on the exercise of his poetical abilities for fortune and reputation, or tempted him to turn up his nose at the more commonplace uses of the pen, the delusion is greatly to be regretted. We believe that none of our Calcutta Dutts has fallen into this ruinous error, but that steadily following their more homely and more profitable vocations, they prudently reserve their poetical powers to amuse their moments of leisure—it will be well if the recreations of Young Bengal were always so innocent.... With this we take our leave of M. M. S. Dutt and his poetry.

Anyone, unless he was a sworn enemy of Madhu, would have been irked by the tone adopted in the review. It is not difficult to imagine what it must have done to an exuberant young man, who had borrowed money to have this book printed, craving recognition as a poet. However, to Madhu's credit, he did not allow it to upset him for too long. Within a fortnight, on 5 June 1849, he wrote to Gour: 'I find that your *Hurkaru* has been somewhat severe with me. Curse that rascal, his article reached me like a shaft which has spent its force in its progress.... Methinks, that after the praises I have received from some whose claims to bestow them are indubitable, I can afford to stand a little abuse.'

Madhu continued to wait eagerly for other reviews, and to hear from his friends. But he had to be disappointed. Some of his friends were said to be angry by the piece in the *Hurkaru*, but there is no evidence that any of them wrote to him at length. Nine days after the review in the *Hurkaru* was printed, the *Hindu Intelligencer* carried a short piece by Kashiprasad Ghosh,[†] the same Indian poet who wrote in English, and whose poem was included in the collection put together by DLR in Hindu College. Ghosh did not say very much about *The Captive Ladie*. Neither did he attack it, nor was he lavish in his praise. If anything, he sounded patronizing:

We have received a book, running into about eighty pages, printed in Madras. There are two poems in it, *The Captive Ladie* and *Visions of the Past*. The writer is called M. M. S. Dutt. Presumably, he is an Indian. This is his first publication and, as such, he deserves every encouragement. He does not lack the qualities that make a true poet. If he applies the skills nature has given him, we have no doubt that, one day, he will reach greater heights in the world of poetry.

Needless to say, these comments did not fill Madhu with great joy and excitement. A third review of his book appeared much later, towards the end of the year (1849), in the *Calcutta Review*. But that was not complimentary, either. It is not known whether Madhu saw it. In any case, by then he had lost his own enthusiasm and eager anticipation to hear what was being said. Several years later, when Madhu was back in Calcutta, he became known for his commitment to his writing, and his diligence. But, as he said in a letter to Gourdas, written on 5 June 1849, 'Diligence can be nurtured only if it is refreshed every now and then with showers of recognition and praise.'

Soon after *The Captive Ladie* was published in Madras and warmly received there, Madhu had started to write another long poem. He was of the belief that this new poem (its title is not known) was going to be even better than *The Captive Ladie*. However, in the absence of any 'showers of praise' from Calcutta, Madhu could not finish it. Nevertheless, he did not see *The Captive Ladie* as a failure. When Gour wrote to him of his own disappointment that it was not better received, Madhu replied to him on 6 July 1849: '...you seem to consider the *Captive* a failure, but I don't.... it has opened the most splendid prospects for me...a short time ago I was sent for by the Advocate-General, Mr Norton. The old man received me as kindly as I could expect...We correspond like friends, and he has given me a most valuable number of classical works, as a "token of his regard".'

When Madhu's book went to the printer, the dedication made was to his friend, Richard Nailor. But by the time the first canto was printed, Madhu was suddenly hit by the idea of dedicating it to George Norton. Norton was a well-known and influential man in Madras. Not only was he the Advocate-General, but also the Adviser and Sponsor of several organizations. Madhu did not know him personally at the time when his poem was being printed. So why did he suddenly think of dedicating the whole book to him? It does appear from this that, although Madhu was not what one might call 'crafty', on occasions he did act with a practical sense. His dedications, made to the right people with enough influence, did sometimes work to his advantage. Although he was very fond of his friends, none of his works is dedicated to them, the only exception being Bhudev Mukhopadhyay. In the case of *The Captive Ladie*, changing the dedication from Nailor to Norton was certainly unfair. Yet it must be admitted that the change did bring him some benefit.

Three months after Madhu's book was published, Norton called Madhu. Not only did he receive him 'kindly', but he also offered him the reassurance he needed. Norton told him that a new college in Madras was soon going to be opened, on the same par as colleges in Dhaka, Benaras, and Hooghly. Madhu might well be given the job of the headmaster or an inspector, he was told.

Sadly, Madhu could not afford to wait until such a college was established. His wife Rebecca was soon going to have a child. He needed a better job immediately. Norton sent him to the headmaster of Madras School, Mr Powell, in the hope that he might give Madhu a job. Powell had been appointed as the headmaster, on the recommendation of the governor, Lord Elphinstone, as soon as Madras School became operational in April 1841. His salary at the time was seven hundred rupees (in 1855 it rose to a thousand), and he was given an additional eighty rupees towards the rent of his house. He was only six years older than Madhu, but he was a powerful man in Madras. Madhu enjoyed meeting him, although he thought that the university was 'a sorry building, and had nothing in the shape of a good library'. Nevertheless, any job at the university was bound to be better than the one he had at the Male Orphan Asylum. Unfortunately, there was no vacant post at the time in Madras School. The college Norton had mentioned did not come into being, either. Madhu was forced, therefore, to stay where he was.

The Captive Ladie did not bring him widespread fame and fortune. But through it, he made some friends in Madras. And more importantly, it did two things for him. Firstly, he learned to exercise the discipline required to write an epic. In future, it stood him in very good stead. Secondly, the criticism hurled at him by certain people in Calcutta gave him food for thought, and made him judge himself and his ambitions more realistically. J. E. D. Bethune was one of the people to whom Madhu had sent a copy of his book as a gift. He had written to Gour, asking him to write these words in the accompanying letter: '(it is) a humble token of the author's gratitude for your philanthropic endeavours in the service of his country.' Bethune's reply,† conveyed to Gour, gave Madhu further food for thought. Bethune said:

...I should take this opportunity, through you, of endeavouring to impress on him the same advice which I have already given to several of his countrymen, which is that he might employ his time to better advantage than in writing English poetry. As an occasional exercise and proof of his proficiency in the language, such specimens might be allowed. But he could render far greater service to his country and have better chance of achieving a lasting reputation for himself, if he will employ the taste and talents, which he has cultivated by the study of English, in improving the standard and adding to the stock of the poems of his own language, if poetry, at all events, he must write.

What Bethune said certainly had some truth in it, but it might be possible that he wrote that letter to Gour after only a cursory glance at the poem. He had offered similar advice to other Indians whose skills and talents were certainly not as great as Madhu's, and had said more or less the same thing in a lecture at Krishnanagar College† just before he received the copy of *The Captive Ladie*.

In any case, well known though Bethune was for his philanthropic work, he was not hailed as a literary critic. There was no reason to treat his as the final word on the merits of either *The Captive Ladie* or Madhu's skills as a poet. Nevertheless, sensitive as he was, Madhu was far more hurt by these remarks than the long, unfavourable review in the *Hurkaru*. His self-confidence was considerably shaken. This is proved indirectly by the words he wrote on the copy of *The Captive Ladie* that he sent to British Museum from Madras. Under his own name he wrote by hand the words, *of Bishop's College, Calcutta.*

He did that possibly because he thought his name alone might not be sufficient to convince the authorities that his book was worth keeping in their collection. If they knew that he was from Bishop's College in Calcutta, they might be suitably impressed. Thirteen years later, when he presented his complete works to the Museum, he did not feel the need to explain who he was, for by then he had heard himself being compared to Milton and Kalidas.

Some of the criticism that came from various people in Calcutta might well have been undeserved. But Madhu did need to be woken up from his dream. It was from this point that he began to realize two things: first, if he continued to hope that his poetry written in English would bring him fame and glory, it would amount to building castles in the air; and second, there was no glory in ignoring one's own mother tongue. In the first letter that he wrote to Gour from Madras (on 14 February 1849), he had said, almost proudly, 'I am losing my Bengali faster than I can mention.' After that, although he spoke modestly at times about his lack of a good grasp over Bengali, he never said anywhere that he was 'losing' it.

Nevertheless, it would be wrong to assume that Bethune's remarks made Madhu stop writing in English at once. He continued to do so, but became increasingly aware of the need to write in his own language. With that end in view, he began to make preparations.

As a matter of fact, almost six months before Bethune's letter was written, Madhu had already asked Gour to send him copies of the Ramayana and Mahabharata, both written in Bengali. Besides, he knew that, even if he wrote in English, he could hardly choose foreign material on which his poetry could be based. The story of the *The Captive Ladie*, as well as the untitled poem that he had begun (but did not complete), were both taken from Indian legends.

The books he asked Gour to send him finally reached him in August, together with Bethune's letter. Only a few days later, on 18 August 1849, Madhu's first child—a daughter (Bertha Blanche)—was born. Madhu's pockets were so completely empty at the time that he hardly knew whether to be happy, or bang his head against a wall. The same day, he wrote to Gour: 'You will be glad to hear that my wife has just given me a little daughter. So I am a father.... I am badly off and have hardly anything to jingle in my pocket. Beg I must not...'.

His financial difficulties continued for a long time. In spite of that, Madhu began studying several classical languages in order to prepare himself for his future writing. In the letter to Gour he mentioned spending two hours in the morning studying Hebrew followed by four hours at the Asylum school, teaching; in the afternoon, he spent another couple of hours learning Greek, which was followed by lessons in Telugu and Sanskrit. In the evening, he studied Latin from five to seven o'clock, and from seven until ten, read English. 'Am I not preparing for the great object of embellishing the tongue of my fathers?' he asked. What is worth mentioning here is that Madhu had started following this strict routine even before Bethune's comments reached him. The importance of knowing more about Indian culture and heritage had already sunk in.

Surprisingly, soon after August 1849, contact with Gour was lost as suddenly as it had been re-established in February that year. Had that not been the case, we would have learnt more about how Madhu continued with his study of all those languages, and how he studied different literature.

What we learn about his life from other sources is that he and Rebecca were very happy with their first child, Bertha.[†] In order to show their gratitude to Charles Kennet, the name 'Kennet' was added to Bertha's name. On 15 November, when she was christened, Charles Kennet and Richard Nailor were both present at the ceremony.

However, after the birth of his child, despite their joy and Madhu's attempts to engage himself in a rigid routine, what drove him to despair was the ongoing battle with poverty. At the time, he was no longer an 'usher' at the Asylum, but the only teacher who ran the school. It is likely that, in order to make ends meet, Madhu wrote in magazines and journals for some extra cash. In fact, the owner of the *Eurasian* magazine appointed him as its editor in 1849. Madhu handled his duties very competently, which indicates that he had had some previous experience in this matter.

The owner of the *Eurasian* was A. P. Simkins. It was his printing press that printed *The Captive Ladie*. Simkins was a capable and shrewd businessman. The journals that were printed by him ran for quite a long time. There was a sizeable Eurasian population in Madras at that time (in 1875 their number rose to twelve thousand). Simkins felt that if a journal could be published that spoke of the needs and interests of the Eurasian community, it was bound to be popular. Although Madhu was an Indian, in his habits and behaviour he was very much a European. He had already proved his command over the English language, and gained some experience in journalism by contributing to other periodicals. To Simkins, he was an ideal candidate for the post of the editor. Since he already had a full-time job, it was possible to hire Madhu at a salary lower than anyone else might have demanded. Madhu started as editor officially from 3 November 1849. It was a weekly journal; a new issue came out every Saturday.

The *Eurasian* helped Madhu in many ways. Not only did it provide him with an extra income, it also gave him the chance to publish his own works. He had spent a lot of time sending his poems to various magazines, and then waiting patiently to see if they were printed. A few magazines in Calcutta did publish some of his works, but neither the *Athenaeum*, nor the *Spectator*—two of the best known journals in Madras—did anything to print his contributions for nearly two years after his arrival there. The only periodical that supported him was the *Madras Circulator*. For this reason, Madhu was happy to accept Simkins's offer. The *Eurasian* was new, and little known. Even so, it was the tool Madhu needed to reach out to a wider readership. It is also likely that Madhu thought this would give him the chance to show senior editors how a journal ought to be run. So he began his job with a lot of enthusiasm and determination.

What the *Eurasian* contained mainly were advertisements, important news from other parts of India as well as local news, letters from readers, and whatever was considered important in those days, such as information about the movement of ships, news related to the army, and events in the courts. Some journals reproduced material from other periodicals. The *Spectator* published a literary supplement on Fridays, which contained material from various magazines in London. Madhu began to fill the *Eurasian* with his own writing. The second issue of the magazine, dated 10 November 1849, carried the first instalment of his play, *Rizia: Empress of Inde*. Between 10 November and 12 January, nine scenes from the play were published.†

The subject and style adopted in *Rizia* were both extremely unusual at the time. No other Bengali writer had thought of using a Muslim source in their writing. The general belief was that no reader would be interested in learning anything about Muslims. Madhu, of course, was different from everyone else. He did not hesitate to walk away from traditional routes, and experiment with new and original ideas. *Rizia* was one of them.

One reason for his choice was that in his childhood, he had studied Persian. Persian literature and the history of the Mughals had made an impression on his mind. Besides, as he said years later in a letter to Keshav Ganguli (dated 1 September 1860), he thought: 'We ought to take up Indo-Mussulman subjects. The Mohammedans are a *fiercer* race than ourselves, and would afford splendid opportunity for the display of passion. Their women are more cut out for intrigue than ours.' When Madhu went back to Calcutta later in his life, he expressed the desire—more than once—to use similar Indo-Mussulman subjects. His friends and sponsors dissuaded him. His thoughts and attitude on this matter made him different not only from his friends, but also from all the intellectuals of those times.

Madhu broke away from his own religion and his own community, to take refuge in a different religion. After a few years, his devotion to the Christian rituals demanded by the church began to weaken. He could never identify himself exclusively with one particular sect or community. He was the only writer in Bengal who was not held back by convention or dogma. In that respect, Madhu was really unique, his writing truly secular.

Madhu's aim in writing *Rizia* was not to sing her praises, or that of all Muslims. In fact, the historical authenticity of the story he describes is also questionable, although he says it is based on Alexander Dow's translation of *History of Hindustan*, originally written in Persian by Mahummad Casim Ferishtah. What Madhu really wanted to do was focus on the human angle of the story. The *Captive Ladie* was no different. There were various dramatic elements in it, but it was basically a love poem. *Rizia*, too, speaks of a love story—the love between two people who, in social terms, live in two different worlds. That is why the story is so full of passion and emotion. In relating this story, Madhu used material from Hindu, Muslim, and Greek legends. At the time, only a handful of Indians could have done that. The difference between the others and Madhu was that even if the others knew something about Muslim history, they did not have the courage and generosity of spirit to use any of it in their writing. Madhu did.

According to the story of the play, Rizia fell in love with one of her own slaves, called Jamal. Naturally, her husband (Altunia, the Sultan of Sindh) was outraged. He plotted against Rizia, eventually dethroning her and presenting her with the chopped head of Jamal. Then he freed Byram, Rizia's brother, who had previously been imprisoned. Byram became the emperor of India. Rizia was captured and finally killed. Obviously, the dramatic rise and fall of fortunes in this story appealed to Madhu, as did the passion, and even the jealousy and violence.

Eight years after he published those nine scenes in the *Eurasian*, Madhu began a new life in Calcutta as a playwright. No doubt writing *Rizia* gave him the experience he needed to be a successful playwright. Sadly, he could not finish the play. The reason was probably simply that he did not find the time to do so. Handling a full-time job and editing a journal must have been very demanding indeed. Nevertheless, Madhu never lost his fondness for *Rizia*. Years later, he tried to rewrite the whole play in Bengali, but did not get beyond fifty lines.

Back in Madras, Madhu was so pleased, even proud, to have written it that he published some shorter poems, without indicating his full name. Instead of the author's name, the words 'by the writer of *Rizia*' appeared under the poems. However, his views about this play are not known in any detail as, for some mysterious reason, he lost touch with all his friends in Calcutta, including Gour. Madhu himself is not to be blamed for this. In the last letter that he wrote to Gour in 1849, on 22 November, he said, 'Are you all dead? Or have I by some unintentional act or other offended you? I really do not remember having received a single letter from you or Bhudeb for the last three months!' There is evidence to suggest that Gour did receive this letter. What is not known is why he did not reply, or why the regular flow of letters between him and Madhu ceased so abruptly. Over the next six years, no letter from Madhu can be traced. But it seems that the two friends did not lose contact altogether. Two letters written by Gour—one in July 1851 and another in April 1852—have been traced. In the first one he complained to Madhu, saying that Madhu had visited Calcutta earlier without contacting him; in the second, he acknowledged that he was receiving the *Hindu Chronicle* that Madhu was sending him from Madras.

To tell the truth, it was not just the letters that stopped. In 1850, Madhu's writing, that was going from strength to strength, particularly after he became the editor of the *Eurasian*, also came to an abrupt halt. The true reason for this is not known. The obvious reason was lack of time. His job, a busier life at home with a small child, learning various languages, and editing a journal—all these must have stood in the way of creative writing. How long he could continue with his language studies is also doubtful.

His wife, Rebecca, had been ailing since the birth of their child. Now, possibly in late February, she and the child went to visit some friends in the Upper Provinces (possibly Nagpur, where she was born), to rest and recuperate. This was the first time since their marriage that they were separated. Madhu missed his family very much. On 9 March, he published in the *Eurasian* a poem called *On the Departure of My Wife and Child to the Upper Provinces*. It said:

> My home is lonely—for I seek in vain
> For them who made its star-light; there's a cry
> Of anguish fiercely wrung by untold pain
> E'en from heart of heart's! Hear it on high.

Not only did he express his sadness in this poem, but also prayed to God for his wife and daughter:

> O Mercy throned thou, Whose eyes of light
> Aye beam with sleepless love—to thee I kneel
> For them—the lov'd—the loving! Yes to thee,
> O Lord—our God of glorious majesty.

During the days of their separation, even as Madhu was thinking of his absent wife and child, something happened that later made their separation a permanent one. Both Madhu and Rebecca knew about this event, but they did not know how it would one day influence their own lives. On 11 April 1850, Rebecca's future rival, Henrietta, lost her mother, Eliza White. It was her mother's death[†] that, in due course, brought her closer to Madhu, although it is likely that Madhu did not know her all that well at the time when her mother died.

It is not known exactly when Rebecca returned, but she was certainly back in Madras by June, for that was when she became pregnant for the second time. At that time, Madhu's chief source of income was his job at the Asylum school. He was the only teacher there, and so he had to handle the duties of the headmaster as well. The directors of the Asylum began to think of appointing someone from England as the headmaster. Madhu felt threatened by this possibility, and decided to speak openly. There was really no reason not to promote him and make him the headmaster permanently. On 29 April 1850, he wrote in the *Eurasian*[†] that he was not just questioning the need for appointing a European teacher in the place of a Eurasian, but was condemning such a proposal unequivocally. He said that the Asylum school was chiefly an East Indian school and that it did not need a European headmaster. He went on to say that the man who had been entrusted with the responsibility of running the school was not inferior to any European in intellect, talent or ability.

The underlying bitterness in these comments indicates that his Westernized behaviour notwithstanding, Madhu was fully aware of the racial discriminations of the British authorities. He had seen plenty of cases of such discrimination, both in Calcutta and Madras. According to his earlier biographers, in Bishop's College, the kind of drink to be offered to a person depended on the colour of his skin and his clothes. Krishnamohan Bandyopadhyay,[†] who encouraged and helped Madhu to convert to Christianity, told of how Madhu himself got into trouble for wearing Western clothes. Therefore, what happened in Madras, that is, the proposed appointment of a European to act as the headmaster, was not Madhu's first brush with racism. It is likely that his comments led to friction between the board of directors of the Asylum and himself. However, Madhu was obliged to spend the next two years in the Asylum school.

A small handful of students in the school were bright and intelligent. But, brought up carelessly amidst want and deprivation, most of them fared poorly in their studies. So there is little reason to believe that Madhu's job as a teacher brought him any great joy. It is also doubtful that his other job, that of the editor of the *Eurasian*, was deeply fulfilling. Madhu was first and foremost a poet. How far his interest ran in pure journalism, keeping abreast of current affairs, is debatable. Perhaps the recognition and respect that went with the job offered him some comfort. Whatever his private feelings, it is true that Madhu did his job as the editor with great sincerity and competence. It was because of this reason that its owner, Abel Simkins, decided to expand its scope to cover a wider readership. On 12 June 1850, the title of the *Eurasian* was changed to the *Eastern Guardian*. The change of name suggests that Simkins wanted his periodical to cater to a wider reading public. In addition to that, he started a new journal for Indians, called the *Madras Hindu Chronicle*. Madhu was asked to edit both. The *Madras Hindu Chronicle* began on 2 October 1850. From the very first issue, Madhu was able to display a high standard. The *Athenaeum* was immediately impressed and wrote that the original articles and the extracts in the paper would create a favourable impression.†

Over the next eighteen months, Madhu performed this task with his customary efficiency. When, at the end of that period, he had to leave it because a new teaching job in Madras School had finally come his way, this is what the *Athenaeum* had to say, on 9 March 1852:

...there is but one paper, The *Hindu Chronicle*, which has any pretensions to merit; and the public will regret to learn that it is likely to be discontinued. Mr Dutt became a writer from the sheer force of ability; and has lapsed into a school master from the force of circumstances. His mental power partakes so much of the nerve and energy of the Saxon spirit, that the distant contemporaries have expressed doubts as to the paternity of the articles in the *Hindu Chronicle*.†

Soon after the *Madras Hindu Chronicle* was launched, Abel Simkins got a good job in the Military Board and left his printing business. The chronicle was then bought by C. M. Pereyra and the *Eastern Guardian* by Lawrence and Company. While Pereyra continued to employ Madhu, the *Eastern Guardian* found a new editor.

Only a few of the articles written by Madhu have been traced. He wrote on such subjects as the education of the natives (March

1851), the remarriage of Hindu widows (May 1851), and on the Mughal rule juxtaposed against the British Raj. His comments were both progressive and fearless, even when they upset not just the British rulers, but also fellow Hindus.

Many of his articles appeared in 1851, which proved to be an eventful year for him. In early 1851, his mother died. She could not have been more than forty-two or forty-three. By that time, Madhu had virtually become a stranger to her. Not only had he become a Christian, but had been living hundreds of miles away, for several years. Even so, he had not forgotten her love for him. When the news of her death reached him, he felt he had to return to Calcutta, however briefly. He had always been short of money, so was unlikely to have had enough to pay for a return ticket and travel in a cabin. His name does not appear on any list of passengers on a ship that travelled to Calcutta from Madras that year. It seems that he travelled as a 'deck passenger'. Names of passengers who travelled on the deck were not recorded in those days.

Strangely enough, it was not Gourdas who told him about his mother's death, but his own father, Rajnarayan Dutt. Whether he informed his son out of a sense of duty, or it was his dead wife's last wish, we do not know. What we do know is that Madhu somehow managed to travel back to Calcutta and face his father, possibly some time in May or June, 1851.

It is difficult to say whether Madhu held himself responsible for his mother's untimely death and all the pain she had had to suffer. As far as Rajnarayan was concerned, he had no compunction about holding his son responsible for most of his misfortunes. The atmosphere at home must have been so awkward that Madhu left as hurriedly as he had arrived. It is likely that he did not have a great deal of respect left for his father. What Madhu could not have known, though, was that this brief meeting with his father in 1851 was to be his last.

During his short stay in Calcutta, Madhu did not meet any of his friends, not even Gour. The only person he did see was Rev. Jodunath Ghosh.† Gour heard about Madhu's visit from Ghosh, and felt justifiably hurt. On 29 July 1851, he wrote to Madhu, 'You finished your work and went back to your favourite city. I was very sorry to hear that, since I would certainly have expected you to have given me the chance to meet you.... It is clear that you have no affection for me.' When Madhu received this letter, he arranged to send to Gour copies of the *Madras Hindu Chronicle*; but whether or not he replied to his friend's letter is not known. What is known is that even after this letter regular correspondence between them was not established.

In 1851, another significant event occurred in Madhu's life. It was the birth of his second daughter, Phoebe.† She was born on 9 March. With her birth, Madhu's expenses went up, which was sure to have cast a shadow on whatever joy he might have felt. It took him a long time to organize Phoebe's baptism, which took place on 3 August. It was attended by the Kennets, and another family friend, J. W. Saalfelt. Once again, Madhu and Rebecca expressed their appreciation for their friends' kindness by naming their daughter after them. Charles Kennet had recently married, and Phoebe was his wife's first name. 'Saalfelt' was also added to the baby's name.

Twenty days later, Charles Kennet died, and was mourned by a large number of people in Madras. On 23 August 1851, the *Athenaeum* wrote that the number of people who attended the funeral of Charles Kennet was unusually high for Madras. He had worked as the honorary secretary of the Orphan Asylum for thirty years and it was not just the orphans who were helped by him. Madhu and Rebecca got a lot of help from him as well. He was indeed a great friend of the Dutts and they therefore must have been very saddened by his loss.

Towards the end of October, Rebecca became pregnant for the third time. Madhu was now desperate for another job with a bigger salary. His domestic anxieties affected his writing so much that, for a whole year, he did not write anything at all. It is possible that he was trying hard for another job and must have asked his mentor, George Norton, to help him. It is difficult to understand why, as the Advocate-General, Norton was unable to find a government post for Madhu—even an inferior post, if he could not offer him the post of a deputy magistrate. A number of Madhu's friends had become deputy magistrates with qualifications similar to his.

Madhu's dream of financial stability was never fulfilled. The reason for that was not just ill luck, but his own inability to be thrifty. When he had any money, he spent all of it without thinking of the consequences.

In early 1852, however, things finally began to improve for Madhu. A post fell vacant in the Madras High School, which was then called Madras University. Mr H. Bowers,† who used to teach English language and literature there, took early retirement at the age of thirty-four, and decided to return to Europe. Madhu's name had already been recommended by Norton to the headmaster of the school. He was chosen unanimously by the board of directors. In their letter to the Governor, they described Madhu as a scholar of high calibre. 'This gentleman's attainments,† as well in classical as in English literature, are of a distinguished quality—and although a young man he has already had considerable experience in Tuition.'

At the time of Madhu's appointment, there were, apart from the headmaster, E. B. Powell, three other teachers (or tutors, as the school called them): George Giles White, J. McLeash, and Adam A. Gordon. McLeash was Anglo-Indian, the others were British. Madhu was appointed at a salary lower than that of his English colleagues. But he accepted it, as it was certainly more than what he was getting at the Asylum. Powell had a salary of seven hundred rupees, excluding eighty rupees paid towards the rent of his house. Gordon, who passed his MA, and then had teacher's training at a college near London, came to Madras in 1846–7 and had a salary of three hundred and fifty rupees. He was the assistant headmaster. White and McLeash were paid two hundred rupees. Madhu was offered a salary of one hundred and fifty rupees only.

His decision to join Madras School made the directors of the Asylum close the boys' school there, although the official reason for the closure was shown as something quite different. It was said that the boys' school was closed only because two other schools in the area had been established. The students of the Asylum school were placed in the care of Rev. Tailor,† who ran one of the two new schools.

The Asylum school was closed on 8 March and Madhu must have joined Madras School within a few days. How far he actually enjoyed teaching is not known, since he never wrote to anyone about his experiences. Presumably, to a degree, he was inspired by the example set by his favourite teacher in Hindu College, D. L. Richardson. In his new job, Madhu was required to teach history, poetry, and geography. Not only was he extremely well-read, but had published his own poetry and a play. It could well be that

Madhu thought of himself as best suited to teach literature. On the other hand, his fellow teachers, who were English, might have undermined his suitability. If this led to occasional friction between colleagues, that is not surprising.

In spite of these minor problems, Madhu must have been very pleased to have finally got the job after waiting so long. The salary and the prestige that went with the new job were both so much more than what the old one could ever offer. Besides, when he started, Madhu was under the impression that he could still continue working as the editor of the *Madras Hindu Chronicle*, thereby earning some extra money. Unfortunately, on this particular issue, things did not work out as he had hoped. In fact, Madhu received quite a severe shock when he discovered that both Norton and Powell—the two men who were so impressed by his talents—were now standing in his way. The school committee told him quite frankly that if he wanted to work as a teacher there, he would have to give up his job as an editor. The argument was that his teaching was bound to suffer if he had the additional pressure of looking after the journals. Perhaps the committee was right. But Madhu could not accept this without protest. He had a number of friends willing to support him. The *Athenaeum* took up the fight. After criticizing a number of local periodicals, it said that the only Indian periodical that could boast of a high standard was *The Madras Hindu Chronicle*. It was in danger of folding up because its most able editor, Mr Dutt, was forced by circumstances to take a job in Madras School. The school board's claim that his teaching would suffer if he continued to work for the journal was not true. It was the Indian periodical that would suffer a loss if Mr Dutt left, the *Athenaeum* maintained.

The *Athenaeum* went on to praise Madhu as a fine example of what a native could achieve as a result of exposure to western education. Sadly, these comments did not work. The school committee was adamant. Clearly, it was not happy about the influence Madhu could wield through his journals. The committee must have been aware of how he gained popular support when he wrote in the *Eurasian* against the appointment of a European teacher in the Asylum school. It was not desirable that a new teacher in Madras School should have such a powerful weapon at his disposal. Madhu was naturally unhappy at the committee's decision, but had no option but to bow before it.

About four months after he started in Madras School, Rebecca gave birth to their first son, on 26 July 1852. By this time, financially they were slightly better off. Madhu arranged for his son's baptism within two months.† On 17 September, his son was christened George John McTavish Dutt. This time, Rebecca and Madhu chose the surname of their benefactor, Dugald McTavish, as the third name of their child.

By this time, Madhu had moved out of Raipuram, and was living in a quieter area called Vapoury Castlet. He had come to know some of his colleagues quite well, and had known one of them— George White†—was known to him since his time at the Orphan Asylum School. White took an active interest in matters related to the orphan Asylum. Now, he began to visit Madhu at home, possibly because he was lonely, and he enjoyed Madhu's company. As has already been mentioned, White had lost his wife, Eliza, two years before he and Madhu became colleagues. By a strange twist of fate, it was his intimacy with White that led to the total disintegration of Madhu's happy home, just when things seemed to be getting better.

At the time, George White had three teenaged children. The oldest among these was Amelia Henrietta Sophia. The younger children were both boys: William John Thomas and Edwin Arthur White. Henrietta was born on 19 March 1836.† When Madhu met these young children, he must have immediately felt a great deal of sympathy for them. When he lost his mother in 1851, his sympathy must have grown deeper. George White remarried less than three years after the death of his first wife.† In itself, that was not a remarkable occurrence. What was remarkable was that White was forty-seven years old, and his new bride— Emily Jane Short—only sixteen. Madhu's father had also remarried, more than once; and his new wives were also very young. The difference between the two cases was simply that Rajnarayan Dutt had had no choice. White did. It was impossible to find older, unmarried girls among Hindus. But White could have found an older woman, had he so wished. Did White feel any regret, or guilt, about the enormous difference in age with his wife? We do not know, but at the time of his wedding, he did not reveal his age. On the wedding documents, he simply wrote, 'of full age'.

Henrietta and her siblings were not happy about their father's second marriage. Henrietta, in particular, could not get on with her stepmother, who was slightly older than her. Madhu, as it happened, had witnessed a similar situation. His relation with his stepmothers was not strained, but he was fully aware of the complexities of the situation. His heart went out to George White's children. Henrietta turned to him for support and sympathy, which was willingly given. Over a period of time, that sympathy turned to love.

It was not just his children that White managed to offend. Waves of scandal spread through the small Anglo-Indian community in Madras, so much so that White was obliged to seek early retirement from Madras School. He was replaced by J. S. Jenkins. How this development affected Madhu's relationship with White and Henrietta, one can only guess.

About the same time, a lot of other changes also took place in Madras School. On 12 July 1852, Norton and five others from the board of governors handed in their resignations. Norton had been president of the Madras University Committee since its formation in 1838. The reason was simply that Norton and the others wanted to minimize the number of students[†] and hence were in favour of charging a higher fee. But their views were disregarded and, on 1 January 1853, the tuition fee was reduced from four rupees to two in the high school; in the primary branch, the fee was only one rupee. Almost at once, the number of students more than doubled. It became 221 in the high school, and 278 in the primary.

Several changes were made to the teaching staff as well, but Madhu remained in his old post, at the same salary. However, he did succeed in getting an appointment for his friend, Richard Nailor, who left his job in a different school and joined Madhu's. This may have brought him some comfort, since it was chiefly on his recommendation that Nailor was appointed. But other events could only have brought him discontent. Among his English colleagues, Jenkins and Bowers had no degree. The latter returned from England to be appointed as professor of English on 26 January 1853. In Madhu's eyes, they were certainly not better qualified to hold higher posts and earn bigger salaries. He found it difficult to accept their promotions. This led to such frustrations that, within two and a half years, he was forced to leave his job. Or it could be that his relationship with his colleagues deteriorated, as a result of which he lost his job.

Be that as it may, having obtained a job in Madras School and being less harried by financial worries, Madhu might have gone back to writing poetry; but he did not. However, in early 1854, he delivered a lecture which was published as a booklet in April. Just before he wrote this lecture, Madhu was injured in an accident and become housebound for several weeks. The lecture was written during that time. Its title was *The Anglo-Saxon and the Hindu: Lecture I*. It is possible that he wrote more than one lecture on this subject, but only one is now available. Those who wish to look upon Madhu as a Hindu will not be happy with the comments he made in this lecture. He said nothing complimentary about the Hindu religion, or its mythology. On the contrary, his words indicated contempt for most things Indian. In fact, the views expressed here are in direct conflict with those expressed through his major poetry. That is why, his admirers are often willing to completely ignore and overlook this lecture.

However, *The Anglo-Saxon and the Hindu* is an essay that should be considered seriously, if all of Madhu's writing is to be considered in its totality. This particular essay is a clear indication of the confusion and contradictions still present in Madhu's mind, caused by his adoption of different values taught by different religions and cultures. It is clear that when he wrote it, the Christian influence on him was predominant. This is what he said in his lecture:

The Hindu!—Alas! Centuries of servitude and oppression; the predominance of a superstition, dismal and blasting; a fatal adherence to institutions whose cruel tendency ever it is to curb and to restrain...and violently repressing every inborn longing to be free; these alas! have rendered that name a name of reproach—an astonishment, a proverb and a byword among the nations!

Then he went on to say, '...it is the Solemn Mission of the Anglo-Saxon to renovate, to regenerate, to civilize, or in one word, to Christianize the Hindu!'

He praised not only the Anglo-Saxon as a post-Renaissance progressive force, but also praised its Christian character:

The Anglo-Saxon is the soldier of the Cross—the Crusader, who has come to the sunny East to carry on a bloodless, though a far more glorious war, than did the lion-hearted Richard, than did the puissant Edward—the first of that name. After quelling the obstinate antagonism, after crushing the stout resistance of European Paynimrie, the victorious gonfalon of the

Cross is now unfurled before the mighty and vast citadel of Brahminism, and it is the hand of the Anglo-Saxon which must plant it on the embattled towers of that citadel.

There can be no doubt that, certainly at this stage, Madhu was a devout Christian. None of his close friends in Madras was a Hindu. From Charles Egbert Kennet to George White, everyone he knew was either European or Anglo-Indian. Even the person to whom he dedicated this lecture—John Henry Kenrick,[†] the secretary of the Madras Polytechnic—was a devout Christian. Whether his faith in the Anglo-Saxons remained unshaken or not, we will learn in due course. But his admiration for the tolerance and some other values taught by Christianity only became stronger with the passage of time.

⁂

The exact date of Madhu's departure from Madras School is not known. His name appears on the list of teachers dated 30 April 1855.[†] It is likely that he left soon after that. His mentor, the principal, Mr Powell, left Madras for Europe on a long vacation after 30 April. It is difficult to say whether after that Madhu was obliged to leave the school, or if he left voluntarily. Nailor's name disappeared from the list of teachers after 30 April. The school also turned into a government school after this date. Luckily, Madhu found another job immediately, that of the sub-editor of the *Spectator*, which became a daily paper from 6 March. Prior to that, it had been published three times a week. Its name was then altered slightly to the *Madras Spectator*. Some believe that although Madhu was known as the sub-editor, it was he who edited the entire paper. This could well be true.

Only a few days after the *Spectator* became a daily paper, Rebecca gave birth to their fourth child—another boy, who they decided to call Michael James.[†] For various reasons, Michael junior could not be baptized for a whole year. As a matter of fact, Madhu did not get to witness this event at all.

On 19 December 1855, Madhu received a letter from Gourdas, after many years.[†] It was written from Madhu's house in Kidderpore, which must have brought back many happy memories for Madhu. In his letter, Gour did not immediately explain why he was in that house. All he did was express regret at having lost touch with his friend, and asked why Madhu had not written to him in the intervening years. Then he mentioned that he had lost his wife.

This must have saddened Madhu, and he may have felt embarrassed by his own silence. But what Gour went on to say in the same letter came as a severe shock:

> I regret I have little good news to give you of your family or rather your father's family. You must have heard ere long that both your parents are dead and that your cousins are fighting over the property left... Two widows survive your father, but they are very near being deprived of their late husband's effects by your greedy and selfish relatives. If you come in time you will yet save it from a ruinous litigation and receive unreserved possession of your own estate to the utter dismay and disappointment of all illegal claimants.

Madhu had lost touch with his father, but did not know that he was dead. This news upset him a great deal. After all, there *was* a time when father and son were very close and proud of each other. Madhu wrote to Gour of his pain, on 20 December 1855:

> Your welcome, though unexpected, letter was put into my hands by Mr Banerjee yesterday. It absolutely startled me. I knew that my poor mother was no more, but I never thought I was an orphan in every sense of that word! My dearest Gour, what am I to do? Your talk of my property—what has he left behind?...Ah! those relatives of mine. Great God! But for you,...I would not have heard a word, about my father's death, for months, perhaps years. O dearest Gour! when and where did he die? I feel distracted. Give me all the particulars.... Yes, dearest Gour, I have a fine English wife and four children.... I am most affectionately your own friend—unchanged and unchangeable.

In the same letter, Madhu told Gour that he would travel to Calcutta by the next available ship that was to sail on 27 December. However, possibly due to financial reasons, he could not board that ship. On 5 January, Gour replied to his letter:

> I am too poor in language to describe the joy and delight I felt at the receipt of your warm and loving letter. The black border alarmed me, but the contents gave me not only unmixed satisfaction but at once dismissed all the cruel fears and misgivings which had filled my mind when your relatives and friends at Kidderpore assured me that you were no more.... Your worthy father died on 16 January 1855.... His last acts prove that he was not in his perfect senses towards the close of his life.... I cannot give you an accurate idea of his property. You know best what his estate

in Jessore is valued at. His personal property cannot amount to much; but his Kidderpore house is said to be worth four thousand rupees. Sufficient no doubt has been left to enable you to defray the expenses of a voyage to and back from Calcutta. I am anxious to see you here because your presence will not only put an end to the litigation pending over the property but scare away the illegal claimants whose sole intention seems to be to profit by the unprotected effects of the intestate deceased.... The first thing that came across me at my new station (Kidderpore) is the investigation of an Act IV case regarding the very house in which I passed many a pleasant day with one of my best friends.

In the same letter, Gour pleaded with Madhu to come back to Calcutta with his whole family. He said that it might not be difficult to find a job in Calcutta—particularly that of a teacher or school inspector—which would certainly be better paid than what Madhu was earning as the sub-editor of the *Madras Spectator*.

Thus reassured, Madhu finalized his plans of going to Calcutta. It took him some time to raise enough funds and make other arrangements. He could finally board a ship to Calcutta only in late January, 1856.

What Madhu did not know then was that he would never return to Madras. During his long absence, a certain aspect of his life which had so far remained a secret, was exposed. It came like a sweeping hurricane, and destroyed the home and marriage that Madhu had built so carefully with Rebecca. Not only did he never see his 'fine English wife' again, but his daughters Bertha and Phoebe, and sons, George and Michael were lost to him as well.

How did it all happen? There is no way of getting all the details, but his relationship with Henrietta (George White's daughter) finally became public knowledge, and eventually Rebecca heard about it. Presumably, when the 'sympathy' he was showing Henrietta gradually turned to something deeper—and there is no reason to believe that it was all entirely platonic—it did not affect his marriage. Madhu led, as it were, a 'double' life. If there was even a hint of trouble in his marriage or home, he would not have written to Gour so happily and proudly, 'I have a fine English wife and four children.' Perhaps he simply thought, 'Why not let things be as they are?'

One reason why he was drawn towards Henrietta could well have been that she was better educated than Rebecca, and had considerable knowledge of literature. In later years, she learnt

Bengali and tried to become a true soul-mate for Madhu. But, at the time, Madhu was certainly not prepared to leave his wife and children for Henrietta. He still loved his wife, and had not forgotten how she had stood up to her friends in order to marry him. He must have made his position clear to Henrietta, who realized that there was no point in expecting Madhu to leave his family and marry her.

When Rebecca learnt the truth, neither could she accept it, nor forgive her husband. She had risked the displeasure of her own people to marry a dark 'native' with no prospects; then she had put up with endless deprivations, just to be with her husband and children. Madhu's act of infidelity wounded her so deeply that she refused to have him back in her life. Did Madhu offer to end his relationship with Henrietta? We do not know. It is entirely likely that he was so deeply involved with her that to leave her was impossible for him, which would naturally have driven the last nail in the coffin, as far as his marriage was concerned.

When Madhu left Madras, his youngest child, Michael James, was only ten months old. Two months after his departure, on 2 April, this child was baptized and, on 21 April, he died.† Even then Madhu did not return to Madras. Neither the bonds of love, nor a sense of duty towards his children could make him go back. Thirteen years earlier, when he had left his home to become a Christian, he had shown a similar determination not to allow anything—not even love for his family—stand in his way. It was a special feature of Madhu's character.

Even so, his behaviour at this stage is difficult to understand. If he had simply left Rebecca, that might have been easier to explain. There are times when a person does things to hurt the people he—or she—loves sincerely. But why did he leave four innocent children? It is not as if he left a lot of money for them. It was difficult enough for him to raise the funds required to pay for his travel to Calcutta. He had asked Gour to let him know if the costs could be recovered from his father's assets. So it would not be wrong to say that by turning his back on his children, Madhu committed an act of cowardice. When he had turned away from his mother, he had declared that in order to worship the Muse of poetry, it was necessary to make a lot of sacrifices, even break one's ties with one's parents. But now, when he broke his ties with his children, he offered no explanation to anyone, not even to

Gour. However, he was not entirely heartless. Later in his life, guilt and remorse for his action ate away into his soul. He could never forget what he had done. But it was too late to make amends. All he could do was express his feelings through his poetry, and utter cries of genuine anguish.

Rebecca could not forget her husband, either. When she died of tuberculosis more than thirty-six years after Madhu's departure from Madras, her name was recorded in the church papers as Rebecca Thompson Dutt.† She was never formally divorced. One reason for this could be that she wanted to make sure that Henrietta—who was responsible for Rebecca's marriage breaking up—should never be able to marry Madhu.

During Madhu's journey from Madras to Calcutta, another strange thing happened. On the list of passengers, his name changed from 'Dutt' to 'Holt'.† His other biographers have speculated a great deal over this, and put forward several theories: (a) that he did not want Rebecca or her friends to discover which ship he was on; (b) that the cabin was reserved in the name of a Mr Holt, who sold his ticket to Madhu at the last minute and there was no time to change the name; and (c) since no Indian could travel in a cabin, Madhu had to assume an English name.

None of these theories is correct. Madhu travelled on a ship called the *Bentinck*, which was travelling from Southampton to Calcutta, via Madras. The *Athenaeum* of 29 January 1856 reported under its 'Shipping Intelligence' that the *Bentinck* was to carry from Madras six 'gentlemen' as passengers, a native, two Indian servants, and two grooms. One of the 'gentlemen' was called Mr M. M. Dutt.

Why, then, did he come to be known as 'Holt'? The main passengers were all European. It took them only four days to travel to Calcutta from Madras. In that short time, Madhu caught everyone's attention as an educated man, who spoke impeccable English. It appears that the others started calling him 'Holt' more or less as a joke. The staff on the ship entered that name in the list of passengers, instead of 'Dutt'.

So, although Madhu began his journey under one name, four days later, he arrived under a different one. In truth, he left his old life behind in Madras, and a totally new chapter began with his return to Calcutta.

Chapter Four

'My dear Gourdas,...I am here. I came this morning in the *Bentinck*. Just fancy, they have given me a new name—"Mr Holt"! If you can *quietly* call over, do so. I do not wish people to know that I am here just now.'

Madhu wrote this letter to Gour from Bishop's College, Calcutta, on 2 February 1856.

Two things about this letter may strike one as odd. It is not clear why he wanted to keep his arrival a secret. Besides, the tone is decidedly light-hearted, hardly the kind of tone one might expect from a man who had left his wife and four small children only five days prior to his arrival. Of course, it could be that the storm over his relationship with Henrietta had not yet broken, and his marriage—as far as he knew—was still intact. But there is evidence to suggest that it was not long after he reached Calcutta that things soured between him and Rebecca. Three months after his departure from Madras, his close friend, Charles Egbert Kennet also visited Calcutta, with his wife. The reason for this visit is not known. But it could well be that they came to act as arbitrators between Madhu and Rebecca. Be that as it may, it soon became clear that Madhu had no plans of going back.

Within a few weeks of his arrival, Madhu asked Gour to help him to get a job, not only because he needed money, but also because he realized that he would have to stay in Calcutta for a long time. It is, however, not clear why he decided to stay in Calcutta for long—to recover his parental properties, or because he discovered that he did not have a family in Madras to go back to. In any case, it was not what he had planned when he left Madras. At that time he must have expected that once his relatives learnt about his return, they would all retreat. He had no idea that reclaiming his property would become a complex and long-drawn affair.

When he arrived, Madhu did not have a great deal of money with him. He had to ask Gour to lend him some. Gour gave him fifty rupees, for which Madhu expressed 'a thousand thanks'. More or less at the same time, he left Bishop's College and moved to Gourdas's place.

It was while he was staying there that Gour invited two of their influential friends for a meal, in the hope that they would be able to find a suitable job for Madhu. These friends were Digambar Mitra,[6] a rich nobleman and Kishorichand Mitra,[7] a magistrate of the police court. Everyone thought Madhu was seeking employment because he would have to spend a long time in Calcutta in connection with his case. But perhaps Madhu knew that after what had happened, there was no way he could go back to Madras.

Finding a job in Calcutta was, naturally, not easy. In fact, the competition there was much tougher than in Madras. Madhu was an experienced teacher and journalist. But he failed to find anything in either area. We do not know whether he approached a journal for a job. But he certainly applied for the post of the

---

[6] Digambar Mitra (1817–79) was a well-known personality of nineteenth-century Bengal. He was a student of Derozio at Hindu College and a member of Young Bengal. He began his career as a junior civil servant, but worked up through different cadres to become a manager of a zamindary estate. It was through share dealings that he earned a fortune and later became a well-known zamindar himself. He was one of the first politicized Indians. He was a patron of cultural activities. Madhu dedicated his best work, *Meghnadbadh Kabya*, to him.

[7] Kishorichand Mitra (1822–73) was also a student of Derozio and a prominent member of Young Bengal. He was a good scholar and became an assistant secretary of the Asiatic Society. Eventually, he became a deputy magistrate and, later, one of the police magistrates of Calcutta. He was associated with a number of periodicals including *Indian Field* and the *Hindoo Patriot*. He was enthusiastic about social reform and supported the movement for the remarriage of widows. He published a number of books.

headmaster in the Hooghly Normal School. He was asked to take a written examination which, sadly, he failed. The post went to his friend, Bhudeb Mukhopadhyay. Bhudeb had been a bright student, and Madhu was genuinely fond of him. Even so, it is reasonable to assume that when Bhudeb got the job, Madhu was disappointed.

Eventually, the job that Madhu did find was in a most unlikely place—the police court. It was Kishorichand Mitra who helped him to get this job. He and Madhu were once fellow students in Hindu College. Not only did Madhu get a job with his help, but also began living in his house in Dum Dum. Kishorichand's wife, Kailashbasini, had known Madhu as a child, in Kidderpore. It could be that she asked her husband to invite Madhu to stay in their house.

Madhu's first job was possibly that of an interpreter. It was rather poorly paid. However, very soon he became a judicial clerk. His salary rose to a hundred and twenty-five rupees. Compared to what he was getting in Madras, it was not too bad. However, many of the Bengalis employed by the police court were then earning a lot more. Kishorichand himself was paid eight hundred rupees per month. The interpreter in another court was paid six hundred.† No doubt, Madhu was disappointed and frustrated to see others far less talented than himself earn far more money. It was for this reason that, eventually, he decided to study law and earn a bigger income.

Madhu spent some time at Kishorichand's house in Dum Dum before finding his own place, possibly in August or September. According to Kailashbasini's memoirs, her husband became seriously ill in August with a damaged liver. The reason for this was excessive drinking. Kailashbasini, naturally, blamed his friends with whom he drank. Madhu was one of them. Since he was actually staying with them at the time, it is not surprising that she blamed him more than anyone else. Madhu must have left their house around that time, though it is not known where he went.

As a matter of fact, it took Madhu a long time to settle down even when he found his own place. His creative urges seemed to have dried up. He did not do any creative writing in 1856. The reasons are not difficult to imagine. His life in Madras was over, his family left behind. He must have continued to feel concerned for his children, if not for his wife. On the other hand, there were anxieties regarding his new love, Henrietta. In addition to all that, he was involved in a court case over his father's property.

Madhu went to Kidderpore soon after his return to Calcutta, with a view to informing his relatives that he was back. He was said to have felt greatly disturbed to see his widowed stepmother. But the relatives who wanted to acquire Rajnarayan's property were not prepared to give up without a fight. They had not even informed Madhu of his father's death. On the contrary, they had spread the word that Madhu, too, was dead. Among others, two of his first cousins—Baidyanath Mitra and Peary Mohan Dutt—told Gourdas about Madhu's death.† If, by sheer chance, Gour had not been appointed to investigate the matter when Madhu's relatives began fighting over who was the rightful heir, Madhu might never have learnt that his father was no more; and all his friends, including Gour, would have assumed that Madhu himself had died.

While Madhu was trying to come to terms with the turmoil in his own life, two major upheavals rocked the country in 1856 and 1857. The first was the introduction of the Hindu Widow Remarriage Act. The Act was passed on 25 July 1856, after a movement led by a large number of progressive people in Bengal and other parts of India. Madhu's friends, including Gourdas Basak, Kishorichand Mitra and Rajnarayan Basu, took part in this movement. The most important leader was Ishwarchandra Vidyasagar. Several years later, he was to become Madhu's great friend and patron. Even Madhu had written in favour of this Act in the *Madras Spectator* and the *Hindu Chronicle*.

Although no widow was remarried for a long time even after the Act was introduced, it created a social upheaval. In the face of strong opposition from the conservative society, no one agreed to marry a widow. Even a cash reward of one thousand rupees declared by Kaliprasanna Sinha, a well-known nobleman and social reformer, failed to motivate anybody. Eventually, Vidyasagar and his friends were successful in persuading Shrishchandra Vidyaratna to marry a child widow. He was a colleague of Vidyasagar at Sanskrit College. Not only did he receive cash rewards, but a year later, became a deputy magistrate. The wedding took place in December 1856. The event was recorded in the diaries of several people, including Madhu's host, Kishorichand. Later, Rajnarayan Basu wrote about it in his autobiography. He recalled that people on that day were so shocked that they considered it was the end of all old values and norms.

Even before the furore over the Hindu Widow Remarriage Act could die down, the Sepoy Mutiny started in 1857. But although this shook the whole of northern India and gathered a lot of popular support, in Bengal it received only limited support. The educated high-caste Hindus in Bengal were the first to be benefited by the British rule. The Permanent Settlement of 1793 also helped develop a middle-class landed gentry in Bengal. These people were able to build a stable society with the help of education, trade, and ownership of land. Most of the intellectuals of the time, including Madhu, were products of that society and social system, established during British times. Moreover, there were hardly any Bengalis in the army. Therefore, members of the Bengali educated and landed middle class did not want to see that stability replaced by the havoc and uncertainty of a mutiny. Indeed, most of them considered it an unfortunate rebellion.

One cannot help wondering how Madhu had reacted to the mutiny, particularly in view of his article, *The Anglo-Saxon and the Hindu* which he had written only three years before the mutiny started. He was not in favour of driving the British out to re-establish the Mughals, or to hand the country over to some Indian raja. But that certainly does not mean that he was entirely pro-British. The truth is that he could, and did, make a clear distinction between the culture and heritage of the British, and the British authorities who ran the country. In his eyes, a race that had produced poets like Shakespeare, Milton, and Byron was worthy of unqualified admiration.

However, his personal experience in dealing with some of the British rulers was not always a pleasant one. In Bishop's College, he had had to face racism. In Madras, starting with the objections raised by Rebecca's 'white' friends over their marriage, to being denied the post of the English teacher in Madras School, as well as being paid less than the others, Madhu was reminded time and again that he was not 'good enough' for the British, just because he was a 'dark' Indian. When he was editing the two journals in Madras with remarkable efficiency, a fellow editor of another periodical called him 'Mr Dirt'.† His views regarding the mutiny, therefore, could only have been mixed, and much more complex than those held by the average educated Bengali.

Soon after the Sepoy Mutiny, another movement started in Bengal. This time, it was directed against the indigo planters who exploited poor farmers. While it has to be admitted that not a large number of the urban elite were aware of the plight of the farmers, there were some who were not afraid to raise their voices against it. If that was not the case, Dinabandhu Mitra would not have written the play *Neel Darpan* (*Indigo Mirror*) soon after the 'Blue Mutiny' started in Bengal. Several farces were subsequently written over the next two decades, highlighting the problems of peasants and the underprivileged in villages. Madhu himself wrote two farces in 1860, one called *Ekei ki Bale Sabhyata?* (*Is this Called Civilization?*) and the other *Buro Shaliker Ghare Ron* (*New Feathers on an Old Bird*). Both reflected a great deal of social awareness on the part of Madhu. Indeed, the Blue Mutiny proved to be an important catalyst for social reform in Bengal.

While these external movements were taking place, changing the course of Indian history, the passage of time was quietly healing wounds and preparing Madhu to return to creative writing. He did not go back to Rebecca, but over the next two years, he found himself gradually coming to terms with his new situation.

It was at this stage, two and a half years after his return to Calcutta, that a certain event suddenly led to a reawakening of Madhu's literary talents. It had to do with a play called *Ratnavali*. Although Bengali plays had been published since 1852 and some of them, based on contemporary social issues including Kulin polygamy[†] and widow remarriage, became popular as reading material, they were not performed. However, in May 1857, a play depicting the sorrows of child widows, called *Bidhaba Bibaha Natak* (*Drama of a Widow's Marriage*), was performed on a private stage. In 1858, another play that focused on the topical and controversial subject of Kulin polygamy, written by Ramnarayan Tarkaratna, was performed; it created a major stir. At the same time, an interest seemed to have developed in ancient classical literature. A second play that caught everyone's attention was *Sakuntala*, also performed in 1858.

Among the patrons who supported Bengali theatre were two brothers called Pratapchandra and Ishwarchandra Sinha. They were wealthy zamindars in Paikpara (Calcutta).[8] They decided to stage *Ratnavali* (adapted from the original in Sanskrit by Ramnarayan Tarkaratna) at their own theatre in Belgachia in July 1858.

It was their intention to invite a number of British dignitaries, including the governor of Bengal (Sir Frederick Halliday), to the third performance of the play. Since none of the British people could understand Bengali, it seemed eminently desirable that the whole play be translated into English. The two brothers were looking for someone suitable for this task, when Gourdas suggested Madhu's name to them. No one had any doubts about Madhu's knowledge of English. The Sinha brothers, however, were not sure about his grasp of Bengali. Gourdas was not sure, either; however, it was on Gour's recommendation that they eventually agreed to appoint Madhu.

One of Madhu's chief characteristics was determination. He heard that doubts were being expressed about his ability to translate the play. It fuelled his determination to do it successfully and silence his detractors. He sent the first two acts to Gour, saying, '...I beg that you will carefully read over *every line* and sentence.... I flatter myself you will at once see how I have tried to write in pure Saxon English, the language of the best dramatists....' However, he was not particularly happy with the quality of the original play. In spite of this weakness, everyone agreed that Madhu's translation was completely successful. The editor of the *Bengal Hurkaru* wrote: 'I did not know there was a Bengali with such a fine command over English. To tell the truth, I am sure the Englishmen in Calcutta would feel proud to be able to write so well.'[†]

Translating *Ratnavali* helped Madhu in two different ways. First, he was paid five hundred rupees, which was an amount he had never earned before. Second, it helped his writing career take a most unexpected turn. What happened was this. Madhu, convinced as he was about the poor quality of *Ratnavali* as a play, was even more disappointed when he attended some of the rehearsals. Gourdas had connections with the theatre in Belgachia,

---

[8] Raja Pratapchandra (1827–66) and Raja Ishwarchandra Sinha (?–1861) of Paikpara were zamindars as well as promoters of literary and dramatic activities. They established a private theatre in Belgachia in 1858. It was through his association with this theatre that Madhu came to write in Bengali.

where *Ratnavali* was performed. Madhu happened to say to him one day, 'The Sinha brothers† are spending so much money on such a worthless play. If only I'd known, I could have written a play myself, worthy of your stage!' Gour laughed at this remark. He said something jokingly, which implied that he did not think Madhu could write anything worthwhile in Bengali.

At once, Madhu spotted a challenge, and wanted to prove him wrong. He went to the Asiatic Society the very next day and returned with a few books on drama, written in Sanskrit and Bengali. Having studied them, he began writing a play and was able to show Gour the first few scenes within a week. A brief look at only a part of the manuscript made Gour admit that what Madhu had produced was drama in its purest form. Pleased and excited, he wanted to take those few scenes to Belgachia immediately and show them to the Sinha brothers. But Madhu stopped him and told him in a letter (undated) to wait until the first act was finished.

Gour had to do as he was told. But he could not help talking about it to another patron of the theatre, Jotindramohan Tagore. Tagore did not know Madhu, but had been much impressed by *The Captive Ladie*. On 16 July 1858, he wrote to Gour, 'I am very anxious† to have a perusal of your friend's manuscript drama, for I am pretty sure that he who wields his pen with such elegance and facility in a foreign language, may contribute something to the meagre literature of his own country, which cannot but be prized by all. I shall feel myself honoured by his visit to my humble garden and shall wait to receive him any evening that he may appoint.'

Gour kept applying pressure on Madhu to finish his play, so that he could show it to his friend. However, Madhu himself was still not a hundred per cent sure about the standard of his language. So he asked Ramnarayan Tarkaratna to have a look at his manuscript and see if he could spot any lapses or grammatical errors. He had met Tarkaratna during the rehearsals for *Ratnavali*. But the corrections that Tarkaratna made disappointed Madhu so much that he decided not to take his help. The fact was that Madhu had expected Tarkaratna to correct only his grammatical errors. Tarkaratna, on the other hand, rewrote virtually every sentence in his own style.

In an undated letter to Gour, Madhu said, 'I did not wish Ramnarayan to recast my sentences—most assuredly not. I only requested him to correct grammatical blunders, if any. You know that a man's style is the reflection of his mind, and I am afraid there is but little congeniality between our friend and my poor self.... I shan't have him. He has made my poor girl talk damned cold prose. In matters literary, old boy, I am too proud to stand before the world in borrowed clothes. I may borrow a neck-tie, or even a waist-coat, but not the whole suit.'

Madhu was aware that as a playwright, he had been influenced by foreign dramatists. There was every chance that those who had been exposed so far only to an inferior style might not like his. In the same letter to Gour, he went on to say, 'I am aware...that there will, in all likelihood, be something of a foreign air about my drama; but if the language be not ungrammatical, if the thoughts be just and glowing, the plot interesting, the characters well maintained, what care you if there be a foreign air about the thing? Do you dislike Moore's poetry because it is full of Orientalism?...Besides, remember that I am writing for that portion of my countrymen who think as I think, whose minds have been more or less imbued with Western ideas....'

The play he was writing was called *Sharmistha*, or as Madhu himself spelt it, *Sermista*. *The Captive Ladie* was written in three weeks. *Sermista* did not take much longer. When his creative urges became active, Madhu always wrote speedily. When he revised and brushed up the first draft and sent it to the Sinha brothers, they were both enchanted. Later, the purists criticized Madhu for the unmistakable Western influences on the style and sentiments expressed in the play; but the modern and young readers, fully exposed to Western education, received it with genuine enthusiasm and appreciation.

Some went so far as to say that such a wonderful play had never been written before in Bengal. To Madhu, personally, what mattered most was the recognition he received from the Sinha brothers and Jotindramohan Tagore. They provided all the financial help Madhu required to have his play published. The Sinha brothers also decided to stage the play at their private theatre. The support of these men, in later years, influenced Madhu's writing to a great extent.

The story of *Sermista* was based on the first chapter of the Mahabharata. One may wonder why he chose this particular story. The answer is not difficult to find. There are strong similarities between the story of Madhu's life and the story that unfolds in the play. The central character is the king, Yayati. He is human but he falls in love with two women, who come from a different race. The fathers of both women are non-humans—the father of one is Shukracharya, the guru of the gods; the other woman's father is Vaka, the King of the Demons. In Madhu's case, he was a native Indian. But both the women in his life were non-Indians. The story of Sermista in the play runs like this:

Yayati marries Shukracharya's daughter, Devyani. Sermista arrives to act as a handmaiden for Devyani. Yayati sees her, is moved by her beauty and marries her secretly. In due course, he and Sermista have three sons. Then, one day, as the king happens to be walking in his garden, hand-in-hand with his first wife, Devyani, he is spotted by Sermista's children. They come forward to greet him, and ask him frankly why he is holding the hand of a woman who is not their mother.

In the play, the king describes the whole episode to his court jester in the following manner:

Raja: My union with my sweet Sermista is no longer a secret to the queen!

Vidushak: (jester) How, my lord? How chanced Her Majesty to discover this secret of years?

Raja: Alas! When Fate frowns, 'tis ever thus! The queen invited me this evening to visit the garden that belongs to her ladies, and 'twas with reluctance I yielded me to her entreaties. We wandered on and as we neared the house wherein the princess dwells with her maids, what anxious and dark thoughts of coming evil filled my heart!

Vidu: And then, my lord?

Raja: Sermista's three dear children ran joyously towards me, but when they saw Her Majesty, they stopped short, as if abash'd by her presence...

Vidu: Proceed, I pray you, my lord!

Raja: The queen graciously said—Draw near, sweet ones! Of what are ye afeard? The youngest child, Puru, frowned at her and cried—Afeard? We fear no one, Madam! Who are you that lean on our father's arm? You are not, O, you cannot be our mother, for you do not kiss and caress us!

It could be that Rebecca had learnt about Henrietta in a similar fashion, possibly through one of her own children. In Madhu's play, things end happily when Devyani and Sermista are both persuaded by Shukracharya (Devyani's father) to live together in harmony as Yayati's two wives. In real life, it was impossible to find such a solution. There was no question of Rebecca and Henrietta coming to an agreement. Rebecca therefore had to remain in Madras. It was Henrietta who joined Madhu soon after *Sermista* was written.

The exact date of Henrietta's arrival in Calcutta is not known. Presumably, she arrived some time in late 1858. Her name does not appear on the list of passengers on any ship that travelled from Madras to Calcutta at that time. It could be that she travelled under a different name, possibly because she did not want Rebecca or her friends to learn of her departure. Her father must have known what she was doing, but could hardly have given her his blessings to go and join Madhu—a married man—in Calcutta. That may have been another reason for concealing her name. But, in those days, the names of female passengers were not always recorded. All that the shipping documents showed was the total number of women and children on board.

The first mention of Henrietta's presence in Calcutta is found in Madhu's letter to Gour, dated 9 January 1859: 'Mrs Dutt desires me to convey to you her best thanks for your letter received yesterday, and for the interest you evince in our affairs.' Madhu and Henrietta's first child, a daughter, was born in September 1859. So it seems reasonable to assume that Henrietta arrived between September 1858 and the first week of January 1859.

With Henrietta's help, Madhu could start his life afresh. He found new enthusiasm, and new inspiration to write again as he did for about a year and a half in Madras, when he wrote *The Captive Ladie* and *Visions of the Past*. After *Sermista*, ideas for embarking on other, even larger, projects came to him, one after another. On 19 March 1859, he wrote to Gour: 'Now that I have got the taste of blood, I am at it again. I am now writing another play.'

He once wrote to Gourdas from Madras that all he wanted to make himself a regular man of letters was a decent situation, with a few hundred a month. 'Who will give it to me? Is there none in India?' He partly found this imaginary patron to support him in the form of the Sinha brothers and Jotindramohan Tagore. Not only were they wealthy, but also educated enough to appreciate

Madhu's remarkable talents. Madhu became friends with them quite quickly. When he published *Sermista* in January 1859 (with some financial assistance from the Sinhas), he dedicated it to them.

Unfortunately, *Sermista* did not bring him any financial gain. On the contrary, it took him a long time to repay the money he had borrowed from the rajas to have it printed. But what he did gain from the play was more important than money. The recognition he received helped to rebuild his self-confidence. A few days before *Sermista* was published, he wrote to Gour, on 9 January 1859: '*Sermista* has turned out to be a most delightful girl, if I am to believe those who have already inspected her. Jotindra says it is the *best* drama in the language, "chaste, classical, and full of genuine poetry!" The Chota Raja writes in raptures about it and swears the "Drama is a complete success!"'

Such a lot of praise from everyone encouraged him to think that this play would probably establish him as the best writer in Bengali literature. 'This *Sermista* has very nearly put me at the head of all Bengali writers,' he wrote to Gour. Such an occurrence must have struck him as incredible. After all, Bengali—though his mother tongue—was a language he had never bothered to learn properly. If anything, he had tried hard not to use it at all. Yet, it was his writing in Bengali that brought him fame and glory. Madhu did not fail to acknowledge it, time and again, later in his life. It brought him the joy that *The Captive Ladie* could not bring, despite the praise it had received in Madras.

One might ask how Madhu achieved so much success in his first literary attempt in Bengali. Apparently he had no pervious experience, but a close look at his literary career shows that writing *Rizia* had given him adequate experience in the dramatization of a story, writing dialogue, and developing characters. Most of his major poetry, including *The Captive Ladie*, was based on a story or a legend. That is what he excelled in. That was the chief reason why *Sermista* was so successful, although it must be admitted that it lacked the dramatic qualities of *Rizia*.

Another major drawback in *Sermista* was the language. The lines spoken by the chief characters are sometimes unnatural, the words and expressions stiff and formal. This is possibly due to the fact that Madhu, as well as Tarkaratna who went through the text, were influenced by classical Sanskrit literature. Besides, Madhu was unable fully to reject the prose style followed by other playwrights of the time. In his later plays, his style is closer to colloquial Bengali, but even there he could not shake off the old style entirely. In these plays, particularly the two farces, only characters from the uneducated lower classes seem to speak freely, using colloquial expressions. Others from the upper classes continue to speak stiffly and formally. Had Madhu not decided to follow the traditions set by Sanskrit drama, one assumes his language would have been more natural and spontaneous, from the very beginning.

In spite of these limitations, *Sermista* brought him huge success, and greatly boosted his self-confidence. No other play had been written in Bengal before this that could compare favourably with *Sermista*. The Western influences notwithstanding, Madhu made a conscious effort to follow Indian traditions, fearing rejection by his audience and readers, if he did not do so. The success of the play convinced the Sinha brothers and Jotindramohan Tagore that it should be translated into English. Madhu started to translate it in January 1859 and finished it in March.

Henrietta became pregnant about the time when *Sermista* was published. Finally united in Calcutta, after carrying on their relationship for nearly six years, presumably they were overwhelmed by tumultuous emotions. However, the old problems—chiefly financial in nature—arose once again to distress Madhu. He was forced to borrow money to make ends meet. In fact, this became a habit with him. In later years, Madhu was known to borrow from local shopkeepers and even his landlord.

His perennial poverty made Madhu think of doing something concrete to earn a higher income. He had once seen his father earn a great deal of money as a lawyer. Even now, all around him were people who earned much more than him, people who were once students at Hindu College and nowhere near Madhu in academic distinction. He, therefore, thought of becoming a lawyer. He had spent two and a half years working in the police court. It had given him a fairly good grasp of legal matters. A qualifying examination, to be taken by prospective lawyers, was going to be held soon. Madhu began preparing himself to take the same exam, in the belief that there was no reason why he should not be able to pass, when only 'half-educated' and 'brainless' people were emerging as lawyers everyday.

On 9 January, 1859, he wrote to Gour, '...I am dreadfully busy, reading up for the Law Examination that is coming.... there is no knowing what is to be my fate.' As it turned out, his fate did not favour him. At first, he was advised by some of his friends not to worry about the examination, or becoming a lawyer. On 19 March, in another letter to Gour, Madhu wrote, 'My friends think that I should keep quiet, till *Sermista* is brought out and makes me "Famous".' What would have happened if Madhu had taken the exam, we shall never know, for it did not take place at all. There were rumours that the questions had leaked out, and the entire question paper had been seen in the Bhowanipore area. In view of this, the examination was cancelled. Madhu could only blame his fate.

His financial situation grew worse, and his debts piled up so high that Gour could no longer do anything to help him. But another friend of his—Sreeram Chattopadhyay—stepped in at this time, and told the Sinha brothers about Madhu's debts. At this, the younger of the two brothers—Ishwarchandra Sinha, who Madhu referred to as the 'Chota Raja'—paid off most of his creditors. Madhu could breathe freely again. In his letter of 19 March to Gour, he said, 'The next time you write to the Chota Raja, pray, don't forget to thank him for having saved your poor old friend from much anxiety of mind by his princely *munificence*—don't tell him that I desire you to do so.'

Madhu's financial worries, his preoccupation with the law examination, and Henrietta's arrival in Calcutta kept him so busy that, for a long time, he could not write anything new. All he could do, between January and May 1859, was complete the translation of *Sermista*. His patrons—the two rajas and Jotindramohan Tagore—were all very pleased with it. It was published in early May, once again with financial assistance from the rajas.

After the publication of *Sermista* in translation, a journal called the *Indian Field* printed a short review. Although the comments it made were on the whole favourable, it did not praise Madhu sky-high. The editor of the journal was Kishorichand Mitra, who had once helped Madhu to get a job and even offered him accommodation in his own house. But now, for some reason, he failed to publish the kind of review that might have satisfied and reassured Madhu. All that the *Indian Field* (25 June 1859) had to say about this play was:

Mr Michael Muddoo Soodun Dutta deserves credit for his laudable and, as far as we can judge, successful attempt to produce in the vernacular a classical drama. Though the Bengali language cannot yet boast of healthy literature, as far as from being perfect, yet it is copious enough for being dedicated to the Drama. *Sermista* is not to lie in the limbo of the 'Manager's' desk, but would soon be acted at the elegant theatre at the Belgachia Villa of Rajah Pertaub Chund and Issur Chunder Singh Bahadur. The work is very appropriately dedicated to those Rajahs, whose munificent encouragement of the native drama entitles them to lasting gratitude of their countrymen.

It was probably because of this lukewarm praise that he received from the *Indian Field* that Madhu made no mention of either the journal or the review to any of his friends. Interestingly, Kishorichand showed a lot more enthusiasm in later years, when Madhu wrote *Tilottamasambhab Kabya* and *Meghnadbadh Kabya*.

※※※

Once he finished translating *Sermista*, it seems that Madhu grew somewhat restless, discontented, and possibly even depressed. At the time, Gour was in Balasore in Orissa. Madhu wrote to him in the same letter dated 19 March, 'How do you like Balasore? I would give anything to be posted near the sea and in a country where I could at times catch glimpses of distant mountains, the two noblest objects in creation! What is the distance of the sea, the sea, the open sea from where you are located? Do you hear the mighty roar, ceaselessly sounding? To me it is a familiar voice, but God knows if I shall ever hear it again.'

It could well be that, having started a new life with Henrietta, Madhu could not help feeling guilty about leaving Rebecca, and missed his children. But he was not one to speak openly about thoughts that disturbed him. He continued to be sad. Six weeks later, he wrote a letter to Gour on 3 May, in which he said, '...you are damnably mistaken if you think that I like Calcutta. I would be *happier* I think, even in the Soonderbuns.' It seems that there were two sides to Madhu's character. On the one hand he was loving, affectionate, fond of company, and certainly partial to sensual pleasures. On the other, at times the same man could become withdrawn, lonely, and isolated. This dichotomy continued throughout his life.

However, despite his emotional turmoil, Madhu began writing a new play. The basic idea on which it was based came from an old Greek myth. Madhu transposed the story, to characters from Indian mythology. Before he started writing the play, he discussed the plot with the two rajas, Jotindramohan Tagore, and Keshab Ganguli, who was the best-known actor in Calcutta at the time. All of them were very impressed by it. In fact, judging by his letter of 19 March to Gour, Madhu had already finished writing the first act. By 3 May, he had finished four acts. He was still undecided about its name, but eventually he called this play *Padmabati*. As always, he was very excited about this new creation. He said to Gour, 'You must wait for some time yet for the new play. All that I can tell you is that there are few *prettier* plots in any drama that you have read!'

The story he used was that of the golden apple. But all Greek characters were replaced by Hindu gods and goddesses. Although Madhu himself was thoroughly familiar with Western classical literature, he was not sure how his Indian audience would respond to it, or whether they would appreciate Western ideas. He had not failed to notice that the Western influences in *Sermista* had upset the Hindu purists. The story of *Padmabati*, therefore, had to be handled very carefully, so that his own penchant for Western literature could be satisfied, and at the same time, his audience would be pleased to find gods and goddesses *they* were familiar with.

In *Padmabati*, Madhu experimented a bit. For the first time, in the dialogue that he wrote, he tried using blank verse. Compared to *Sermista*, in this new play he was far more successful in characterization, creating a dramatic atmosphere and using a language that was less formal and more natural.

Everything was going well, but after 3 May (by which time Madhu had finished writing four acts), he suddenly stopped working on the play. This was probably because the Sinha brothers wanted him to write a farce, which forced him to abandon *Padmabati* for the moment. On 8 May 1859, Ishwarchandra Sinha wrote, 'I am thinking† of some domestic farces to follow immediately after the first representation of the *Sermista* and before it is repeated just to show the public that we can act the sublime and the ridiculous both at the same time and with the same actors.'

Madhu wrote the farces in response to this. The first was *Is this Called Civilization?*, and the second was *New Feathers on an Old Bird*. At the time, Madhu was extremely busy with his office work.

But the sheer joy of creation made him write two farces, instead of one. It is reasonable to assume that both manuscripts were sent to the rajas well before September 1859, when *Sermista* was performed. When Madhu wrote these farces, that is, in mid-1859, none of his plays had been performed, despite all the praise he had received from his readers. But he had a tremendous desire to see his plays—particularly *Sermista*—performed. It was for this reason that, when one of the rajas renewed his promise to put *Sermista* on the stage, Madhu could not refuse his request to write a farce.

Both the farces were written about contemporary issues. At the time, a number of farces were being written about problems that contemporary society was having to deal with, such as the remarriage of Hindu widows, Kulin polygamy, and child marriage. For more serious plays, dramatists were still turning to mythology and themes related to nationalism. Madhu, too, chose topical issues for his farces; but, unlike other writers, he did not choose a social theme linked to religion. Making social reforms was not his aim. What he chose had a much wider appeal; it was applicable not only to a small section of Hindus, but the entire Hindu society. As a result, purely through his humour, he could attack the fundamentalists who were basically frauds using religion as a shield behind which they could hide.

But Madhu did not stop there. He also lashed out—with a degree of self-mockery—at those who had had some exposure to Western education, and had started to ape the West, choosing to scoff at their own traditions. It is clear from these two farces that he knew very closely the two sections of society which he held up for ridicule.

However, what is striking about these farces, even more than their subject matter, is Madhu's style. For the first time, he did not have to worry about Sanskrit literature and classical themes. The language he used was much more modern and natural, and if the Western influences in these farces showed, it was not regarded as a problem. It does seem that, while writing the two farces, Madhu felt totally free and relaxed, and enjoyed the experience immensely. In *Is This Called Civilization?*, the mixture of Bengali and English spoken by the young babus must have been particular fun to write.

Unfortunately, successful though he was in writing them, Madhu's luck did not favour him when it came to having them performed. Those that Madhu attacked reacted swiftly. The so-called 'modern' and educated class saw themselves caricatured in *Is This Called Civilization?*, and the Hindu traditionalists saw their double standards being exposed ruthlessly in *New Feathers on an Old Bird*. In an attempt to protect themselves, modernity and tradition joined hands and condemned Madhu's efforts in no uncertain terms.

As soon as rehearsals started for *Is This Called Civilization?*, the influential Western-educated classes learned about it. They were the very people who Madhu lampooned in this play. They urged the two rajas not to perform this farce and thus ridicule the whole of Western-educated society. These people had substantial influence over the rajas. So the rehearsals were stopped, and the rajas were so put off by the whole experience that they refused to go ahead with the other play (*New Feathers on an Old Bird*), in case objections were raised again. The only play that did go ahead and was finally performed was *Sermista*.

No doubt Madhu was happy to see his *Sermista* enacted on stage. But any joy it brought him was overshadowed by his disappointment over the two farces. By stopping them from being performed, the Sinha brothers did a great disservice, not only to Madhu, but also to Bengali drama. Had Madhu been allowed to write something else on similar lines, the new spontaneity he had found in his language would have undoubtedly improved. Eventually, he would have shown the same spontaneity in his serious plays. If that had happened, drama in Bengal would have taken far less time to attain maturity.

The rajas, however, did him one great favour. They bore all the costs of having the two farces published, even if they could not have them performed. The farces came out in early 1860. But the intensity of the criticism that greeted them, from both 'modern' and 'conservative' segments of society, weighed on Madhu, and he began to regret even having published them. On 24 April 1860, he wrote to Rajnarayan Basu: '...I half regret having published those two things. You know that as yet we have not established a national theatre, I mean we have not as yet got a body of sound, classical dramas to regulate the national taste, and therefore we ought not to have farces.'

When he finished writing the farces, Madhu was able to turn his attention once more to *Padmabati*. But by then his earlier enthusiasm had waned. A few critics have commented on the fact that the spontaneity easily visible in the first four acts is absent in the fifth. Madhu himself never commented on why he appeared to have lost interest. But he had been known in the past to behave in a similar fashion. The unnamed poem he started to write after *The Captive Ladie* remained incomplete, as did *Rizia*. At least, he did complete *Padmabati*, in 1859. Moreover, *Padmabati* opened up a new interest for him. It was in this play that he first used blank verse. He was so successful in doing this that it boosted his self-confidence enormously. In the same letter to Rajnarayan Basu dated 24 April, he said, '...is not blank verse in our language quite as grand as in any other?'

What made him think of using blank verse? Apparently, the idea grew from a conversation he had with Jotindramohan Tagore and a few others, while rehearsals for *Sermista* were in progress. Tagore, Madhu, and the two rajas were talking about drama in Bengal. Madhu happened to mention that he thought Bengali drama would never improve unless blank verse was used to write the dialogues. Tagore, however, was of the view that it was impossible to write blank verse in Bengali. The argument continued until Madhu said, 'If I can prove† that Bengali is perfectly suitable for writing blank verse, what will happen?' Tagore replied, 'If you can produce poetry set in blank verse, I will have it printed at my own expense.' Madhu clapped his hands and said, 'All right. I will send you a few stanzas in two or three days.'

Two or three days later, what Madhu sent Jotindramohan were not just a few stanzas, but the first canto of a long poem called *Tilottamasambhab Kabya*. He wrote *Sermista* because Gour had teased him and declared that he could never write anything in Bengali. Now, what Jotindramohan said about the use of blank verse became a challenge, and Madhu felt he had to rise to it. The truth was that Madhu did not always feel motivated to exercise his own creative powers. It was often a chance remark that appeared as a challenge, and it was his determination to meet it that brought his extraordinary skills to the fore.

A question that rises here is how did Madhu succeed in writing blank verse so well, when no one had done it before in Bengal? The fact is that it did not happen as suddenly as it might seem. He had experimented with blank verse before, starting with a sonnet that he wrote while he was still in Hindu College. That was followed by *Visions of the Past* and *Rizia*. Although those attempts were made in English, Madhu had a fairly good idea of what was required in Bengali. He was well aware of the rhythmic rigidity of traditional Bengali metre. In an undated letter to Keshab Ganguli (written sometime in 1859-60), he said, '... the blank verse form of verse is the *best* suited for poetry in every language. A *true* poet will always succeed best in blank verse as a bad one in rhyme.... a truly noble mind will always wither away under restraint.... In China, they confine the feet of their women in iron shoes. What is the result? Lameness!'

Once he had discovered the joys of using blank verse, Madhu's writing flowed unrestrained, and he finished the second canto of *Tilottama*, despite a heavy workload in his office, Henrietta's advanced pregnancy, as well as his other commitments. Like most of his other writing, the story of *Tilottama* was based on Hindu mythology. As with *The Captive Ladie*, he changed a few details and added his own original ideas. A few months after its completion, he wrote to Rajnarayan Basu, on 15 May 1860, '...though, as a jolly Christian youth, I don't care a pin's head for Hinduism, I love the grand mythology of our ancestors. It is full of poetry. A fellow with an inventive head can manufacture the most beautiful things out of it.' There could be no doubt about Madhu's 'inventiveness'. No other poet until then had written something that told the story of the gods and the demons in such a fashion. In style as well as in theme, *Tilottama* was totally unique.

Although people were not familiar with blank verse and Madhu's completely original style, it did not take them—or, at least, many of them—long to realize that *Tilottama* was an extraordinary arrival in Bengali literature. It was not just Jotindramohan Tagore and the Sinha brothers who praised it. The editor of a monthly journal called *Bibidhartha Sangraha*, Rajendralal Mitra,[9] was well known to Madhu as an old friend. Mitra pounced upon the first canto of *Tilottama* as soon as he saw it and published it in August 1859. The second canto appeared in the same journal the following month. What is surprising is that the poet's name was not mentioned

---

[9] Rajendralal Mitra (1822-91) was one of Madhu's friends from his school days. He later became a well-known linguist and historian. He was the first Indian secretary of the Asiatic Society of Bengal. Eventually, he became its president. According to Max Müller, Mitra was the greatest Indologist of his time. He edited two journals, *Bibidhartha Sangraha* and *Rahasya Sandarbha*. He was given the title 'Raja' by the government.

anywhere. It may be that the objection to disclosing the poet's name was raised not by the editor, but by the poet himself. He was not altogether sure about the readers' response to his use of blank verse. Besides, he had not forgotten the adverse criticism of *The Captive Ladie*. Perhaps that was the reason why Madhu wanted to gauge the reaction of his readers before telling them who the writer was.

It is not known whether he did hear any adverse comment about his work. However, he broke off from writing *Tilottama* half way through, just as he had done with *Padmabati* and *Rizia*. *Tilottama* was completed about six months later. At first, Madhu intended to write five cantos, but in the end wrote only four. At one stage, he changed his mind and would have stopped after the third canto, but Jotindramohan encouraged him to write the fourth. It could well be that Madhu, by then, was beginning to lose his interest in the poem.

For various reasons, *Tilottama* took a few months to appear in the form of a book, although Madhu completed it in early 1860. On 1 July 1860, he wrote to Rajnarayan Basu, 'The *Tilottama* is out.' The reviews that followed in various journals were all, on the whole, favourable. Within two months, a journal called *Somprakash* published a review by Dwarakanath Vidyabhushan. He was a Sanskrit scholar, but not a traditionalist. He praised Madhu for his new ideas regarding the verse. The only thing he criticized was his choice of subject, and somewhat difficult language. Rajendralal Mitra wrote a review in *Bibidhartha Sangraha* in late 1860. He praised *Tilottama* very highly, and declared that it would one day be considered as one of the best poems ever written in Bengali.

Whenever he wrote anything, Madhu felt the absence of someone amongst his friends capable of doing a just and fair evaluation of his work. In *Tilottama*, the new verse form as well as a juxtaposition of Eastern and Western ideas made it difficult for many readers to grasp its essence. It must be remembered here that, at first, even someone as scholarly as Vidyasagar failed to appreciate the beauty of blank verse. It was some months before he changed his mind and was prepared to admit that what Madhu had produced had 'great merit'. In a letter to Rajnarayan Basu (undated, written possibly in early 1861), Madhu said, 'You will be pleased to hear that the pundits are coming round regarding

Tilottama. The renowned Vidyasagar has at last condescended to see "great merit" in it.' The truth was that what Madhu wrote was very much ahead of the times in which he lived. The Romantic poets that he had once so admired had one another, or older poets like Wordsworth and Coleridge, to inspire and, motivate them. Madhu had no one.

The only friend who knew something about English poetry, and was a poet himself, was Rangalal Bandyopadhyay. The two had known each other through their families. Madhu renewed his contact with Rangalal when he returned to Calcutta from Madras. Rangalal, at the time (in 1860), was teaching in Presidency College. He was also the sub-editor of the *Education Gazette*. Madhu could relate to him as a fellow poet; but Rangalal's knowledge of classical literature was not as profound as Madhu's. Madhu read out portions of *Tilottama* to his friend, which Rangalal appreciated very much, and was even said to have been influenced by the work. But Madhu was not wholly satisfied with his response.

Madhu's patrons, Jotindramohan and the two rajas, gave him the support he needed, but they were in no position to either understand or influence Madhu's thinking. None of his other friends—Gourdas, Rajendralal Mitra, and Kishorichand Mitra—were authorities on literature. Their knowledge of Western literature was certainly limited.

One person who gave Madhu reason to feel encouraged was Vidyasagar. Once he got over his initial reservations regarding blank verse, Vidyasagar became a great supporter of Madhu and his writing. Madhu was well aware that Vidyasagar was an extraordinary man. Praise from him, therefore, was highly valued. Madhu mentioned in several of his letters that Vidyasagar had uttered words of appreciation for his works. Two years later, he dedicated one of his books to Vidyasagar. However, even Vidyasagar could not provide him with adequate inspiration for, pundit though he was, he was not a creative writer.

Under these circumstances, the only person Madhu could turn to for a correct evaluation of *Tilottama* was Rajnarayan Basu. He was well versed in English literature. They were once classmates in Hindu College, but at that time they were not very close. After reading *Tilottama* in *Bibidhartha Sangraha*, Basu wrote a letter, praising Madhu's efforts, which led to a renewal of contact and the formation of a new friendship between them. Encouraged by

Basu's comments, Madhu wrote to him: 'As I believe you are one of the writers of the *Tattvabodhini Patrika*, will you review the poem in the columns of that journal? That would be giving it a jolly lift indeed.' Later, he even sought Basu's help to have *Tilottama* included in the existing school syllabus—not with any intention of selling more copies, but to make his poetry easily accessible to readers. Perhaps he thought that ordinary people would never get to glimpse the beauty of his poetry unless *he* could somehow bring it to them. As it happened, Basu failed to write a review in the *Tattvabodhini*, though he published one later in English in the *Indian Field*. But, to Madhu's amazement, the book sold so well that within a year, it became necessary to print a second edition.

Although some purists did criticize him for departing from all established norms in the matter of versification, the comments Madhu heard from younger readers, that is those familiar with Western thought and education, were all favourable. This boosted Madhu's confidence a great deal, and made him write to Basu, 'I began the poem in a joke, and I see I have actually done something that ought to give our national poetry a good lift, at any rate that will teach the future poets of Bengal to write in a strain very different from that of the man of Krishnanagar—the father of a very vile school of poetry, though himself a man of elegant genius.'[10] It was this confidence that helped him find the inspiration later to write two poems that were even more successful—*Meghandbadh Kabya* and *Birangana*.

Soon after he started writing *Tilottama*, an important event took place in Madhu's personal life. In fact, that may well have been a reason why Madhu abandoned *Tilottama* for a while. On 15 September 1859, Henrietta gave birth to their first child, a girl.[†] Henrietta had no previous experience of taking care of a baby. Madhu, on the other hand, had seen four of his children grow up. It is not unreasonable to assume here that, after the birth of

---

[10] The reference here is to Bharatchandra Ray. Bharatchandra Ray (1712-60) was a major poet just before the advent of British rule in India. He learnt both Sanskrit and Persian, in addition to Bengali, and came to be known as an urban poet. He became the poet laureate of the Raja of Krishnanagar. Among his poems, *Annadamangal* and *Bidyasundar* are still considered good. However, *Bidyasundar* was considered obscene by many nineteenth-century critics, which is why Madhu called the school it created 'vile'.

Henrietta's baby girl, Madhu spent most of his time helping her to look after the child. The names they chose for her were Henrietta Eliza Sermista. Eliza was Henrietta's mother's name. 'Sermista' was added because only twelve days before she was born, Madhu had witnessed a most successful performance of his play. Although it was not her first name, in later years, Madhu called his daughter 'Sermista', which was further evidence of how much his play meant to him.

When Henrietta joined him in Calcutta, Madhu introduced her to his friends and neighbours as his wife. He never disclosed to anyone that he and Rebecca were not officially divorced, and that he and Henrietta were not married. It could be that both he and Henrietta were afraid that embarrassing questions might be asked at the time of Sermista's baptism, which was why they kept postponing it. Eventually, they overcame their fears on 2 February 1860 and had their first child baptized, five months after she was born. *Tilottama* was about to be printed at the time, and the two farces had either recently been published, or were going to be published within a few weeks.

The birth of his daughter must have filled Madhu's heart with joy, especially as he was then in the process of earning fame, if not fortune. However, it must have brought pain and anguish as well. A new baby would certainly have reminded him of his other children, who he had not seen for almost four years. An ordinary man might have been able to bury his past and forget previous ties. But Madhu was no ordinary man. He was sensitive, loving, and affectionate. Guilt and remorse must have weighed heavily upon him, but he could not share his pain with anyone, not even with a close friend like Gour.

It is likely that Gour and his other friends talked among themselves about Madhu's previous marriage, and wondered what had happened to Rebecca and her children. Many years after Madhu's death, Rajnarayan Basu said in a letter to Gour[†] that although Gour did not say anything about this, he (Basu) had suspected all along that Madhu had run away with Henrietta. His friends knew Madhu very well. It is unlikely that they asked probing questions. Even if they did, Madhu would only have given them evasive answers.

Be that as it may, the fact remains that the birth of little Sermista stopped Madhu from writing anything new for almost three months.

It was only in January 1860 that he finally completed *Tilottama* and, in so doing, realized afresh the powerful potential of blank verse. He also saw, far more clearly, how Hindu mythology could be used to create tales suitable for modern times, highlighting their humanistic aspects. In that age, so fondly called 'the Bengal Renaissance' by historians, Rammohan Roy and Ishwarchandra Vidyasagar had already done this before him, unearthing and reinterpreting old Hindu *shastra*s for the reformation of the Hindus of modern times. But only in Madhu did the spirit of the Bengal Renaissance take a poetic shape. For *Tilottama*, he had chosen a tale of 'the Gods and the Titans'. Tales from the Ramayana, he knew, were more dramatic and far more popular. But before he started on *Meghnad*, he wrote something else. It was a cluster of short poems called *Brajangana*, based on the love of Radha and Krishna.

It is clear from *Brajangana* that Madhu was familiar with Vaishnava texts. He was always fond of listening to kirtan. Becoming a Christian and even going to England later in his life did nothing to affect his fondness for such songs. But in the stories of Radha and Krishna, it was the human angle that appealed more to him than any religious significance. To him, Radha was not a symbol of spiritual love; she was merely Krishna's consort, 'Mrs Radha'. It was the beauty and depth of her love that moved Madhu. The way in which he viewed the relationship of Krishna and Radha was very different from the way it was viewed by others, especially the Vaishnavas. It was probably for this reason that he did not discuss *Brajangana* with anyone before he began writing it. Perhaps he was afraid that others would not understand his different approach. He began slowly, but wrote as many as eighteen modern *padabali*s (or 'odes', as he called them). These were sent for printing in March–April 1860.

The true poetic merits of *Brajangana*, particularly seen in the context of Madhu's other writing, may be questioned. There is a marked absence of bhakti in the poem, whereas devotion is the life and soul of Vaishnava *padabali*s. What stands out, however, is his lyricism. Besides, his new experiments with language and rhythm reached extraordinary heights in this poem. In setting out the stanzas, and maintaining a uniform rhythm in every line, he displayed a new aspect of his genius, which is not often talked about.

> Why, O helpmate, have you filled your basket
> with so many flowers?
> When covered with clouds does the sky at night
> wear a garland of stars?
> Shall a daughter of Braj take care any more
> with her flowers and jewels?
> Shall a flower of the forest wear once again
> her necklace of blooms?
> Why is the tree bereft of the creeper
> that adorned its beauty?
> Bees still befriend it, but who can now comfort
> Miserable Radha?

These lines are likely to remind one of the lyric poets of Bengal, who came a few decades later. At any rate, it is difficult to recognize them immediately as something written by Madhu.

※

Madhu now started writing *Meghnad*, possibly in February 1860. As with *Brajangana*, initially he told no one about it. The reason could simply have been that his style of viewing Ram and Lakshman on one side, and their opponents Ravan and his supporters on the other, was entirely different from anyone else's that he knew, even those known for their modern and Westernized thinking. Besides, he was still not altogether sure about how well he had mastered the use of blank verse. So he wanted to wait before he could show any of his friends what he had written. The first mention of *Meghnad* is in a letter to Basu, dated 24 April 1860. In it, Madhu said, 'I enclose the opening invocation of my *Meghnad*—you must tell me what you think of it. A friend here, a good judge of poetry, has pronounced it magnificent.'

At the time, his old friend, Rangalal Bandyopadhyay used to meet him often. It could be that it was he who had called *Meghnad* 'magnificent'. Even so, Madhu wanted Basu's views. Basu, he knew, was a well-read man, and likely to do justice to his work. But there was one other reason. Madhu was not really one to follow the values held very dear by Hindus, who regarded Ram as a god. Basu's views were important to him, since Basu was a Brahmo. He did not believe in Hindu gods and goddesses. In a letter dated 14 July 1860, Madhu said to him, '...my position, as a tremendous literary rebel, demands the consolation and the encouraging sympathy of friendship. I have thrown down the gauntlet, and proudly denounce those, whom our countrymen have worshipped for years, as impostors, and unworthy of the honours heaped upon them!... If you think the *Meghnad* destitute of merit, why! I shall burn it without a sigh of regret.'

Before he began writing *Meghnad*, Madhu had asked Basu to comment on both *Padmabati* and *Tilottama*. He clearly thought Basu had the ability to emerge as a serious literary critic. He wrote to Basu a number of times saying that he considered Basu's criticism more valuable than loud praise by others. At the time, as Madhu knew, the genre of literary criticism was virtually unknown in Bengal. That was why he wanted Basu to produce before his countrymen well-judged and enlightened critiques. In a letter, he reminded Basu of the high quality of literary criticism in English and asked him to develop that genre in Bengali.

However, it must be remembered that Madhu did not write simply with a view to being noticed by a critic, but because writing was what gave him the greatest pleasure. But in the case of *Meghnad*, he needed reassurance from the very beginning, since he knew that he had made a major departure from established norms and beliefs, not only by presenting the two heroes from the Ramayana as 'impostors', but also in the matter of language and the structure of his verse.

Many of his letters to Basu written in 1860 speak of his joy and excitement over *Meghnad*. He knew, even without any reassuring endorsement from his friend, that what he was in the process of creating would be hailed as something completely unique.

A number of letters written to Basu have been recovered, in which Madhu speaks freely and frankly about his work. What is surprising is that there is very little mention of his personal life. It is only in the letter dated 15 May 1860 that he mentioned two things about Henrietta. The first was that she had lost a relative: '...I am in mourning for a relative of my wife's—who died in England five months ago.' It is not known which relative he was referring to. Perhaps Madhu did not wish to reveal every detail about his 'wife's' family, in order to protect her. After all, *he* knew better than anyone else how delicate her position was. He did not even tell his children anything about her true identity.

The second fact that he mentioned about Henrietta in the same letter was that she had read *Tilottama*. That meant that she had learnt to read Bengali and was trying to understand her husband's work, so that she could understand the whole man.

When talking of himself, Madhu once said to Basu (in a letter dated 14 July 1860): 'I am at times as lazy a dog as ever walked on two legs; but I have fits of enthusiasm that come on me occasionally, and then I go like the mountain torrent!' As a matter of fact, Madhu was not in the least lazy. When he was not actually writing, he was known to spend anything up to twelve hours a day, studying various languages, in addition to doing his office work. He did not spend much time visiting friends, or keeping up with current affairs. 'I read no newspaper and seldom stir out of home,' he said to Basu. This was partly due to the fact that Henrietta needed his help at home, and he did not have too many close friends, in any case. In Madras, there had been a few British or Anglo-Indian friends; but in Calcutta, there was a rigid class distinction between the educated Hindus and the Anglo-Indian community.

In summer, Madhu was known to drink glass upon glass of cold beer, or sherry. However, when he started writing, he would stop drinking altogether. In the letter dated 14 July, he said to Basu, '...though by no means a saint and teetotal prude, I *never* drink when writing poetry; for, if I do, I can never manage to put two ideas together!' It is not known if Henrietta used to drink when she was in Madras. It is likely that she did not, for she was a single young woman with no income of her own. In a household where relations between the father, stepmother, and the children were strained, it is hardly likely that any of the children were allowed to consume expensive alcoholic drinks. But when she began living in Calcutta, Henrietta soon became Madhu's drinking companion.

1860 proved to be the most fruitful year in Madhu's life. He finished *Padmabati* early in that year, then *Tilottama*. He started on *Meghnad* almost immediately. It took him a little over a year to complete it. It was *Meghnad* that became the jewel in his crown.

He started with the intention of writing five books, but eventually produced nine. The challenge it posed, and the sheer joy of creation, made him spend several months on it, which was most unusual for Madhu. It was customary for him to start something with great enthusiasm, then abandon it to start something else. Then, a long time later, he would go back to it and finish it. It is true that he did the same with *Meghnad*, but only after he had worked steadily at it for more than three months.

In August 1860, he stopped writing *Meghnad* and started a new play, called *Krishnakumari*. Why he did so is not clear. The well-known actor, Keshab Ganguli, had asked him to write a play based on a Rajput tale. But it does not seem possible that that was the only reason why Madhu left his beloved *Meghnad* and turned his attention to something else. Perhaps something in particular had happened, or someone had made a comment—as they had before *Sermista* was written—that appeared to Madhu as a challenge. Or, perhaps his patrons, the two rajas, had sent in a request for a new play. Madhu wrote to Keshab Ganguli shortly after he found a suitable story on which to base his play. It is clear from this letter (undated) that he expected the new play to be performed: 'I have made the list of dramatis personae as short as I could, for I wish to have no loophole for our manager to escape through. Fancy, only five or six males, and but four females in a historic tragedy! If the Chota Raja should grumble about the females, please tell him I undertake to find three out of the four!'

By the time he wrote this letter to Ganguli, Madhu had already submitted a synopsis of his play. This is how he explained the manner in which he found the story in Tod's *The Annals and Antiquities of Rajasthan*: 'For two nights, I sat up for hours poring over the tremendous pages of Tod and about 1 A.M. last Saturday, the *Muses smiled*! As a true realizer of the dramatist's conceptions, you ought to be quite in love with Krishnakumari, as I am. Lord! What a romantic tragedy it will make!'

This was briefly the story described by Tod:†

Krishnakumari was the very beautiful daughter of Rana Bhim Singh of Mewar. She was only sixteen. Two men decided to seek her hand in marriage: Jagat Singh of Jaipur, and Man Singh of Marwar. To make matters worse, Sindhia got involved in the matter, when Jaipur denied 'a pecuniary demand' made by Sindhia. Affronted, he instructed Bhim Singh to reject Jaipur's offer of marriage. Bhim Singh refused, at which Sindhia decided to attack Mewar. A bloody battle was fought, but the situation remained unresolved even after it was over. Neither Jaipur nor Marwar would give up their demand for Krishnakumari's hand.

In the end, the only option left for Krishnakumari was death. If she died, only then would honour be saved all round. A poisoned drink was handed to her. She drank it bravely, but did not die. 'The nauseating draught refused to assimilate with her blood.' Another drink was prepared, then another, and another. It was the fourth cup that finally put her into a deep sleep...from which she never woke.

It is easy enough to see the dramatic possibilities in such a story. Madhu was keen, from the very beginning, on the play being performed. He wanted Ganguli to put some pressure on the two rajas to hold performances in their theatre in Belgachia. 'I wish you would stir them up, my friend,' he wrote. 'It is a downright shame that such a theatre, as that at Belgachia, should be the abode of bats, or what is tantamount to it, the gaze of bat-like men!' Sadly, the rajas did not show a great deal of interest in the performance of a new play. Jotindramohan Tagore offered his support by saying that he would help in having it published, but such an idea did not appeal to Madhu. He wrote to Ganguli, '...I am not particularly interested in the question of getting the work printed.... What I want is to have it acted....'

It seems that Ganguli did offer him some reassurance in this matter. Madhu began writing *Krishnakumari* after 15 August 1860 and, in his usual way, wrote like a 'mountain torrent'. He finished the fourth act before the month was over. Since Henrietta had read *Tilottama*, presumably Madhu showed her his manuscript and discussed the new play with her. To Ganguli, he wrote with rare humility, 'Here is the Fourth Act. As a humble member of the noble Belgachia Amateur Company, I am doing what I can to promote its glory. If the other members won't stir themselves, it is no fault of mine. By Jove! Here is a play—if meritorious in no other respect, at least *brimful* of acting, acting, acting!'

After reading the fourth act, Ganguli wrote a detailed analysis. He praised Madhu's efforts on the whole, particularly his language. But he compared it with Shakespeare's writing, and made some critical remarks as well. Madhu accepted his views, for he respected Ganguli as an actor. What he said in his own defence, on 1 September, was this: 'Some of the defects you point out, are defects indeed, but it does not fall to the lot of everyone to rise superior to them, and even Shakespeare himself does not do so often.' Eventually, he dedicated the play to Ganguli.

Although he took the basic plot from Tod, the story—as it unfolds in the play—was entirely Madhu's own. A story of greed and lust for power among kings, in Madhu's hands, became a story of love, affection, and one's sense of duty. He portrayed with immense sympathy the conflicting emotions of his characters. It is very clear that he was thinking of Shakespeare when writing this play. In fact, Madhu admitted this himself, in a letter to Keshab Ganguli, dated 1 September 1860. Naturally, he had to make several changes, bearing in mind the contemporary society, the Bengali language, and drama as it then existed. In addition to Shakespeare, another influence may have worked on his mind. The tragic story of Krishnakumari—who had to give up her life simply because she became a victim of circumstances—comes as a reminder of the Greek play, *Iphigenia in Aulis*. Tod, too, mentions Iphigenia in his *Annals*.

It is not difficult to see why Madhu was so eager to see this play performed. He wrote time and again to Ganguli, imploring him to speak to the rajas. Unfortunately, Madhu's dream could not be fulfilled. *Krishnakumari* was eventually published in 1862, but never performed. Madhu was very disappointed, particularly so because not long before this episode the rajas had asked him to write the two farces. Those farces were not performed, either.

When he began writing *Krishnakumari*, Madhu had warned Ganguli not to play the same trick again. In a letter to Ganguli, he said, '...You all broke my wings once about the farces; if you play a similar trick this time, I shall foreswear Bengali and write books in Hebrew and Chinese!' In the end, a frustrated Madhu realized that he was 'born an age too soon'.

Having finished writing *Krishnakumari*, Madhu turned his attention once more to *Meghnad*. His old enthusiasm returned as soon as he began writing the third book. He had made a conscious decision to write an epic. With that purpose in mind, he read classical literature carefully, in order to make a study of how epics were written. He knew that it was customary to write ten 'books' in an epic. At first, he was not altogether sure that he could write as many as ten; but now, with his imagination soaring high, he decided not to stop until all ten were written. He wrote to Basu, '...I intend to lengthen this poem to ten Books and make it as complete an epic as I can. The subject is truly heroic; only the monkeys spoil the joke—but I shall look to them.'

One reason why Madhu was feeling so enthusiastic about *Meghnad* was that, at this time, his earlier poem *Tilottama* was receiving a lot of praise. Even Sanskrit pundits, including Vidyasagar, who had not been able to appreciate blank verse before, were now prepared to admit that *Tilottama* contained various points of merit. This praise boosted Madhu's confidence. His mood was reflected in one of his letters to Rajnarayan Basu: 'Blank verse is the "go" now. As old Runjit Singh [the leader of the Sikhs] used to say, when looking at the map of India—"sub lal ho jaga" [every place will turn red], I say "sub blank verse ho jaga.".'

A few weeks later, in September 1860, Madhu decided to publish the first five books of *Meghnad* in one volume, instead of waiting until the remaining five were complete. Digambar Mitra had already offered to meet all costs of publishing it, so Madhu did not have to worry about money. He said in the same letter to Basu, 'Did I tell you babu Digambar Mitter...has promised to coach the work through the press in a pecuniary point of view? In this respect, I most thankfully acknowledge, I am singularly fortunate. All my idle things find patrons and customers.' More than a hundred years later, it seems that his patrons were more fortunate than him. At the time, they had to spend only a little money. But, by doing so, they attained immortality through Madhu's creations.

Madhu finished writing the fifth book of *Meghnad* in December 1860. Henrietta became pregnant for the second time in October, which may have caused some concern, but it did not slow him down. Madhu always wrote with the speed of lightning, producing new lines, as well as checking and revising what was already written. In this matter, he was a perfectionist. It seems he finished the fifth 'book' while the other four were being printed. It is not known when he completed it, but the first volume of *Meghnad* was published on 4 January 1861.

As always, Madhu became anxious to hear what his friends had to say about his latest creation. Basu was the first he approached to seek his comments. He wrote to him (letter undated): 'Pray write to me about *Meghnad*. I am looking out with something like suspended breath for your verdict.' He did go on to point out in the same letter that 'The poem is rising into splendid popularity. Some say it is better than Milton—but that is all bosh—nothing can be better than Milton; many say it licks Kalidasa; I have no objection to that. I don't think it is impossible to equal Virgil,

Kalidasa, and Tasso. Though glorious, still they are mortal poets. Milton is divine'.

Despite Madhu's entreaties, Basu did not immediately send his comments. This disappointed Madhu, but both to his delight and amazement, he discovered that recognition was coming from other sources. On 12 February 1861, he was given a reception by a well-known literary association called *Bidyotsahini Sabha*. Amongst others, there were three men present at this function, who knew Madhu well. They were Krishnamohan Bandyopadhyay, Kishorichand Mitra, and Jotindramohan Tagore. It was a simple function, at which Madhu was presented with a silver claret jug. No other poet in Bengal is known to have been given such a gift. No doubt the decision to choose it was influenced by Western practices. Madhu was naturally very pleased, but more amazed by the fact that he was expected to speak in Bengali. Although he chose to write in his mother tongue, perhaps he truly believed that he was different from his fellow men. This is how he described the event in a letter to Basu: 'You will be pleased to hear that not very long ago the *Bidyotsahini Sabha*...presented me with a splendid silver claret jug. There was a great meeting and an address in Bengali. Probably you have read both address and reply in the vernacular papers. Fancy! I was expected to speechify in Bengali!'

What gave him greater pleasure was the knowledge that *Meghnad* was gaining popularity even outside the circle of the educated elite. In a letter to Basu, he wrote of a shopkeeper in Chinabazar who praise *Meghnad* very highly, without realizing that he was speaking to the author. Madhu did not reveal his identity, but asked him 'if he thought blank verse would do in Bengali'. The man replied, 'Certainly, Sir, it is the noblest measure in the language.'

In another letter to Basu, Madhu said, 'Many Hindu ladies, I understand, are reading the book and crying over it.' This must have brought a great deal of encouragement to him, although how many Hindu women in Bengal had enough education at the time to appreciate *Meghnad*, is questionable.

Meanwhile, Basu's article on *Tilottamasambhab Kabya* was published in the *Indian Field* and Madhu was delighted at its favourable tone. The article included some comments on the first volume of *Meghnad*. It appears that Basu also commented on *Meghnad* in a letter to Madhu. The letter has disappeared, but it seems from

Madhu's tone that it was full of praise. If he did find flaws, they were few. Madhu said to him: 'Your "feeling" is anything but uncomplimentary.... But you must wait, old boy, before you allow this feeling to become settled and permanent. You must read the whole poem through.'

Although he praised Madhu's works in a private letter, Basu disappointed Madhu by not reviewing *Meghnad* in the *Tattvabodhini Patrika*, just as he had failed to review *Tilottama* there. However, based on that letter, Basu did write an article in Bengali many years later. By that time he had turned into a nationalist and his attitude to everything Hindu had undergone a profound change. His praise was therefore mixed with criticism. In 1878, five years after Madhu died, Basu delivered a lecture on Bengali literature. In this lecture he was even more critical. A one-time Brahmo and a staunch critic of Hinduism, he was now critical of the way Madhu had treated the divine Ram and Lakshman.

Madhu's letters to Basu written during the writing of *Meghnad* are not dated, but it seems that almost immediately after the first volume was published in January 1861, he began writing the sixth book. However, he fell ill and remained out of action for more than a week. He explained: 'A few hours after we parted, I got a severe attack of fever and was laid up for six or seven days. It was a struggle—whether *Meghnad* will finish me or I finish him. Thank Heaven, I have triumphed. He is dead, that is to say, I have finished the sixth book in about seven hundred and fifty lines.'

The seventh and the eighth books were written at Madhu's usual speed, and sent for printing by the end of March. But even by the end of May, he could not finish the ninth book and contrary to his earlier plans, he decided to end with nine, not ten books. It is not known when he finally finished the ninth book. However, it was still being printed on 23 July. In a letter written in August, he informed Basu that a copy of the second volume had been sent to him.

It took him more than a year to finish *Meghnad*, but his interest in it remained consistent. Unlike his other creations, he did not abandon it every now and then to write something else. The reason for that is perhaps the fact that he started writing *Meghnad* not because someone threw him a challenge, but because of his own strong feelings about the subject. In addition, the story was truly appropriate for an epic, and based on the great Ramayana.

There were various elements in the story of *Meghnad* that appealed to Madhu—its dramatic qualities, the inherent spirit of heroism and, above all, the opportunities it gave him to form and develop his own originality of expression. He worked very hard to achieve perfection. This becomes clear from his letter to Basu, after the second volume was ready:

I believe you will like the second part of *Meghnad* still better, at least I have been finishing it with more care. I shall not conceal from you that some parts of it fill my heart with adulation. I had no idea, my dear fellow, that our mother tongue would place at my disposal such exhaustless materials, and you know I am not a good scholar. The thoughts and images bring out words with themselves—words that I never thought I knew.... I think I have constructed the poem on the most rigid principles and even a French critic would not find fault with me.... Comparatively speaking the work is wonderfully popular and commands a very respectable sale. It has silenced the enemies of blank verse. A great victory that, old boy.

What is a little surprising is that although he started writing the eighth book in February, the ninth book was not written till May. Could he have been preoccupied with something else in the intervening period? An answer to this question lies in some of the letters written to Gour and Rajnarayan Basu during this time. At least two of the cases that he was fighting regarding his father's property and mother's jewellery reached their final stages in February–March 1861. Towards the end of February, Madhu won a case in Jessore. The other one was being fought in Calcutta. Gour was required to give evidence, both as the deputy magistrate who had started the investigation, and as an old friend of the family. He was posted in Balasore in Orissa at the time, but for some rason, he returned to Calcutta, and Madhu's lawyer wanted to take advantage of his presence there. Gour was therefore asked to appear as a witness. However, on the appointed day, he failed to turn up. Madhu was naturally upset by this. On 30 March 1861, he wrote to Gour, '...For Heaven's sake, my dear fellow, do let me know what you intend doing. If you do not go, I shall run every risk of losing my poor mother's jewels.' Fortunately, another date for the hearing was fixed, and it seems that Gour did turn up this time, for Madhu won his case.

There were two other things that might have kept Madhu from writing the concluding part of *Meghnad*. The first was the death of one of his patrons, Ishwarchandra Sinha. Sinha died on 29 March

1861. The second might have been his translation of Dinabandhu Mitra's play, *Neel Darpan*. But there is no concrete evidence to prove that it was Madhu who did the translation. The work was commissioned by James Long, a renowned missionary who turned into a social worker and a champion of Bengali language and literature. However, nowhere did he mention the name of the translator. When he published the translated version, it led to a few problems; cases were lodged by some indigo planters, since the picture drawn in the play of British planters was most unflattering. It has since been assumed that not only did Madhu translate the play, but he was also reprimanded by his superiors for doing so. Neither assumption can be said to be correct, for Long had the work translated and then arranged to have it despatched to various people, with the full knowledge and approval of the authorities, including the chief secretary and governor of Bengal.

Another factor that most undoubtedly affected Madhu's work was related to his family and other personal circumstances. To start with, he had to move from his house in Lower Chitpur Road to a house in Kidderpore (though not his father's house where he had spent his childhood). At first, he thought the move was temporary, since the house in Chitpur Road was under repair; but eventually, he decided to stay on in Kidderpore. Then, on 23 July, Henrietta gave birth to their second child, a son this time.† Madhu called him Frederick Michael Milton Dutt. The inclusion of 'Milton' shows how much Milton had been on his mind when he was writing *Meghnad*.

Apart from Ishwarchandra Sinha, another man that Madhu knew and respected highly died before Madhu could complete the final book of *Meghnad*. He was Harishchandra Mukherjee, the editor of a weekly newspaper called the *Hindoo Patriot*. He was known to be an outspoken journalist and he had played an important role during the Sepoy Mutiny by exposing the wrongdoings of Company officials. He then did the same during the revolt by the indigo farmers. He firmly criticized the indigo planters in his periodical and gave evidence against those cruel planters who exploited the farmers. Madhu respected him for his courage and wanted a statue built in Mukherjee's memory. He also contributed some money to the Harishchandra Mukherjee Memorial Fund. One cannot be sure whether the deaths of Sinha and Mukherjee slowed him down in any way as far as writing

Meghnad was concerned, but he must have felt considerably distressed. After Sinha's (the 'Chota Raja') death, Madhu did not write another play.

❧※❧

With *Meghnad*, Madhu reached the climax of his writing career. He himself did not see it as such, for he still thought there was still some way to go before he could write poetry that might be seen as truly great. He was capable of producing something bigger and better than *Meghnad*, he felt. Yet, in his letters to his friends, he sounds quite satisfied and content with all the praise showered upon *Meghnad*. It is almost as if he thought: 'That's enough, I don't need anything more. After all, I *have* been compared to Milton and Kalidas. What else could I want?' The truth about Madhu was that although he craved recognition, once it came his way, he had no wish to continue to grasp it. Before he left for England to become a barrister, he wrote a letter to Rajnarayan Basu which bears evidence of his detachment. Deep down in his heart, Madhu had perhaps realized that, with the success of the blank verse that he had introduced, there was no pressing need for him to continue to write. He was happy to leave the field to younger writers, and leave his motherland, not to serve his Muse, but to seek his fortune.

A lot of questions have been raised about how far the events in the life of a creative artist are reflected in his works. Some, including no less a personality than Rabindranath Tagore, did not think there was any need to know much about a writer's life in order to understand his works.[11] Others—Henry James,† for instance—felt that however hard he might try to hide, a writer was always present in every page of his book. When a novelist writes a novel, or a playwright produces a play, the characters he describes may all be different from his own self. But the essential spirit that underlines his work, the feelings he expresses can come from no one but the writer himself. They are what he feels deep down in his heart.

---

[11] Tagore wrote a number of short and long autobiographies covering different phases of his life, but thought quite strongly that a poet's life was not important to understand or appreciate his works as he says in one of his poems *Kabire pabe na tahar jeeban charite* ('You will not find a poet in his biography').

The theme and subject matter of *Meghnad* have led to endless debate. Madhu seems openly sympathetic not to the traditional hero, Ram, but to his opponent, Ravan. In fact, in an undated letter to Basu, Madhu said, 'I despise Ram and his rabble; but the idea of Ravan elevates and kindles my imagination; he was a grand fellow.'

Certainly at the time, such an idea was unheard of. How did it come to Madhu? Was it simply his exposure to Western education? Perhaps, but that alone would not have encouraged him to think so completely differently. It was also his conversion to Christianity that helped him to look at traditional beliefs with new eyes.

Those who are keen to uphold Madhu as a 'modern' thinker often maintain that when he wrote about a battle between Ram and Ravan, what he was really doing was writing about the spirit of nationalism among Indians that was rising in the wake of the mutiny in 1857. This appears to be a somewhat simplistic analysis of a view that was unique to Madhu. One look at history would tell us that in mid-nineteenth century, Bengal was not showing any sign of rebelling against the British. No one from the educated class welcomed the mutiny; no one wanted the security and tranquillity of their lives destroyed.

Madhu's response to the mutiny could not have been very simple. He was a Christian, the two women in his life were both half-English.† Moreover, he had a deep regard for Western literature and culture. In *The Anglo-Saxon and the Hindu*, he wrote of how superior Western culture was to Hindu civilization. He could hardly have responded to something like the mutiny by simply deeming it as 'good' or 'bad'. It was only when he went to Europe later in his life that he suffered an identity crisis, which made him look upon his motherland in a completely new light. He wrote a few sonnets at the time that reflect this new outlook. This is a factor worth keeping in mind when discussing *Meghnad*.

Another view is that the only reason for Madhu's support of Ravan was his opposition to Hinduism. That, again, is far too simplistic a view. What must be remembered is that Madhu was rejected not just by Hindus, but by Christians as well. At any rate, he was reminded by both Europeans and Eurasians that the colour of his skin made him different and less acceptable. Therefore, Madhu belonged to no religious or social group. He became a truly secular man, simply a member of the human race. That, naturally, broadened his outlook. Added to that was his knowledge of world literature, which helped him to rise further above religious or communal confines. In his eyes, therefore, characters from the holy epic—be they Ram, Lakshman, and Sita; or Ravan, Meghnad, and Birbahu—lost their godliness and superhuman features. Each became earthly, endowed with qualities that were entirely human.

It was this purely humanistic outlook that enabled Madhu to produce a new interpretation of the story of Ramayana.

The celebration of *vira ras* (the heroic mood) that started in Madhu's writing with *The Captive Ladie* and *Rizia*, found its culmination in *Meghnad*. However, a detailed analysis of the story of *Meghnad* would show that from its title to the main event it describes, the whole epic is shrouded in tragedy. It is a story of how a happy and prosperous household was destroyed totally as a result of an attack by outsiders and betrayal by those within; and how a responsible king, and loving husband and father like Ravan lost all his glory in trying to combat a severe blow of misfortune.

When he started to write *Meghnad*, Madhu knew very well that it was the tragedy in this tale that would rise above all heroism, or *vira ras*. It is true that there are long descriptions of Lanka's wealth and prosperity, the valour of Birbahu, Meghnad, Ram, and Lakshman, and the devastating conflict between them. But at the heart of the epic lies Meghnad's tragic death and Ravan's heart-rending loss of glory. On 24 April 1860, when Madhu sent the opening invocation of *Meghnad* to Basu, he said, '...I am going to celebrate the death of my favourite Indrajit. Do not be frightened, my dear fellow, I won't trouble my readers with *vira ras*.'

The truth was that no matter how much he talked of battles and the heroism of men, deep down in his heart Madhu was a Romantic and a lyric poet. His lyricism is very much in evidence in *Meghnad*. As it happened, Madhu was fully aware of it. In another letter to Basu (undated), he wrote: 'Perhaps the episode of Sita's abduction (Fourth Book) should not have been admitted since it is scarcely connected with the progress of the fable. But would you willingly part with it? Many here look upon that book as the best among the five....' The reason why Book Four continues to appeal to readers is simply the spontaneity that runs through this very emotional scene, and the compassion with which the subject is treated.

It seems that when Madhu eventually finished writing *Meghnad*, he was quite relieved. Perhaps he was getting tired of tales of valour. On one occasion, he wrote to Basu, 'I shall not attempt anything in the heroic line.' On another, he said, '...I must bid adieu to Heroic poetry after *Meghnad*.... there is the wide field of Romantic and lyric poetry before me, and I think I have a tendency in the lyrical way.'

Having finished writing *Meghnad*, Madhu was at a loose end for a while. He had taken a break when he was still writing it, and produced *Krishnakumari*. In addition to that, he had also written sonnets in Bengali—again, a feat never accomplished before by any other poet in Bengal. The first of these, called *Kavi-matribhasha* (*The Poet's Mother tongue*), was later revised and retitled as *Bangabhasha* (*The Bengali Language*). It has become one of the best known poems written in Bengali, because of the poet's frank admission of remorse for having neglected his own language and looked for fame and glory through another. In the end, in a dream, his motherland appears as a goddess and urges him to return to what is his own:

> There were countless jewels beyond price in my own
> Storeroom; neglecting them all, I wandered
> From country to country in greed for wealth,
> Like a merchant ship from port to port.
> I denied myself pleasure, spent too long
> In this quest, like a hermit in a hermitage
> Who despises food and bed in relentless
> Dedication of body and mind to his god.
> In a dream one night, the goddess of the race
> of Bengal said to me: 'Child, the Goddess Saraswati,
> Seeing your devotion, looks kindly on you.
> You have wealth at home; so why have you turned
> Yourself into a beggar, rich as you are?
> Why are you joyless today in a mansion of joy?'

When he finished writing *Meghnad* in June 1861, Madhu wrote another poem for the *Tattvabodhini*. This poem was called *Atmavilap* (*Self-lament*). Like *Bangabhasha*, it earned a permanent place in the hearts of his readers for its lyricism and the sincerity of his emotions.

Only a few weeks before he wrote this poem, he had written a lament for Ravan in *Meghnad*. It is now difficult to say whether it was Ravan's lament that gave him the idea of writing *Atma-vilap*, or whether it was Madhu's own feeling of guilt and remorse that poured out through Ravan's lips. Perhaps each was a reflection of the other. The difference was that Ravan could not see what sin he had committed to deserve such grief. In his eyes, the abduction of Sita was not a sin. But, in Madhu's case, he knew very well what his own 'sin' was.

When he wrote *Atma-vilap*, Madhu was only thirty-seven. He was too young, therefore, to worry about his advancing years, or that his time on earth was going to waste. If anything, by this time he had achieved the three things he had always dreamt of: love, fame, and money. He was not wealthy by any means, but a steady job, and victory in some of the cases he had been fighting to regain his father's property and mother's jewellery, had brought a certain amount of financial security. Yet, it was at this moment that he chose to write *Atma-vilap*, accusing himself of running after a mirage, turning his back on his duties and responsibilities:

> You long to shackle your feet   with the chains of love:
>   What fruits have you gained?
> Yearning for fire's bright flame   you flutter down
>   Into death's snare:
> Lured like an insect, alas,   you rush in blithely,
>   Seeing not, hearing not, and now your heart aches.

It is clear how deep his feeling of guilt ran. Perhaps it was not just the thought of having abandoned Rebecca and her children. Maybe he also felt guilty about having caused pain and sorrow to his parents and others who had loved him. Whatever the reason, in this poem the voice that speaks is not simply that of a gifted poet, but of a man whose heart is heavy with pain and anguish. The sincerity of his feelings is unmistakable. It is for this reason that this poem has been hailed with so much sympathy by his readers and is better known than any of his other short poems.

After *Atma-vilap* was written, Madhu was once again unsure of his future. He even thought of writing prose once again, but could not settle down to anything. In the meantime, Henrietta's health broke down after the birth of their second child. Madhu had to suffer many an anxious moment, and did everything the doctors advised him to do, including nursing his wife. In a letter written to Basu, possibly in February 1862, he said: 'I have suffered a great deal of mental anxiety of late on account of my wife's ill health. I have been a wanderer on water and land. I took her on the river and then to Burdwan. Thank God, her health appears to be quite re-established now....'

It was only after Henrietta recovered that Madhu could finally settle down to writing poetry again. What he wrote this time was a number of letters, from various women either to their husbands or lovers. He called the collection *Birangana*. It was inspired by the Roman poet Ovid's *Heroides*. Although each one is a letter, it reads like a dramatic monologue. The women Madhu chose were all from Hindu mythology. There are eleven 'letters' in *Birangana*, from (1) Shakuntala to Dushyant; (2) Tara to Som; (3) Rukmini to Dwarakanath; (4) Kaikeyi to Dasharath; (5) Surpanakha to Lakshman; (6) Draupadi to Arjun; (7) Bhanumati to Duryodhan; (8) Duhshala to Jayadrath; (9) Janhabi to Shantanu; (10) Urvashi to Pururava, and (11) Jana to Niladhwaj.

Although the title of this work is *Birangana*, the mood that runs through it is not one of valour or heroism, but of romance, love, and longing. Every woman speaks freely, baring her heart and soul, talking of her pain, anxiety, and sorrow. Much of what they say bears further evidence of Madhu's guilt. The words these women speak might well have been spoken by Rebecca. For instance, Shakuntala says to Dushyant:

> Have you, Lord of Life, abandoned me now
> In my fresh youth? For what sin, O Husband,
> Tell me, is your servant Shakuntala guilty
> At your feet? The bird of delight that had built
> Its nest in my heart, what kind of hunter were you
> To come and kill it?

The lines spoken by Draupadi to Arjun also seem quite appropriate for Rebecca:

> You might keep on forgetting, but how
> Can Draupadi forget?

~ ~ ~

> Poet of poets that you are, send
> To the one who adores you a song
> Coated with sweetness!

~ ~ ~

What is your reason, pray, for this deception?
Come back, jewel of men! Who roams abroad,
Leaving his young wife on her own at home?

It is not known whether Rebecca did indeed write to him, expressing her feelings in such terms. But certainly, Madhu imagined her to be complaining thus, and longing for the return of the man she had loved and lost. Hindu mythology certainly enthralled him, but the same sense of guilt that had moved him to write *Atma-vilap* also inspired him to write these poems. The final result was that Madhu punished himself through his own poetry. When he started to write *Birangana*, he wanted to write twenty-one such 'letters'. Eventually, only the first eleven were published. What he wrote afterwards remained incomplete.

But what makes *Birangana* very special is not simply the autobiographical elements in it. In terms of style, structure, and versification, it shows the maturity Madhu had attained. The new verse-form—that is, blank verse—he introduced in *Tilottama* was much improved when he wrote *Meghnad*. In *Birangana*, it reached new heights. If Madhu had continued to write, no doubt he would have left further evidence of his extraordinary talents. But, only four months after *Birangana* was published (in 1862), Madhu removed himself from the world of literature. Eight months earlier, he had written that famous letter to Rajnarayan Basu, in which he had prophesied that he would, one day, 'come out like a tremendous comet'. He had mentioned a comet because its speciality is the suddenness of its appearance. Then it disappears, perhaps just as suddenly; but its extraordinary arrival—and brilliance—is recorded in history for ever.

Having reached the pinnacle of his success as a poet and dramatist, and having obtained a certain measure of financial stability, Madhu was now lured by a different temptation. In the course of time, it proved to be no less dangerous than the golden deer that had lured Sita in the Ramayana. Madhu decided to mortgage some of the property he had regained from his relatives, and go to England to become a barrister. He had spent years watching others, with far less intelligence and skill, earn a great deal more than he ever could. His attempts to study law in India, and take the qualifying examination, had failed a number of times for various reasons. Now, if he could go to England, not only would his most cherished dream be fulfilled, but he would well be on his way to amassing wealth. There were about thirty barristers in Calcutta at the time, but they were either British or Anglo-Indian. If Madhu could return from England as the first Bengali barrister, fame and fortune would both be easy to attain, he thought. Henrietta might have objected to his going alone, but there is no evidence to suggest that she did.

In this venture, Madhu was encouraged by his friends. But the person who helped him the most, in sheer practical terms, was Ishwarchandra Vidyasagar, to whom Madhu had dedicated *Birangana*.

Vidyasagar was one man whose feet were firmly planted in the real world. He was a writer, a scholar, and possibly the best-known social reformer of nineteenth-century Bengal; but he was fully aware of the importance of material success in life. Besides, it must have caused some distress to the patriot in him to watch educated and intelligent Bengalis fall behind and fail to attain the success that English and Anglo-Indian barristers did. Virtually no Indian had the means to study law in England, but Madhu had. He also had the linguistic ability required for this purpose. It was, therefore, important to Vidyasagar that Madhu be given the opportunity to do so. It was not just Vidyasagar who thought in this vein. A feeling of nationalism was rising quickly among the educated people in Bengal, and the desire to vie with the British, and be on an equal footing, was gathering force. It was partly from this feeling that, in March 1862, Satyendranath Tagore and Manomohan Ghosh left for England to return as ICS officers. The entire community was proud of the men that they became.

When Vidyasagar and other friends helped Madhu to mortgage his property and raise enough funds to go to England, it was with the noble intention of seeing another fellow Bengali gain as much status as an Englishman. What they did not know then was that their well-meant action would effectively push Madhu into a dark cavern of misfortune, from which he would never escape.

The first indication of Madhu's plans for going to England appears in a letter to Basu, written in early February 1862: 'But I suppose my poetical career is drawing to a close,' he wrote, 'I am making arrangements to go to England to study for the Bar and must bid adieu to the Muse! You will be pleased to hear that the great Vidyasagar...has taken great interest in my proposed visit to England...and has undertaken to raise a sufficient sum for me on easy terms on the mortgage of my property. The thing will cost me about twenty thousand rupees and I can spare that. No more Modhu the *kavi*, old fellow, but Michael M. S. Dutt Esquire of the Inner Temple Barrister-at-law! Ha! Ha! Isn't that grand? But I hope I shan't be disappointed.' But Lady Luck had other plans. Eventually, Madhu did go to England and return as a barrister. But he could never put his knowledge to good use. The hardships he had to suffer destroyed him completely.

However, all that was in the future. At the time of writing that letter, Madhu was busy making arrangements to ensure a regular income while he was away. The manager of two of his father's estates was Mahadeb Chattopadhyay, who Madhu had known for a long time. Although initially Mahadeb had joined the relatives who had tried to deprive Madhu of his rights, Madhu was prepared to trust him in the belief that he had realized his mistake and would now remain loyal. So he allowed Mahadeb to lease the two estates. These two areas, situated in the southern part of the district of Jessore, were called Chauk Munkia and Gadardanga. It was agreed that Mahadeb would pay him an annual rent of three thousand rupees, over the next seven years.

In order to raise ready cash for going to England, Madhu did several other things. Selling his ancestral home was one of them. He had moved to Kidderpore, but not to the house where he had spent his childhood. The reason why he did not move back into his old home is not clear. Either the location of the house was no longer convenient for him, or it could be that it was in a state of disrepair. Madhu sold it for seven thousand rupees to Harimohan Bandyopadhyay, the younger brother of his friend, Rangalal. He could possibly have got much more had he waited for another buyer, but clearly he was in a hurry, and selling his old home was not as much of a trauma as it might have seemed.

There was a plot of land attached to the house, which was also sold, but not to Harimohan. It went for one thousand and six hundred rupees to an Anglo-Indian called James Frederick, an employee of the Oriental Bank. Still, the money raised was not enough. Madhu was forced to borrow from his friends. Vidyasagar lent him a thousand rupees. Three others gave him a total of three thousand.

Even while he was making these preparations, some of his friends imposed a serious responsibility on him. He was roped in to edit the *Hindoo Patriot*. Its former editor, Harish Mukherjee, had died in June 1861. Since then, no one suitable could be identified to take over as a full-time editor. The journal was about to become extinct, when Madhu was approached, among others, by Vidyasagar and Jotindramohan Tagore, in the hope that with his previous experience of running journals, he would be able to save the *Hindoo Patriot* from such a fate. Although Madhu wrote to Rajnarayan Basu that he was being 'burdened', it seems that he was quite enthusiastic to start with. But as things turned out, he did not work for this journal for more than two months. The chief reason why he left seems to have been that he was not paid regularly.†

In any case, in view of his impending departure, it is doubtful that Madhu would have continued to work for this journal for any length of time. His primary concern at this time, naturally, was for Henrietta and their children. He wanted to leave as much money as he could for his family, and ensure their safety. Unfortunately, there were still a few unresolved problems.

In early March 1862, Madhu wrote to Basu, 'I don't think I shall be able to go to England quite so soon as I had expected. I do not like to leave the country before extinguishing the flames of litigation with my relatives and they, I am sorry to say, are either the greatest rogues or fools under the sun!'

About three months after this letter was written, Madhu did leave for England. How did he feel as the time of his departure approached? This is what he said to Basu, in a letter dated 4 June 1862:

You will be pleased to hear that I have completed my arrangements, and...propose starting on the morning of 9th instant.... You must not fancy, old boy, that I am a traitor to the cause of our native Muse. If it hadn't been for the extraordinary success the new verse has met with, I should have certainly delayed my departure. Or not gone at all. But an early triumph is ours, and I may well leave the rest to younger hands, not ceasing to direct their movements from my distant retreat. *Meghnad* is going through a second edition with notes, and a *real* BA, has written a long critical preface, echoing your verdict—namely, that it is the first poem in the language. A thousand copies of the work have been sold in twelve months.

In these lines, two things become apparent. The first is a sense of guilt and betrayal that he is leaving his motherland to equip himself for a better life; and the second is a sense of pride and contentment regarding *Meghnad*. The 'real BA' was Hemchandra

Bandyopadhyay. No doubt Madhu felt proud that such a man had written the preface and the notes.

But, having achieved fame and recognition, having served Saraswati (the goddess of learning), Madhu was now free to pursue Lakshmi (the goddess of wealth). It must be remembered here that although Madhu had a passion for good living—and to do that, one naturally needed money—he had no wish to earn vast sums just to build up large savings. Money, on its own, held very little appeal for him. He always spent more than he earned.

In the letter to Basu dated 4 June, Madhu included a poem. It was called *Bangobhumir Prati* (*To Bengal*). 'I hope the thing is—if not good—at least *respectable*,' he said. It began with a line from Byron, 'My native land! Good night!' Then he went on to say:

> Keep me, Mother, loyal as I am, in your mind.
> I implore you at your feet: if disaster prevents me
> From achieving my desire, do not banish
> My sweet name from the lotus of your heart!
> If in exile, by the power of fate,
> My life's star falls from my body's sky,
> Do not grieve at that. Those who are born
> Must one day die: who, where, can be immortal?
> What water lasts forever, alas, in life's
> River? But if you remember me, Mother,
> I do not fear death; even wax
> Doesn't melt, if dropped in a lake of nectar.

What is most striking about this poem is its simplicity. The 'scholar' Madhu is absent here. What he says seems to come straight from his heart. The sense of guilt that he expressed earlier in his letter at leaving his motherland seems to be present also in this poem. There is the fear of losing his life (which, in those days, was justified and understandable, before embarking on a long voyage by sea). But, most of all, there is the prayer that he be remembered by his countrymen.

That, in fact, was the final thing that he wrote to his friend before he set sail:

Here you are, old Raj, all that I can say is—*modhuheen koro na go tabo mano kokanade* [do not banish my sweet name from the lotus of your mind].

Come rain or shine, Madhu simply wanted to bloom like a lotus in the memory of his native land.

Chapter Five

'Believe me, my dear fellow, our Bengali is a very beautiful language.... Such of us, owing to early defective education, know little of it and have learnt to despise it, are miserably wrong.... I wish I could devote myself to its cultivation but, as you know, I have not sufficient means to lead a literary life and do nothing in the shape of real work for a living. I am too poor, perhaps too proud to be a poor man always.... Make money, my boy, make money! If I haven't done something in the literary line, if I do possess talents, I have not the means of cultivating them to their utmost content and our nation must be satisfied with what I have done.'

This is what Madhu said in a letter to Gourdas, written from Versailles in France, on 26 January 1865. Nowhere did he speak more plainly about the real reason behind his departure for England.

Two and a half years before that letter was written, Madhu had finally set sail from Calcutta on the *Candia*,† on 9 June 1862. His ship reached Madras on 12 June, and remained there for the next two days. Madhu left no written record of his feelings upon reaching Madras. Did he think of Rebecca and his children? Did he want to go and see them? Did he see anyone at all in those two days? It is impossible to say with any certainty what Madhu did in Madras, since there is no evidence to support any assumption; but a sensitive man like him would certainly have felt a great deal of pain to be back in a place that was filled with so many memories.

The *Candia* left Madras and eventually reached Port Syed, via Aden. The passengers had to disembark at Port Syed and board another ship called the *Ceylon*, and then go on to Alexandra. A letter that Madhu wrote to Gourdas on 11 July 1862 from this ship gives an indication of his state of mind:

I sit down to scribble a few lines to you, my good friend, from on board the good steamship *Ceylon*—quite a fairy castle afloat, my Boy.... The saloon is worthy of a palace, the cabins fit for princes.... I am at this moment floating down the famous Mediterranean sea with the rocky coast of North Africa in view! Yesterday we were at Malta, last Sunday at Alexandria. In a few days more, I hope, we shall be in England. Just 32 days ago, I was in Calcutta! Is not this travelling with wonderful rapidity?... But the journey has its dark side also.... I wish I had half a dozen of our countrymen on board. We would form a party by ourselves....

One thing becomes clear from this letter. Madhu was suffering from an identity crisis. Back in his own country, he had thought of himself as different, even superior, to his fellow men. But now, thrown into the company of white English people, he began to think much more of his own country and society. More than six years earlier, he had travelled from Madras to Calcutta. The English passengers on that ship had noted his Westernized attire and behaviour, and decided to give him a new name—Mr Holt. Madhu had then seen it purely as a joke. Now, travelling together with English people returning to England, he began to view them differently. It is not surprising that he felt isolated, and wished there were more Indians on board.

The problem that Madhu had to grapple with all his life was a dichotomy of mind. He had a simple nature, but the manner in which he viewed life was far from simple. Although born and brought up in the East, his mind and intellect were shaped by Western values. Yet, even when he tried to embrace the West with all his heart, his natural ties with, and sympathy for, the East stopped him from becoming an integral part of the Western society. This eternal conflict in his mind never let him find peace. It was as if he was born to suffer by being driven in two different directions.

On 14 July, Madhu's ship reached Gibraltar. Then, on 19 July, before dawn broke, it finally docked at Southampton.† By the time he reached London—the city of his dreams—it must have been past noon. The people who initially offered him hospitality in London were Manmohan Ghosh and Satyendranath Tagore,† the two men from Bengal who were already there. Over the next four weeks, Madhu saw the various sights of London. But he lost no time in securing his admission in Gray's Inn.† This shows how serious he was about his quest. The next term did not start until November. Madhu could well have arrived three months later. But he was very keen to be in London and complete all the formalities well before his studies began.

Prospective barristers could study at any of these institutions: Lincoln's Inn, Inner Temple, Middle Temple, and Gray's Inn. They were collectively called the Inns of Court. The largest was Lincoln's Inn. Gray's Inn was the smallest.

It is interesting to note that on his application form, Madhu spelt his name slightly differently.† He wrote it down as Michael Madhusudana Datta. This somewhat old-fashioned and Sanskritized spelling could be another indication of Madhu's identity crisis. Having spent his entire life emulating the English, he was suddenly reminded of his own roots when he actually found himself in England. Clinging to those roots, and what was his 'own', became very important.

From a letter written to Manomohan Ghosh on 16 September 1862, it appears that Madhu was staying with him and Satyendranath until shortly before that date. From his application for admission to Gray's Inn it seems that he moved out to 54 Bernard Street, not far from Gray's Inn, before joining. Judging by the tone of Madhu's letter, he was feeling very lonely: 'I feel very dull and sad...I need scarcely say that I miss both of you very much.' Nevertheless, he mentions in the same letter that he had gone out with a fellow lodger to visit the Kew gardens, Richmond and Hampton Court. 'I can scarcely describe to you the wonders I saw. What a pity you don't stir out of London and see these wonderful places. These places add an air of romantic reality to the dry historical facts we learnt in our younger days. I am quite in love with Hampton Court....'

This shows that Madhu was making a determined effort to rise above his loneliness and misery. Besides, he never allowed himself to forget the real reason why he was in London. He reminded his two young friends about it, on 14 November: 'Work on, my boys, win all manner of honours; we are all of us in for it.... We three, I dare say, are the theme of frequent discourse among our countrymen.'

'Work on' seemed to have become his own ruling principle in life. There is no indication in his letters written at this time that he was doing any creative writing or, for that matter, reading any contemporary literature. Madhu's only mission in life appeared to be to study law, become a barrister, and then return to his own country.

Initially, everything went as Madhu had planned. Indeed, all would have been well, and he would have achieved his goal, had his arrangements back home not gone awry. What happened was totally unexpected. Madhu learnt about it from a letter sent by Henrietta. It turned out that Mahadeb Chattopadhyay, who was supposed to pay nearly three thousand rupees every year—some of it to Henrietta, and the rest to Madhu—had not paid any money to either of them. According to their agreement, he was to pay one hundred and fifty rupees to Henrietta every month. A certain portion of that money was paid to her in advance before Madhu left. But, after his departure, Mahadeb paid Henrietta only a hundred rupees in November 1862, fifty rupees in January, and ninety-five rupees in February 1863.[†] To Madhu, he did not pay a single paisa. Moreover, Madhu's relatives, who were expected to return his mother's jewellery to Henrietta, did not do so. In fact, they joined hands with Mahadeb and harassed Henrietta in whatever way they could. Perhaps they thought that if both Madhu and his wife could be driven out of the country, they could regain possession of his property.

Under these circumstances, after much deliberation, Henrietta took the only decision she could take, since she was without friends or a mentor to advise her. She decided to leave for London with her children to join her husband. At this point, a few well-wishers (including Vidyasagar and Digambar Mitra) must have helped her, for before she set sail (possibly on 23 March 1863), she managed to recover thirteen hundred rupees from Mahadeb on 22 March 1863.

Having recovered the money, if she had so wished, Henrietta could have stayed on in Calcutta. Why did she insist on taking the extreme step of making such a long journey with two small children? One obvious reason is that she had no wish to face the same problem again with Mahadeb and Madhu's relatives. But there might have been another reason which cannot be overlooked. Over a period of time, certain rumours about Madhu had been afloat. It took a while for Madhu to realize what was happening; when he did, he wrote to Gourdas and Vidyasagar, begging them not to pay any attention to what they might hear. But nowhere in his letters was he specific about the precise nature of these rumours. Some thought Madhu had got involved with another woman. If this particular rumour had reached Henrietta's ears, it was not surprising that she was alarmed. Besides, Madhu's relatives were harassing her so much that, even without any worrying rumours about her husband, she would probably have decided to leave Calcutta.

Back in London, Madhu was facing an old familiar problem—lack of money. He had to borrow from Manmohan on occasions to make ends meet. Although Mahadeb was to pay three thousand rupees a year, and according to a later verbal agreement two thousand rupees, Madhu had instructed Mahadeb to send him two hundred and fifty rupees every month, and pay one hundred and fifty to Henrietta. That came to four thousand and eight hundred rupees a year. Even if Mahadeb had made this payment regularly, there would have been a shortfall of one thousand and eight hundred rupees. So it seems that it was Madhu's judgement that was faulty. He himself had sown the seeds of his future deprivations.

Henrietta reached England on 2 May 1863, almost ten months after Madhu's arrival the year before. It is not known where Madhu took his family. Presumably, they found someplace cheap, using some of the money that Henrietta had brought with her. A few weeks later, when they were feeling a little settled, Madhu wrote to several people in Calcutta, to chase his overdue payments. In addition to Mahadeb, he wrote to the two guarantors who had been appointed at the time of drawing up the lease. They were Digambar Mitra and Baidyanath Mitra. The latter was Madhu's cousin. He worked in the Alipore Court, and had agreed to look after Madhu's interests for the payment of three hundred rupees a year. Surprisingly, neither Digambar nor Baidyanath responded.

In June 1863, Madhu finished the first four terms of his course. In every term, six dinners were held, which every student was expected to attend. Normally, once a student had attended seventy-two dinners, that is, completed twelve terms, he would qualify as a barrister. Madhu, therefore, had to wait another two years before he reached that stage.

However, it soon dawned upon him that it would be impossible to live in London, depending purely on the money Henrietta had brought from India. Not only was London an expensive place, but there were people there who knew them. It hurt his pride to be seen as someone who was living in abject penury. He decided to move to Versailles in France, at least for the time being. Why he chose that place is not clear. Perhaps Versailles was cheaper than London and, of course, it was devoid of people who might recognize him. But why, instead of going to an unknown place far away from his place of study, did he not simply move to the countryside in England? One likely explanation is that he was tired of the English weather. In many of his letters, Madhu complained about it. (To Manomohan Ghosh, on 8 January 1863, he said, 'London has been dreadfully foggy these two days. What a brutal country is this, by Jove!' Three years later, on 17 January 1866, he wrote to Vidyasagar, 'We are now in the midst of a rigorous winter. For a poor man like myself London is dreadful.') Those familiar with the vagaries of English weather will understand why Madhu wanted to escape it.

The real reason, however, might have been racism in England, far more prevalent in those days than is commonly known. In recent years, quite a few in-depth studies have shown that in the 1860s, a few thousand black and Asian people lived in England. The poverty they had to endure was horrific. The upper classes treated them with a marked lack of sympathy. A student wrote a letter in *The Times* in 1865, describing the pathetic conditions in which two hundred Indian beggars lived in London. Henry Mayhew also described the condition of these beggars in his *London Labour and the London Poor* (1861-2). In 1873, another book called *The Asiatics in England* spoke of the dreadful condition of Indian sailors who were living on the streets of London.

Sensitive as he was, Madhu probably felt quite overwhelmed by what he saw and read. France, he knew, was different; nor was he disappointed. On 26 October 1864, he wrote to Gour from Versailles: 'Everyone, whether high or low, will treat you as a man and not a "damned nigger".' Sixteen years after Madhu's arrival in London, the young Rabindranath Tagore also visited England.[†] But, unlike Madhu, he stayed with an English family. His letters written during that time give humorous (but accurate) accounts of how he was treated. He heard a young girl speaking to her mother, referring to him as 'blackie'. Even the two girls in the English household where he stayed were so scared when they heard that he was coming to live with them that they left home and stayed in a relative's house for a few days, before being reassured by their eldest sister that he was 'all right'. But his hosts—Dr John Scott and his wife, Mary—were affectionate people, and very soon Rabindranath began to be treated by everyone with warmth and friendliness. Madhu was not so fortunate.

It is likely that someone known to Madhu gave him the idea of going to Versailles, just as, in 1847, the idea of going to Madras had come from his friend, Charles Egbert Kennet. But it is not known who in England might have given Madhu such an idea. Madhu knew before setting out that his stay in Versailles would have to be for more than a few weeks. It was obvious that the complexities that had arisen over his financial situation in Calcutta were not going to be easily resolved. As things turned out, it took far longer than Madhu had anticipated.

It was Madhu's belief that in France he could manage on far less than what he would have needed in London. Perhaps he also hoped to earn a little money by teaching English. But this hope was never fulfilled. Before he left London, Madhu had to borrow twenty pounds from the hundred pounds he had paid as a deposit at the time of his admission to Gray's Inn.†

Some of his earlier biographers appear to think that Madhu stayed in Paris before moving to Versailles. This does not seem likely, in view of Madhu's limited resources and the expensive living conditions in Paris. What happened probably was that Madhu stopped in Paris for two or three days enroute to Versailles. It is unlikely that he had visited Paris before. Now, he may simply have taken the opportunity to see the city and its sights, in spite of his stretched means.

Versailles is fifteen miles from Paris. It is famous for the palace that was built there by King Louis XIV in the seventeenth century. It was so large and so opulent that nearly a thousand officials and four thousand assistants were required to look after it. All these workers lived in the palace. For more than a hundred years, Versailles was the capital of France. When the French Revolution started, its first waves swept across Versailles. Twenty-six years before Madhu went there, Louis-Philippe had turned the palace into a museum. However, in spite of all its glory, Versailles was like a small town in the 1860s when it had a population of about forty thousand. A few years after Madhu left it, it became politically important again as the Germans occupied it, and the coronation of the German Emperor was held there in 1871.

Madhu spent two and a half years in Versailles. He could not get any job during that time. He and his family survived simply by stretching their resources to their farthest limit. They arrived in Versailles in June, 1863. By January, 1864, they were penniless. All they could do after that was borrow from whoever they could, and watch their debts mount.

Madhu rented a flat at 12, Rue-des-Chantiers. Eighteen families lived in that building. Twelve of those received financial help from government charity funds[†] during 1864–5. It is not hard to imagine how cheap and lowly that area must have been, and what kind of people Madhu must have acquired as neighbours. That might have made him unhappy, but he had no choice. Luckily, Versailles was a beautiful place. Once he could get out of his house, Madhu felt happy enough. He fell in love with the palace, just as he had with Hampton Court in England. In some of his letters he mentions visiting the garden of the palace, and feeding the fish and ducks in a nearby pond. The palace was only half a mile from his house. Since it was summer when Madhu arrived in Versailles, he and his family could enjoy the warm weather, which made a huge difference after cold and foggy London. Besides, fresh flowers were blooming everywhere, and the whole of Versailles was looking gloriously colourful.

All that natural splendour soon awoke the poet in Madhu. He decided to write another epic. The subject he chose this time was from the Mahabharata—Draupadi's *swayamvar sabha* (the assembly where Draupadi chose her husband). He began writing it on 9 September 1863.

In the opening invocation, Madhu promised his readers that it would be a tale set in a 'new rhyme'. Sadly, he abandoned the project after writing only thirty lines. At first, he wrote in blank verse, very much like *Meghnad*. But then he revised it, and rewrote the same lines using a truly new verse form. Years later, Tagore gave this form a finite shape, and it came to be known as the 'rhyming couplet'. Why Madhu could not write any further is not clear. An obvious reason is his poverty and great uncertainty over his future. Besides, as he admitted to Gour a year later in his letter of 26 October 1864, 'The fit has passed away and I do not know if it will ever come back again. You know I write by fits and starts.'

But the 'fit' returned briefly after his first abortive attempt, and Madhu tried again, choosing the story of the abduction of Subhadra, also from the Mahabharata. This time, he wrote sixty-one lines before he lost interest. Yet, the desire to experiment with a new verse form and tell a new tale would not leave him completely. So, for the third time, Madhu turned to the Mahabharata and began telling the tale of the Pandavas. Only seventeen lines later, he stopped again.

It would not be fair to speculate on how these poems might have turned out, had Madhu finished writing them. But it would perhaps not be unreasonable to assume that the experience and skill that he had gained while writing *Meghnad* would have helped him to produce something more mature, more effective. His new experiences in Europe had taught him a lot about life and people, and had, no doubt, affected his outlook.

Obviously, poetry was a difficult Muse to pursue, when a grim battle had to be fought just to survive. Madhu's money was running out. The many letters he wrote to his friends in Calcutta, particularly to Digambar Mitra, remained unanswered. By October 1863, it was time to return to London to start the Michelmas term at Gray's Inn. Luckily, that term lasted just twenty-four days.

Madhu left his family in Versailles and paid a quick visit to London. He attended six dinners during that term (between 2 and 25 November 1863), and returned to Versailles. Before he came back, he applied once more to Gray's Inn to borrow another twenty-five pounds from his deposit.† In his application, he described his situation quite candidly. The pension committee in Gray's Inn considered his application on 22 December 1863, and granted him the money he had asked for. By this time, the little money that Henrietta had brought with her was almost all gone. Moreover, she got pregnant again. Madhu resumed writing desperately to Digambar Mitra and Baidyanath Mitra, begging them to help him to retrieve the money Mahadeb owed him.

From January 1864, his debts in France began mounting. He could not pay his rent, nor settle the unpaid bills at the local grocery. Their few valuable possessions made their way, one by one, to a pawn shop. Still no help came from India. All that Madhu learned from Baidyanath Mitra, in February 1864, was that Mahadeb had been instructed by Digambar to send him a thousand rupees. Baidyanath himself owed a thousand rupees to Madhu. He reassured him that the money would be sent very soon. But it did not arrive.

If Madhu and his family managed to survive during this period, it was only because his neighbours and friends took pity upon them, and he received occasional help from the church near his house. In a letter dated 18 June 1864, Madhu admits: 'I have been obliged to appeal to the generosity of the English clergyman here to save us from starvation....' Nagendranath Som, one of his earlier biographers, describes how his neighbours used to leave food outside his front door. Normally, a proud man like Madhu would never have accepted charity. But hunger and deprivation had left him with no choice.

What Madhu could not imagine was that none of his friends in India would come forward to help. He kept borrowing money, or buying provisions on credit, in the hope that someone or the other would soon send him money from home. By May 1864, he was so deeply immersed in debt that it began to look as if he might have to go to prison. His creditors ran out of patience and either lodged an official complaint against him, or threatened to do so. Driven out of his wits by poverty and anxiety, Madhu could think of appealing once more only to that one person in whom he had any faith left—Ishwarchandra Vidyasagar.

On 2 June 1864, he wrote: 'I am going to a French jail and my poor wife and children must seek shelter in a charitable institution, tho' I have fairly four thousand rupees due to me in India. The Benchers of Gray's Inn, from whom I was compelled to draw four hundred and fifty rupees have suspended me and this is the third term I am losing this year.... You are the only friend who can rescue me from the painful position to which my confidence in Digambar has placed me, and in this, you must go to work with that grand energy which is the companion of your genius and manliness of your heart.' When Madhu sent this letter, he was too unwell to write himself. He dictated the whole letter to Henrietta, who was not in good health, either.

At the time, mail sent from France used to take five weeks to reach India. So Vidyasagar could not have received this letter before mid-July. Madhu, however, could not wait that long to see if Vidyasagar would reply. He continued to write to him, perhaps in the hope that if somehow one of his letters was lost, the others would reach him. Over the next four weeks Madhu wrote four letters to Vidyasagar, describing his situation in detail. On 9 June, he wrote: 'I always thought Digambar a generous, warm-hearted sincere man. God alone knows what we have done to change his feelings towards us.' But he went on to say: 'You will be pleased to hear that I have been saved the disgrace of a French jail by a young, beautiful, and gracious French lady, whose acquaintance I made in a railway carriage, and who has ever since taken great interest in us, consoled us in our misfortunes and assisted us with her purse.'

In spite of this help that came so unexpectedly, Madhu was nowhere near settling all his debts. In his earlier letter of 2 June, he had instructed Vidyasagar to mortgage his land: 'I have got landed property which gives me at present fifteen thousand rupees a year. All lawsuits have been extinguished and my rights are undisputed. The Land Mortgage Society in Calcutta lend money at ten per cent. You will thus be able to raise fifteen thousand (15,000) rupees for me.' Now, in his second letter, he reminded Vidyasagar of what had to be done, and added, 'Perhaps people will try to throw impediments in your way, but I hope you will overcome everything.' Three paragraphs later, he said again, 'People in Calcutta will, no doubt, tell you *lies* about us; do not believe them and have faith in me, I pray you!' This last comment is a clear indication that, by this time, Madhu—who had once been trusting and simple—had become suspicious of the motives of others. Certainly, his own faith was badly shaken.

On 18 June, Madhu ended his letter to Vidyasagar by saying, 'I hope you will write to me in France, and that I shall live to go back to India and tell my countrymen that you are not only Vidyasagar, but Karunasagar [Ocean of Mercy] also!' As it happened, Vidyasagar put things in motion to help Madhu even before he received this letter. It was not in his nature to remain indifferent if anyone appealed to him for help.

A week after he had despatched his letter to Vidyasagar, that is, in the last week of June, Madhu finally received eight hundred rupees from Digambar Mitra, although by then, according to Madhu, Mahadeb Chattopadhyay owed him something between three and five thousand rupees. No one has been able to explain why the amount was reduced to eight hundred, when a thousand had been promised in February. Nevertheless, it brought a certain measure of relief. About the same time, Madhu also wrote to his publisher, Ishwarchandra Basu. It is likely that Basu sent him some money in due course. In the following year, between January and June 1865, Madhu earned a thousand rupees as royalty from his books. But now, in June 1864, the eight hundred he received from India was soon spent.

On 2 August, Madhu wrote to Vidyasagar again, although he knew that even if Vidyasagar had sent him any help, it was too soon for it to have reached France. But things were worse than before. Henrietta was about to give birth to their third child. In his letter, Madhu said: '...you must excuse the anxiety which induces me to inflict another letter on you. You cannot imagine how unhappy I am!...if you do not send me *all* the money I want by October next, I shall lose another Term and remain buried in France as I am at this moment.... My poor wife expects to be confined every day and I haven't got more than twenty rupees in the house!...God help me! My great hope now is in you, and I am sure you will not disappoint me. If you do, I must work my way back to India to commit one or two murders—*wilful*, premeditated murders and then be hanged!'

The language Madhu uses in this letter shows what agonies he was suffering. The following day, Henrietta gave birth to a baby girl, but it did not live.[12] Still struggling to cope with want and grief, Madhu wrote to Vidyasagar again on 18 August. Perhaps, by this time, he had started to hope that Vidyasagar's reply to his first letter would arrive any day. Or perhaps he wanted to keep up the pressure on his friend. So he reminded him once again of the seriousness of the situation: '...we are again in distress—in worse distress than before...and I am absolutely without a penny. The money with which I have bought postage stamps for this letter has

---

[12] It is not clear if Henrietta gave birth to a dead child, or the child died soon after her birth. Madhu wrote to Vidyasagar on 18 August that his 'poor wife gave birth to a dead child on the morning of the third instant'. However, on 26 October, he wrote to Gour that they 'had a beautiful daughter born here but she did not live long.' According to the birth document at the Versailles Municipal Archives (No. 671, 3 August 1864), the child 'was presented dead to the Alderman'.

been raised from a pawn broker's office!...you must not forget, my dear friend, that unless you send me several thousand rupees on the mortgage of my property, I shall continue to be a prisoner in France and cannot possibly join Gray's Inn next November.'

Ten days later, on 28 August, Madhu's prayers were answered. In his next letter to Vidyasagar, dated 2 September 1864, this is how he described what happened:

...as I was seated in my little study, my poor wife came to me with tears in her eyes and said, 'The children want to go to the Fair, and I have only three francs. Why do those people in India treat us this way?' I said, 'The Mail will be in today and I am sure to receive news, for the man to whom I have appealed, has the genius and wisdom of an ancient sage, the energy of an Englishman and the heart of a Bengali mother!' I was right; an hour later, I received your letter and the fifteen thousand rupees you have sent me.

At the time, the total amount that Madhu owed was two thousand and six hundred rupees. With the money he received from Digambar Mitra and Vidyasagar, he repaid half of his debts. It was still his intention to leave his family in France and return alone to London to finish his studies. In the same letter dated 2 September 1864, Madhu told Vidyasagar: 'When I go to London, I must live apart from my family till July next, after which I can live on in France.... Besides, I wish to leave my children behind, they being too young to go backwards and forwards....' Later, however, Vidyasagar tried to make him see that if his family lived with him wherever he happened to be, it would be far more economical.

Madhu knew, of course, that before he left France—alone or otherwise—he would have to repay every penny he owed. To that end, he was not yet out of the woods. Between May and September, in every letter that he wrote to Vidyasagar, he raised the question of mortgaging all his property. He did not seem to mind doing this possibly because, at one time, he had no hope of getting any of his father's assets and, in any case, he himself had not had to work hard to acquire any of it. So his attachment to his father's property was minimal. Vidyasagar, on the other hand, had far more practical sense. As Madhu's well-wisher, he wanted to explore other possibilities of raising funds. At first, Madhu was not inclined to listen to his advice, but eventually he came to accept the idea. As a matter of fact, by then Vidyasagar had received an assurance from his friend, Anukulchandra Mukhopadhyay, that money would be forthcoming. Mukhopadhyay was a lawyer in the High Court. He agreed to lend some money to Madhu. Having received such an assurance, Vidyasagar then went on to contact Baidyanath Mitra and Mahadeb Chattopadhyay, and tried to recover the money they owed Madhu. It was Madhu's belief that part of the money that Vidyasagar sent him in the first instance came from Baidyanath. Since the letters Vidyasagar wrote to Madhu are no longer available, it is impossible to say exactly how much he recovered from these individuals. What *is* known is that Madhu was perfectly satisfied with the action taken by Vidyasagar and was happy to leave the matter to him.

Another thing that Vidyasagar tried to do was to make Madhu see that getting angry with Digambar Mitra and Mahadeb Chattopadhyay, and using strong language against them, was not going to serve any purpose. After having received some money from Mitra, Madhu was prepared to relent towards him, but he still saw Chattopadhyay as a villain. 'I am afraid that of late the state of my feelings has imparted great bitterness to my language with reference to M—C—[Mahadeb Chattopadhyay]: but I must candidly confess to you that I am still far from thinking myself deserving of the reproof, which you so gently and elegantly administer.... I see plainly that Master M—C—has suppressed facts and taken advantage of your ignorance of our affairs to make out a nice little case for himself,' Madhu wrote on 18 September 1864.

Whether or not he was right about Mahadeb, it eventually turned out that Madhu was right about the need to get a large sum of money in a lump sum. That might have been possible if Vidyasagar had mortgaged his property. But since he tried to raise the necessary funds through other means, acting purely as Madhu's well-wisher, everything got more complex and there were inevitable delays. On 18 December 1864, Madhu wrote to Vidyasagar: 'I am quite ready to go back to London with my family, but you must help me do so. I shall want... altogether two thousand and nine hundred rupees. I hope your friend will put this sum in your hands for my use *at once* and in *one lump*.... Alas, this sending of money by dribs and drabs does more harm than good.'

As things turned out, it took Vidyasagar fifteen months (from the time he received Madhu's first letter) to find the money Madhu required to pay all his debts in Versailles and return to London. In these fifteen months, Madhu must have spent at least four thousand rupees; and he still needed to attend five terms before he could qualify as a barrister.

※※※

It is clear from Madhu's letters to Vidyasagar that he was clinging to him exactly as a drowning man would clutch at a straw. He explained in every letter why and how it was essential for him to have a lot of money. Yet, even when he was penniless and facing starvation, he could think of other things to write about. Madhu did not waste his time in France, although he did not—or could not—do much creative writing. In his second letter to Vidyasagar (dated 9 June 1864), he said: 'Though I have been very unhappy and full of anxiety here, I have very nearly mastered French. I speak it well and write it better. I have commenced Italian and mean to add German to my stock of languages.... The French do not generally love foreign languages; yet our Sanskrit is not a stranger here; and you see half a dozen fellows even in this Provincial town eager to know something about it.'

His preoccupation with his own problems did not affect his interest—and pride—in the achievement of other Bengalis who were in London, particularly Satyendranath Tagore. When Tagore passed his ICS exam, Madhu was quick to inform Vidyasagar (on 11 July 1864): 'You will be pleased to hear that Satyendranath has passed and will go out in the course of a few months.' Then Madhu went on to write a sonnet, as a tribute to Satyendranath:

> Like that hero of heroes Arjuna, returning
> To the city of the gods in his own shape, having
> Finished his work by the strength of his virtue,
> Return now in joy to the world of India...
> Through distant Bengal the news of your glory
> Will quickly flow...

Manomohan Ghosh, who was also striving to become an ICS officer, was less fortunate in passing the exam. But Madhu was genuinely fond of him, and wanted to help him in whatever way he could. In spite of his own hardships, he invited Manomohan to visit him in Versailles, so that Madhu could help him gain a better grasp of Greek and Latin. Manomohan visited him in Versailles in September 1864. By this time, Madhu had received some money from Vidyasagar. The second instalment arrived from Calcutta while Manomohan was staying with Madhu. The enormous pressure he was under eased somewhat, and Madhu began to think once again of his own studies and other subjects.

With a little money in his pocket, his old habit of bragging returned. He managed to convince his landlord and the shopkeepers in Rue-des-Chantiers that he was actually a wealthy man who was just going through a difficult time. Around this time, Madhu received a letter from Gourdas. What he wrote in his reply (on 20 October 1864) bears unmistakable echoes of the past. The voice is very much that of Madhu who had once paid a gold mohur to have a haircut:

I am writing this letter to you...from a room elegantly fitted up with all the comforts (if not luxuries) of European civilization.... You are, no doubt, anxious to know why I am here in France. I will tell you. London is not half so pleasant a place to live in as this country, and its brutal climate does not agree with Mrs Dutt's health, though I am strong enough for any country under the sun.... This is unquestionably the best quarter of the globe. I have better dinners for a few francs than the raja of Burdwan ever dreams of! I can for a few francs enjoy pleasures that it would cost him half his enormous wealth to command—no, even that would be too little.... Here, you are the master of your masters! The man that stands behind my chair, when I dine, would look down upon the best of our princes in India. The girl that pulls off my muddy boots on a wet day, would scorn to touch our richest raja in India.

There is no mention at all in this letter of the torment, the anguish, even the humiliation he had had to suffer for more than a year. If one were to look at him critically, one might be tempted to label him a liar. But that was not really the case. It seems that, in this letter, Madhu simply described a dream he had secretly cherished in his heart all his life. An exaggeration it certainly was, but to one whose mind often soared on flights of fancy, it was all real.

Besides, there is reason to believe that, despite his poverty and deprivations, Madhu did get the chance to move in literary circles. In the nineteenth century, France was known for the circles formed by patrons of art and literature. Socialite women often became members of such groups. It could well be that Madhu met some of these people. After all, if he was learning French, Italian, and German and gaining fluency in each language, he could hardly be doing so without mixing with the speakers of those languages. Those interested in Sanskrit must have been learned and educated people, who might have befriended Madhu. On 26 January 1865, Madhu wrote another letter to Gourdas, in which he mentioned having written a sonnet in Bengali and translated it for some European friends, who 'very much liked it'. So there is a strong possibility that, at least on one occasion, Madhu was invited to a dinner given by some elite and cultured group of people. A waiter might have stood behind his chair, and a girl might have dragged his muddy boots off. What he wrote to Gour, therefore, need not necessarily be wholly untrue.

Moreover, Madhu had seen the difference in attitude between the English and the French, where foreigners were concerned. He felt that the French treated him with far more respect than the English. He wanted his children to grow up as Europeans, without ever encountering the insularity of either the English or Indians. 'Sermista is already quite French,' he wrote. 'If you should hear her rattle away, you would not believe that she was born on the muddy banks of the Hooghly.... I am going to leave my family behind in Europe for the education of my children.'

It was around this time that Madhu went back to poetry, although what he wrote were short poems for children, each with a moral. His inspiration came from Jean de La Fontaine (1621–95). Madhu wrote three poems: *The Peacock and the Goddess, The Crow and the Vixen,* and *The Mango Tree and the Creeper.* It is difficult to say why he decided to write moralistic poems. In his letter to Gour (26 October 1864), he referred to his writing thus: 'I have not been doing much in the poetical line, of late, beyond imitating a few Italian and French things.'

The 'Italian' poetry was a series of sonnets, which Madhu wrote in the style of Petrarch (1304–74). He had written sonnets in English before, when he was a student in Hindu College. But those early efforts were made in the Shakespearean style, taught by his favourite teacher, Richardson. Many years later, he wrote *Kabimatribhasha* in Bengali, after which he wrote no more sonnets. Now, having learnt to read Italian, his interest in sonnets was revived once more.

One may wonder why he was influenced by Petrarch. The

reason is not difficult to see. There were certain similarities in their situations. Petrarch's poetry was rooted in ancient classical literature, despite the romance that run through all the sonnets that were written about his lady love, Laura. Madhu's poetry was no different. Like Madhu, Petrarch was the son of a lawyer. His father insisted on his studying law, but Petrarch did not ever work as a lawyer. He devoted most of his time to reading classical writers. He did so not with the intention of going back to ancient times, but using the age-old traditions to enrich contemporary literature and language. Madhu had done the same, long before he went to Versailles. The humanism that is the hallmark of all renaissance literature, is visible in everything that Madhu wrote, from *Tilottama* to *Birangana*.

Five hundred years before Madhu's arrival in Versailles, Petrarch had produced *Canzoniere* (which contained around three hundred sonnets, addressed to Laura). Over the next four or five centuries, poets all over Europe followed the ideal set by Petrarch, in a movement that came to be known as Petrarchism. Baudelaire—a French poet of Madhu's time—was also influenced by Petrarch, albeit to a limited degree.

Petrarch fell in love with Laura when he was twenty-three. His love for her was purely platonic. As it happened, Laura died young, and Petrarch lived on for several years. His sonnets and other short poems talked about love, friendship, faith, separation, death, grief, even Laura's eyes and hair. Surprisingly, in Madhu's sonnets, love plays a minimal role. What he took from Petrarch's sonnets was more their structure, rather than their theme, although Madhu made variations even in the rhyme-scheme. In the octave of a sonnet, Petrarch almost always used *abbaabba*. His sestet varied, from *cdcdcd*, to *cddccd*. Madhu followed the Petrarchan style in the octave, but not in the sestet. Besides, many of Madhu's sonnets were written in the Shakespearean form.

In December 1864, Madhu received some more money from Vidyasagar (it was the third instalment), which eased his financial strain once more. Madhu relaxed, and became quite nostalgic, particularly after hearing from Gour. His heart longed for the motherland he had left behind.

Eventually, the sonnets he wrote numbered a little over a hundred. The subjects on which they were based fall into five categories: (a) nostalgia; (b) personalities (such as Tennyson, Hugo, Dante,

Vidyasagar, Kalidas and many others); (c) conflict in Madhu's own mind between his desire for wealth (pursuit of Lakshmi) and producing good poetry (pursuit of Saraswati); various moods (*rasas*) such as pathos, valour, fury; (e) the mystery of creation, and others.

In November–December 1864, it was nostalgia that prompted most of his sonnets. He wrote to Gour that he was hoping at some stage to have a collection of his short poems published. Perhaps that is why he wrote so many. At times, it does appear (particularly in those sonnets that are based on, or addressed to, well-known personalities) that they were written merely as a formal exercise. They do not seem to have been prompted by any spontaneous powerful feelings.

More deeply felt, however, are the sonnets on places he remembered from his childhood. This famous one, for example, is about the Kapotaksha river at Sagardari:

> Always, O River, you return to my mind.
> Always I think of you in this isolation;
> Always I imagine I am soothing my ears
> With your murmur (like the phantom music that people
> Hear in dreams). I have seen many rivers
> In many lands, but which can satisfy
> This thirst for love that I feel?
> You are like a stream of milk flowing from the breast
> Of my birthplace. Shall I ever see you again?
> Till the end of time, you will give your
> Water to the sea, like a subject paying taxes to his king.
> This is my prayer, that you will sing in the ears
> Of the people of Bengal, friend, the name (as of a friend)
> Of one who in exile sinks now in love for you
> As he takes your name in Bengali verse!

Only five of his sonnets were written with a woman in mind: nos 13, 14, 26, 58, and 100. Out of these, 13 and 14 (jointly called *Parichay: The First Meeting*), no. 26 (called *Kushume Keet: Canker in a Flower*), and no. 58 (untitled) appear to be written for or about the same woman. He introduces himself to her in sonnet no. 13. Nos 14, 26, and 58 describe his love and their coming together.

One may wonder who this woman was. Was she real or imaginary? Was she the same lady who had offered him financial help? That, however, does not seem likely for she was wealthy and well-bred. The woman described in sonnets 14 and 26 is beautiful, but not from a distinguished background. 'The lotus has left the lake and bloomed on land,' says the poet. In sonnet no. 26 he says, 'You are the moon of the garden. Which ill-star has cast its shadow over you?' Perhaps this line is an indication that this 'sylvan beauty' was being oppressed by a cruel man. It seems that the poet got to know this woman quite closely, but she expressed doubts over the sincerity of his affections. In sonnet no. 14, he offers her reassurance: 'I shall love you, in this matter/why have unnecessary doubts?' In no. 26, he expresses sympathy for her.

According to Nagendranath Som, one of the earlier biographers, sonnet nos. 13 and 14 were originally written in French. Then Madhu rewrote them in Bengali. It is not known how Som came up with this idea. But if what he says is true, there can be no doubt that the woman described was real, not imaginary. In the final sonnet (no. 58), he describes their physical union:

> I am not, O lovely-eyed one, leonine Lakshman;
> So why should I not be vanquished in battle?
> You drive, formidably, a moon-crested chariot;
> By Kama's gift, you have learnt the skills of Meghnad.
> Concealed behind a mountain, O beautiful one,
> You bind up your enemy with snakes; you cut his cheek
> With love's ten arrows, attack him with your lips;
> You repeatedly stir him with earthquakes!
> What a strange battle this is! At the sound of your conch,
> My strength is shattered. With the arrows of your breath,
> You blow away the armour of patience, lady,
> Pierce my soul with the sharp spear of your glance.
> If in this, O lovely-faced one, you take
> The naked form of Kali, who is not terrified
> Enough to immediately admit defeat?

The unquestionable sincerity of these emotions also suggests that it is more than just a flight of fancy. In fact, this particular sonnet is almost certainly indicative of an extramarital relationship between Madhu and another woman. Nevertheless, it must be admitted that although he was intimate with her, it was no grand passion that might have swept him off his feet.

No one has been able to unearth the true identity of this woman. Madhu might have met her through his acquaintances in the literary circles. Or she might have been an inhabitant of 12 Rue-des-Chantiers, where people from lower classes lived. But no matter who she was, by writing so openly about a 'fallen woman'—one looked down upon by society—Madhu created a new milestone in Bengali poetry. Ancient Sanskrit literature abounds in references to sex or carnal desire. But those references are impersonal in nature. In Madhu's case, there was an autobiographical element in it.

At the time, the educated Bengalis' attitude to sex in literature was somewhat ambivalent, partly because they were influenced by Victorian England. On the one hand, many educated Bengalis would not mind visiting prostitutes or keeping a mistress; on the other, they would not only show their disgust towards such women, but also a disapproval of extramarital love. Vidyasagar and Shibnath Shastri were known as champions of the cause of women and zealous theatre-goers; but when prostitute-actresses were introduced to Bengali professional theatre in 1873, they both abandoned the theatre. In nineteenth century Bengali literature, including autobiographical literature, it was only Dewan Kartikeya Chandra Ray, who gave a hint of his love for a prostitute. So by writing these two sonnets, Madhu certainly entered forbidden territory.

However, the true 'love poem' in his collection of sonnets was no. 100 (untitled). A few critics are of the view that it was written with Henrietta in mind. But a closer look shows that it was written for Rebecca. Or else, why should the poet say:

With the golden colours of love, O woman
With lovely eyes, you have painted a picture
In this heart of mine; who has the power
To wipe it out, however long
I wander through this mortal world?

There was no need to write these words about the woman with whom he was living. What he appears to be saying, really, is that although there is a chance that the 'golden colours of love' may be wiped out by someone else, he would not let that happen. Two lines later, he says: 'Far or near/wherever I am, I shall worship you always.'

Henrietta was living with him, there was no question of her being 'far'. That applied to Rebecca. In the penultimate line, he says: 'You will live forever in the temple of memory.' Henrietta was very much alive then, most certainly she was not just a 'memory'. What the other critics seem to emphasize is the final line of the poem: 'You are my constant companion in this world.' They believe that the words 'constant companion' can refer to no one but Henrietta. However, if the final line is seen together with the line that precedes it, the poet seems to be saying, to Rebecca, that it is her memory that keeps him constant company.

In some of the remaining sonnets, Madhu paid homage not to a woman, but to his mother tongue and motherland. In the sonnet written earlier (*Kabi-matribhasha*, later renamed *Bangabhasha*), he had already expressed his regret and remorse for having neglected his own language in his youth. The last sonnet in this collection reinforces this particular feeling. Even in some of his letters, Madhu expressed this same view regarding his mother-tongue. A careful analysis of everything he said, set against certain events in his life, highlights one single fact: his attitude towards Bengali was essentially ambivalent. On the one hand, there was genuine regard; on the other, there was supreme indifference. In other words, it was a 'love-hate' relationship. In the last sonnet, he says:

> Mother, I failed to recognize you
> In my childhood, stupid that I was!
> In my youth, you called out to me
> (Can a mother forget even her lowliest son?);
> Now, like the Pandavas, I leave the city I have built
> And go into the wilderness!

Madhu knew that under the present circumstances, there was really little that he could do for his motherland. Yet, he prayed that she be 'filled with light'. It is a clear indication of his love for his own country and language. But perhaps it also shows that he was still suffering from an identity crisis.

In his sonnets, Madhu also expressed sorrow, more than once, that India was being ruled by a foreign power, and that Indians—despite their glorious past—were helpless in the present situation: 'we are...in this weak, faint, infamous world...(like) pygmies among giants, a jackal born to a lion.'

Apart from these love poems and sonnets written about his country, there is one other that always gets a special mention from his critics. It is the one that he wrote to mark the five hundredth birth anniversary of Dante.[†] Madhu sent it to the king of Italy.

He became familiar with Dante's poetry when he was a student in Hindu College. Besides, when he was writing *Meghnad*, he consciously borrowed ideas from Dante. So it is not surprising that he wrote a poem to mark this famous poet's five hundredth anniversary. Moreover, the fact that he sent it to the king of Italy shows how important it was to him to impress royalty. And Madhu was rewarded to the extent that the king of Italy acknowledged receipt of this sonnet with gratitude. It was the same Madhu who had written proudly to Gour (on 26 October 1864): 'I have had the honour of bowing to, and being bowed to, by the famous Emperor and Empress of the French.' One wonders why he did not try to bow to Queen Victoria, or write a poem on her. Perhaps he thought that a bow or a poem from a humble subject from India would not be appreciated. He might have also felt bitter at the racist attitude that he had encountered in London.

The sonnets showed a spurt of creative activity towards the end of 1864, but Madhu could not spend a great deal of time on them. Financial problems raised their heads once more. Madhu knew that if he kept sending reminders to Vidyasagar, the latter might well lose his patience. Still, he wrote to him on 16 November, and then again on 2 December. Both letters show how helpless he was feeling, and how desperate he had become to hear from Vidyasagar: (a) '...I feel reluctant to trouble you; but my apology is that of a desperate man.... If you abandon me, I must sink!' and (b) '...I know how wise, thoughtful and kind and considerate you are; and how precious your time is. But you must allow me to deplore my bad luck. I have lost a whole year in Europe; and that is no trifling loss to a man, in my time of life, going to begin a new career.'

In mid-December, Vidyasagar sent him a thousand rupees (two thousand four hundred and ninety francs). It was not enough to repay all his outstanding debts, but naturally Madhu felt a little reassured. It became clear, however, that after having settled some of his debts, buying warm clothes for his family, and keeping five hundred francs aside to survive another month, Madhu could not return to London to continue his studies.

It also appears that in his letter to Madhu, Vidyasagar had made it plain that he could not help him unless Madhu gave him a Power of Attorney. Initially, Madhu was a little hesitant in this matter, partly because he was not well. After Manomohan Ghosh's departure from Madhu's house in Versailles, Madhu wrote to him on 30 October 1864: 'After you left I had been laid up with an inflammation of the bowels and I believed that the comedy was going to end, and the curtain fall; but here I am, my part is not finished yet.'

The tone here is light, but it seems that he was seriously ill. Later in October, his eyes began troubling him, so much so that he thought he might be going blind. Under such circumstances, it was difficult for him to go to Paris to draw up a Power of Attorney. However, it now became clear that unless Vidyasagar could be given greater freedom and power to handle his affairs, Madhu and his family would most certainly starve. So he did what was required, and wrote to Vidyasagar on 18 December: 'You will see that I have availed myself of your friendly suggestion with reference to a "Power of Attorney".... The document I send ought to invest you with sufficient power to do anything necessary on my behalf.'

Later in December, Vidyasagar sent him some more money. The following month, Madhu heard from Gourdas again. True to his nature, in his reply Madhu said nothing of his hardships. However, from some of the things he said, it does appear that by now he had gained a little wisdom. On 26 January 1865, he wrote with surprising candour: 'You can scarcely conceive how Europe has changed me in my habits, in my tastes.... I am no longer the same careless, impulsive, thoughtless sort of fellow...of course I am still romantic, for that you know is my nature.... I have my dreams and aspirations and vague longings, but I am growing wiser.'

Madhu had hoped to return to England in April, so that he could start a new term (the Trinity Term) at Gray's Inn on 27 May. That was not to be. It turned out that the Power of Attorney Madhu had sent was not adequate for Vidyasagar to borrow more money on Madhu's behalf. A revised document could be sent from France only by the end of April 1865. It was another three months before Madhu received enough money to settle all his debts in Versailles. The intervening months brought more anxiety, more humiliation. On one occasion, he had to appeal to a British charitable fund in Paris for the meagre sum of five hundred francs. 'You cannot imagine how degraded I felt,' he wrote to Vidyasagar on 18 May 1865.

By the time he could afford to go back to England, it was late September 1865. He missed the term that started in May. The next one would start in November. On his return, Madhu rented a house in Shepherd's Bush for a year, starting from October. At the time, it was a suburb of London; there were large areas of woodland, as yet undeveloped. Rent was therefore cheap. (Today, on the same site where Madhu's rented house had stood, stands the training centre of London Transport and a car park).

For the first time in his life, Madhu acted sensibly by choosing to live in a place where the rent was low. Then he went a step further and took in a paying guest, so that it became easier to pay the rent and other bills. In theory, the idea was a practical one. But the person Madhu chose to be his lodger turned out to be most unsuitable. He was a Bengali, called Khetramohan Dutt. He had arrived in England with the intention of going in for higher studies, but could not decide on a subject. Eventually, he studied medicine. At first, both Henrietta and Madhu were very fond of him. In fact, Henrietta took such good care of him that Khetramohan jokingly referred to her as 'Ma'.

However, by February 1866, their relations had soured. Over the next few months, Khetramohan began making slanderous comments about Madhu. As it happened, Khetramohan himself was no saint. Eventually, he moved in as a lodger with an English family and married one of the daughters.† Madhu heard about his activities and mentioned it, in confidence, to Vidyasagar in a letter dated 10 June 1866: '[Khetramohan] is living somewhere in London and has apparently cut us, his friends. I understand that he is *speculating in the matrimonial market*!' On his marriage certificate, Khetramohan is described merely as a 'gentleman'. It is clear that he was reluctant to reveal too much about himself, even to his betrothed. Madhu's suspicion (expressed later to Vidyasagar), that the source of all the malicious gossip about him was Khetramohan, seems justified.

※※※

For a couple of months after his return to London, Madhu appeared to be financially stable. By February 1866, he was running out of money once more. So he began writing to Vidyasagar again, reminding him how expensive London was and why he still needed a large sum of money. Vidyasagar heard his pleas with great patience and sympathy, and sent him one hundred and one pounds in February, and one hundred and fifty-one pounds in April. But Madhu continued to spend more than he could afford. In June 1866, he wrote again to Vidyasagar, asking for twelve hundred pounds to cover his expenses for the next six months, including fees at Gray's Inn, and expenses for travelling back to India. At the same time, he and Henrietta made a decision, which later proved to be perfectly disastrous. On 18 June, he wrote to Vidyasagar: '...we have come to the conclusion that it would be better that I should go out alone and that (Henrietta) should follow me some months after, when I have acquired a sort of professional footing.'

Although Madhu asked Vidyasagar to send him more money, he knew that even for Vidyasagar, it would be impossible to raise such a sum without selling Madhu's property. At the same time, he knew that if he lost what property he had, he would become a laughing stock. People were already making fun of him, for no one else appeared to need as much money as him to study law in England. It was even being said that Vidyasagar was spoiling him by giving in to his demands. On 26 June 1866, Madhu wrote to Vidyasagar: 'I have every right to do what I like with my own [property]. No sensible man would say that *you* have helped me to ruin myself.... If any good Samaritan should come forward to help us, well and good, if not you must raise money on the sale of property....'

Vidyasagar came to his rescue once more. It is not known exactly how much he sent after receiving the letter quoted above, but the amount must have been substantial. As it happened, he did not have to sell Madhu's property. Vidyasagar's friend, Anukulchandra Mukhopadhyay, lent him the money against the mortgage of some of the land owned by Madhu.

Over the next few months, Madhu was able to pay whatever he owed his landlord in Shepherd's Bush and move close to Russell Square (7, Bedford Place) in central London. It was a far more expensive area than Shepherd's Bush. In choosing to live there, Madhu displayed his old snobbery and habit of squandering money. Nevertheless, he managed to pay all outstanding fees at Gray's Inn, and requested the authorities to call him to the Bar even before he could finish attending all the seventy-two dinners.

The total number of dinners he went to was sixty, that is, he missed a couple of terms at Gray's Inn. Luckily for him, his request was granted and he was called to the Bar in the middle of the Michelmas Term, on 17 November 1866.

Once he emerged as a full-fledged barrister, the first person Madhu informed was Vidyasagar. On 18 November 1866, he wrote: 'I am sure you will be highly delighted to hear that I was called to the Bar last night by the Society of Gray's Inn and that I am at last a Barrister-at-Law. All this I owe to God and to you under God, and I assure you I shall ever think of you to be my greatest benefactor and truest friend.'

Three days later, Madhu had his name included in the list of British barristers, although he knew he would never practise in Britain. It is not difficult to imagine the joy he must have felt at this time. At last, he could truly afford to dream of gaining not just social distinction, but also the material comforts and luxuries that had always eluded him.

Madhu returned to Versailles with Henrietta and the children soon after this, possibly within two weeks. But when he sailed to India at the beginning of 1867, he left them in Versailles. The reason that he mentioned to Vidyasagar was simply that he wanted to establish himself as a barrister in Calcutta before getting his family to rejoin him. This was perhaps not the real or the only reason. It was Madhu's wish to see his children grow up as Europeans. In his letter to Gour dated 26 October 1864 (written from France), he had expressed joy and pride that his son and daughter were both fluent in French. But when he made the decision to leave them in Europe, he clearly did not think of every possible consequence. More than anything else, he should have thought of Henrietta, who was pregnant once more at this time (November–December 1866). To leave a pregnant wife and two small children in an alien land, where they knew no one, was a thoughtless and foolhardy act, to say the least. Yet, Madhu did not hesitate to take that step, not on an impulse, but only after careful deliberation, and consultation with his wife.

Clearly, in spite of the hardships he had to suffer there, Versailles held a strong attraction for him. On his previous visit, Madhu was forced to live among the poor. This time, he rented a house in a far more posh area, next to the lake behind the royal palace. Perhaps he thought nothing less would be appropriate for his new status as a barrister. Besides, he must have felt the urge to prove a point to those who had once mocked or insulted him.

On 9 December 1866, he wrote to Vidyasagar once more, informing him that he was going to leave for India by the 'Bombay Steamer of the 5th January'. This was his last letter from Europe. He spoke at some length about why he had decided to leave his family in France, stressing once again that it would be cheaper to do so. He had no doubt that as soon as he reached Calcutta, he would be able to establish himself as a successful and wealthy lawyer.

But rosy dreams about the future were not the only things he mentioned in this letter. 'I must now proceed to draw your attention to a much serious subject,' he wrote, '...I am about to undertake a long voyage by sea. Life is uncertain.... Should anything happen to me, my wife and children will have no one to look to but yourself.' What followed were Madhu's instructions regarding the distribution of his assets among his children. Effectively, this letter was an informal will.

The language and tone of this letter clearly indicate the conflicting emotions in Madhu's mind. On the one hand, there was joy, relief, and excitement. After years of grim struggle, he was now on the brink of putting all that behind him and acquiring the wealth that would bring him both material comfort and social recognition. On the other hand, there was some uncertainty about life itself. Even the impractical and unrealistic Madhu knew that there might be many a slip between cup and the lip.

In this final letter to Vidyasagar that he wrote from Versailles, Madhu did not hide his doubts. 'I cannot conceal it from myself,' he said, 'that in order to get into the profession, I have well-nigh beggared myself. It now remains to be seen "what fruit this tree will bear".'

Chapter Six

'My passage, my outfit to India, the setting myself up there as a British Barrister, the expenses of living as a Gentleman (in the European sense) till I get practice will cost a great deal, however economically we might manage these things.'

'...I am likely to be in distress for money soon. I have to pay a great deal every day for carriages and my servants want their pay for March. Hotel bill can be put off till the end of the month. Good God, what will become of me?'

These are lines from two letters written to Vidyasagar, the former from London, on 17 January 1866; and the latter from Spence's Hotel in Calcutta, on 11 April 1867. Clearly, even before he returned home, Madhu was concerned about the way he might live to suit his status. Only two months after his return, however, he had reason to start worrying about his finances.

He left for India from Marseilles on 5 January 1867. The ship was bound for Bombay. On reaching Bombay, he most probably took another ship to Calcutta, but the exact date of his arrival there is not known. His name cannot be traced in any of the passengers' lists published either in the *Bombay Almanac* for 1867, or the *Bengal Almanac* for the same year. However, there is no doubt that he reached Calcutta by the end of the first week of February.

What is more important than the date of his arrival is his state of mind when he reached Calcutta. The days of his bitter struggle were over. His most cherished dream was now fulfilled. He was a barrister, and all the comforts and joy life could offer—he thought—would now be within his grasp. He drew a blueprint of his future in his mind: he would live in the most fashionable area in the city; own an expensive vehicle; be surrounded by servants and others to obey his every command; when he walked down a road, people would salute him with respect.

His letters to Vidyasagar show that with the passing of time, his dreams had become increasingly rosy. A few months before he left London, he had written that he would be happy to stay in a room in Vidyasagar's house, and be content with whatever simple food—even plain rice and *dal*—that he could get. However, in the letter that he wrote just before his departure, he was more optimistic. He expressed his hope that he would 'hire the upper storey of some house with an Attorney's or other office below, furnish a few rooms decently and live with a cook and *khidmutgar* till briefs begin to come in'.

By the time he set foot in Calcutta, he was even more conscious of his newly acquired status. He knew he could hardly afford the luxury of renting a couple of rooms in Spence's Hotel, the most expensive hotel in Calcutta, which was situated quite close to the Government House. But he could not think of any other place suitable for a barrister, especially when the junior-most barrister of the Calcutta High Court—Manomohan Ghosh—had set up his office there. Madhu was convinced that, for the sake of his status, some sacrifices had to be made, even if he had to do it with borrowed money.

Vidyasagar came to visit him there—or perhaps it would be more appropriate to say that he came to receive Madhu with great honour. Only about seven weeks prior to that, Vidyasagar had been seriously injured in a road accident, from which he had not quite recovered (in fact, he never really recovered fully after that). Even so, he was eager to see his friend, of whom he was undoubtedly very proud. Madhu, too, was overcome with emotion when he saw Vidyasagar, the only man who had stood by him in his hour of need. It is said that he kissed Vidyasagar on his cheeks several times!

Knowing that Madhu would require somewhere to stay, Vidyasagar had rented a house on his behalf. It belonged to a friend of his, called Rajkrishna Bandyopadhyay. Situated near Cornwallis

Square, it was a perfectly suitable house, in a good locality. But Madhu refused to go there. The scenes of luxurious opulence that he had seen in Europe had so dazzled his eyes that he preferred to remain in Spence's Hotel. Nothing less, he felt, was befitting for a man of his standing.

This was certainly not the first time that he had taken a decision without thinking of the possible consequences. But it was one of the most foolish decisions that he ever took. What made him do it is a mystery. He had not yet started to earn, and he was still dependent on Vidyasagar. Over the next few months, he borrowed more money with Vidyasagar's help. Not only was it foolish, it was also unnecessary. At the time, there were only two other Bengali barristers in Calcutta. Had Madhu acted a little more sensibly, he could have established himself as a barrister and gradually started to earn a reasonable amount. But he could not wait to see himself settled in a practice; he decided to spend the money he had not yet earned, simply under the assumption that the day was not far when he would be a rich man.

Soon after his return to Calcutta—on 20 February 1867—Madhu sought permission from the authorities to start practising as a barrister in the High Court. The authorities were all British, but the name of Michael Madhusudan Dutt was not unknown to them. Many of them had heard of his fame as a writer, and knew something about his life. As a result, while some of them were prepared to support him, others were not. This eventually led to a huge conflict, which was quite unforeseen.

At first, Chief Justice Sir Barnes Peacock supported Madhu's application. Other judges, such as G. Lock, Bailey, J. P. Norman, and F. B. Kemp, endorsed Peacock's view. However, strong opposition came from Justice A. G. McPherson:[†]

I think that Mr Datta ought not to be admitted as an Advocate without further and more satisfactory evidence of his being a person whom it is proper to admit. Mr Datta's antecedents and former position as Interpreter of the Calcutta Police Court are not suggestive of his being such a person. While the letters annexed to his application are quite insufficient to lead me to suppose that he is, the opinion expressed by Babu Digambar Mitter (if worth anything in itself) is to my knowledge opposed to that entertained by many persons. It is remarkable that Mr Datta produces no letter from anyone in England, and none from any of the government officers with or under whom he served before he went there.

Justice J. B. Phear also raised queries about Madhu's character:[†]

> In view of the short number of terms and general bad reputation of Mr Datta, I cannot consent to his admission, until his qualifications have been made to appear by definite testimony and his character has been satisfactorily cleared.

It became clear to Madhu that Lady Luck was still not prepared to smile on him. But he was not one to give up easily. He retaliated by gathering support from his friends, starting with Shambhunath Pundit, who was the only Indian judge at the time. Pundit saw the whole thing as a British conspiracy against Indians. He advised Madhu to collect as many certificates of merit as he could. On 11 April 1867, Madhu wrote to Vidyasagar: 'This morning I called on the Punditjee who...says that our enemies seem to have won the judges and that the antidote must be as strong as the poison.... Shambhunath said, '*e bishoye na jitle ar maan thakbe na*' [we shall lose our prestige if we don't win this case]. He has great hopes of success if he be properly backed....'

Eventually, more than fifty very well-known and influential men in Calcutta, including Kalikrishna Bahadur, Ramanath Tagore, Jotindramohan Tagore (his old patron), Rajendralal Mitra, and Vidyasagar, came forward to speak in favour of Madhu. They praised not only his talents as a writer, but also his character and his knowledge. In view of this overwhelming response from famous and well-established citizens of Calcutta, the British authorities were obliged to withdraw their objections and confirm Madhu's admission to the High Court as an advocate.[†] This was done on 3 May 1867. On 7 May, Madhu began his new career as a barrister.

One can only imagine the joy and the relief Madhu and his friends must have felt on that day. There was absolutely no doubt in Madhu's mind that he would be a success. The question was, how soon that success would manifest itself.

Once again, Madhu had to face disappointment. He continued to stay at Spence's Hotel and also opened his chamber there, without thinking of the expenses. But the great throngs of clients that he had expected did not show up. One reason for this was that not only was Madhu new and inexperienced, he also lacked the goodwill of people that was necessary to find new clients. He had alienated himself from his own community by becoming a Christian and behaving like a European, preferring to speak

English. On the other hand, the British or the Anglo-Indian community could not trust him completely, either. As a result, his business suffered; no one wanted to hire him.

While he waited to see clients crowd his office, his debts continued to mount higher. He was under considerable pressure to pay the interest accrued on most of his debts. On 8 April 1867, Anukulchandra Mukhopadhyay, to whom Vidyasagar had mortgaged Madhu's property, wrote to Vidyasagar: 'I am in urgent need of money at this moment. Please arrange repayment of three thousand rupees, and the payment of twelve thousand in addition, as the interest on the mortgage. You are aware that, so far, no interest has been paid. Since Mr Michael is now here, these matters should be settled without delay.'†

It was not just Anukulchandra Mukhopadhyay who was anxious to see his money repaid. Spence's Hotel, where Madhu was initially received with great enthusiasm, began to show its displeasure when several bills remained unpaid. To tell the truth, Madhu had gone totally overboard in trying to live in style in the hotel. He had taken three rooms just for himself. It is said that at every meal, he would order as many as six dishes. Quite often, he would invite his friends to dinner, and offer them sherry, champagne, whisky, and beer. It is hardly surprising that he found it difficult to pay every bill on time.

However, what distressed and embarrassed him more than anything else was the fact that he was unable to send any money to Henrietta in France. Desperate once more, he wrote yet again to Vidyasagar. The letter is undated, but it is easy enough to see how much stress he was under at this time. It starts with the words 'Private—I hope you will destroy this letter after perusal.' Then he goes on to say: '...My poor wife is almost as badly off as I was when I first wrote to you, and I am perfectly helpless. What money I am making this month, I am paying to my hotel people, for I do not like the idea of being indebted here.... I have been very thoughtless perhaps, and have not managed matters well, but don't punish innocent people for my folly. If you don't get me this money before the French mail on the 25th, they will nearly perish in Europe.'

Vidyasagar did not destroy that letter. Gentleman though he was, perhaps keeping this letter was not a particularly gentlemanly thing to do. But it goes a long way to show Madhu's state of mind.

There were several other letters written to Vidyasagar. The few that have been traced are undated, but it becomes clear that from November 1867, Madhu's health began to fail. In one letter, he says, 'You know I have no money and have been getting on very indifferently since last November on account of my throat and general health.' Eventually, the problem with his throat began to hamper his performance in court. It appears from the reminiscences of those who knew him that he never took care of his health. Not only did he drink excessively, but also neglected to eat properly. The severe stress and anxiety he had to suffer for many years left him with high blood pressure and cardiac problems. He did not allow himself to take enough rest. Whenever he had the time, no matter how adverse his circumstances, he either wrote, or read extensively. Even now, after his return to Calcutta and still struggling to make ends meet, he began writing something new, a prose version of Homer's *Iliad*, called *Hektor-badh* (*The Slaying of Hektor*). Judging by his experiments with a new style of prose, he spent a long time working on it. But the final result of all that hard work was loss of health.

Another person whose health was causing some concern was Vidyasagar. It was for this reason that he had to spend months on end out of Calcutta, in the hope that a change of air might improve his health. It was partly the physical distance between them, and Madhu's continued inability to repay his debts that eventually began to create a rift between Madhu and Vidyasagar. The fault was certainly Madhu's, Vidyasagar cannot be blamed in any way.

Among those from whom Vidyasagar had personally borrowed money in order to help Madhu was Srishchandra Vidyaratna. Like Anukulchandra Mukhopadhyay, Srishchandra had agreed to part with his money only because the person asking for it was Vidyasagar, who had never been known to go back on his word. Now, he began to put considerable pressure on Vidyasagar for the repayment of his loan. At the time, Vidyasagar was in Burdwan. He wrote to Madhu from there, possibly in July/August 1867:

Many believe that if I give my word, I will most certainly keep it. It is for this reason that they act in good faith, without ever questioning what I say. There is no doubt that being so trusted by people is a very good thing. However, there are indications that I may soon lose their trust.

When I took Anukul's money, I had promised him that it would be returned as soon as you came back. Then, when you needed more money, I could see no other way but to take a loan from Srishchandra. The promise I made to him was that it would be repaid without delay. In both cases, I have had to break my promise. If Srishchandra and Anukul babu do not get their money soon, most undoubtedly, I shall be further embarrassed and humiliated....†

Such a letter from his closest friend and well-wisher naturally distressed Madhu profoundly. 'Your letter which reached me a few minutes ago, has given me great pain. You know that there is scarcely anything in the world that I would hesitate to do for you,' he wrote in reply. Then he added, 'Of course you have full permission to adopt any steps you think proper to relieve yourself of the unpleasant burden. Sirish has written to me offering twenty-one thousand rupees. But don't you think Onoocool would advance fresh money enough to pay off that man and hold the property by way of mortgage...?' It was clear to him now that the time had come to take the only step that would bring him a certain amount of money—sell his property.†

As it happened, despite Srishchandra's offer of twenty-one thousand rupees, Madhu did not sell his property to him. Or perhaps Srishchandra withdrew his offer. Surprisingly, the person to whom Madhu did sell it, a few months later (in February 1868), was none other than Mahadeb Chattopadhyay. It was the same man who had apparently cheated him when he was in Europe and caused him a lot of grief. Mahadeb now paid him twenty thousand rupees for his property, although it was worth thirty thousand. Why did Madhu turn to Mahadeb, and why did he settle for an amount less than what he deserved? No one has been able to find a satisfactory explanation.

It could perhaps be that since Mahadeb had looked after this property for many years, going back to Rajnarayan Dutt's time, the tenants who lived on it had started to look upon Mahadeb as the landlord. It was easy for him to manage the affairs of the estate. A new buyer would have found it much more difficult to come to grips with the existing situation. So, no one else came forward to make an offer, and Madhu—desperate as he was—was forced to sell his land to Mahadeb. Gourdas confirms in his own reminiscences (quoted by Jogindranath Basu) that Mahadeb Chattopadhyay took advantage of Madhu's position and bought his property for much less than what Madhu should have been paid.

Having sold his land, Madhu was able to pay Anukulchandra Mukhopadhyay what he owed him, which was about eighteen thousand rupees, including interest. It is entirely likely that Srishchandra was also paid his dues, perhaps even before the land was sold, since no more letters have been found regarding money owed to him. Vidyasagar must have felt immensely relieved, when Madhu's debts to these two men were settled. However, when Madhu ran into financial difficulties again only a few weeks later, Vidyasagar refused to get involved. On 18 March 1868, he wrote to Madhu: 'I am still very unwell and confined to bed, and in consequence utterly incapable of mental or physical exertions of any kind. You will therefore be good enough to excuse my inability to work in furtherance of your object.'

A pertinent question here is, what *did* Madhu do as a barrister? Did he not get any work at all? The truth is that not a great deal is known about the work that Madhu did. What is known is that it was only in 1868 that he received a certain amount of success. He fought for the zamindar of Serampore, Gopikrishna Gosain,[†] and won his case. There were other cases that he fought successfully. Then he was appointed, as a part of a legal team that included a number of established barristers, to fight a case for Gyanendramohan Tagore, who was a barrister himself. This particular case came to be known as Tagore vs Tagore.[†] Madhu and Gyanendramohan had been fellow students in Hindu College. Like Madhu, Gyanendramohan had become a Christian; however, unlike Madhu, he had been disinherited by his father, Prasannakumar Tagore, who was one of the best-known lawyers of nineteenth-century Bengal and a very influential person.

Just before his death in August 1868, he changed his will and disinherited his only son and left his enormous estate mainly to his daughters and Jotindramohan Tagore, his nephew. He also left a sizeable portion of his property to different charities. He took help from a number of barristers to draw up his will, since he wanted to leave no loopholes for his son to exploit. Therefore, in spite of employing a strong team, the verdict did not go in Gyanendramohan Tagore's favour. Madhu was perhaps included in the legal team because of his first-hand knowledge of the Inheritance Act of 1849, which dealt with the rights of children converted to another religion. It is likely that Gyanendramohan thought Madhu's experience in fighting a case with his relatives and regaining his parental property would prove useful. However, it is doubtful that Gyanendramohan, or anyone else, was prepared to consider Madhu as one of the best barristers at the time. In fact, that he was not re-employed by Gyanendramohan for his appeal, indicates just that lack of trust.

During 1868-9, Madhu was sometimes required to go out to district towns away from Calcutta. On one occasion, he went to Baruipur, where the magistrate was Bankimchandra Chattopadhyay, tha famous novelist. According to some of his earlier biographers, at the time Madhu was earning something between a thousand and two thousand rupees. On 30 July 1869, Madhu wrote a letter to Gour, which starts with, 'You cannot imagine how sorry I was to be obliged to let you leave Town without a chat on account of my chamber being full of interesting clients!'

However, it was certainly not every day that Madhu's chamber was full of clients. At one point, Madhu even began to think of giving up trying to become a successful barrister, and do something else related to law. In October 1868, he heard that the judge of the Court of Small Causes—G. S. Fagan—was going to retire and go back to Britain. Madhu turned to Vidyasagar once more, in order to get himself recommended for the post. Vidyasagar happened to know the governor of Bengal. So Madhu asked him to request the governor to give him the job. Fagan's salary at the time was two thousand and five hundred rupees. Madhu must have thought that anything around that figure would ensure a comfortable living. But only a few months before that, his relations with Vidyasagar had become strained over Madhu's unpaid debts. The very fact that he wrote to Vidyasagar again shows how desperate he was to get Fagan's post.

At the time, Madhu's health was also causing him some anxiety. He must have realized that he could not continue forever with a bad throat and a hoarse voice, when his job involved cross-questioning witnesses, and speaking at great length. Besides, his tendency to speak contemptuously and arrogantly did not endear him to the magistrates and judges. On one occasion, it is said that Judge Jackson felt annoyed with him and remarked, 'The Court orders you to plead slowly, the Court has ears.' Always a ready wit, Madhu replied instantly, 'But pretty too long, my Lord!' Some of those present in the court might have felt amused by his comment; but it is doubtful whether the judge was pleased with being compared to a certain animal.

As for being considered for Fagan's post, Madhu's luck played another cruel joke. Vidyasagar might have tried to help him, but Fagan did not retire, after all. He merely took some time off, and went to Europe on holiday.

❦

Madhu's penury continued as before. A major reason for this was his reckless decision to leave his family behind in France. Henrietta, perhaps unaware that her husband was not doing as well as she had expected, was still living in Versailles—this time, away from Rue-des-Chantiers, and in a more expensive area, adjacent to the palace. Moreover, she had a baby boy—the youngest she gave birth to, called Napoleon Albert.[†] But the money she received from Madhu (and that, too, irregularly) was not enough to meet her expenses. Henrietta was lonely, worried, and still having to count every penny.

Stressed and strained by all this, Henrietta began drinking heavily. She used to drink with Madhu even before they left Calcutta. But now, she became an addict. According to one of her bills that has been found, a local hotel used to supply her with two bottles of wine every day. It is not known whether she drank all that wine every day by herself, or whether she had company. What *is* clear is that no normal and healthy person would drink that much wine every day and, if they did, they would not remain normal and healthy for long.

However, despite her problem with alcohol, Henrietta did not lose her practical sense. She realized that it was time to go back to India, instead of continuing to live in France, simply in the hope that things would work out one day. So, on 13 March 1869, she wrote to a French gentleman that she knew, begging him to speak to the Steam Navigation Company in Paris. She could raise a thousand francs by selling her few possessions. Would the company allow her to travel back to India with her children, if she paid them a thousand francs? The fare from Marseilles to Calcutta, at the time, was nearly two thousand five hundred francs. The shipping company refused to give her a ticket for a thousand francs, but agreed later to lower the price marginally. Luckily, Henrietta received some money from Madhu soon afterwards. She bought the cheapest ticket she could get, and left for India with her three children, some time in early April 1869.

Exactly when she reached Calcutta is not known, but she was certainly back by mid-May. She and Madhu were reunited after two years and four months. One can only guess Henrietta's thoughts on seeing the man she loved. All her dreams of wealth and a comfortable life as a barrister's wife must have shattered quickly. Besides, she must have felt concerned by the state of Madhu's health. By this time, Madhu had put on a lot of weight, and was looking much older than his forty-five years. His voice had changed, too.

The first thing that Henrietta did was persuade Madhu to give up his chamber at Spence's Hotel, and move to a house in Laudon Street. It was a large house, where, according to *Thacker's Directory for Bengal (1869)*, as many as four families had lived in the past; and, just before Madhu moved to that house, the Assistant Accountant General of Military Accounts had lived there. Its monthly rent was four hundred rupees, which was a lot of money in those days. Fortunately for Madhu, it was a time when he was doing slightly better. But, instead of saving what he could, he began spending all that he earned on doing up his house in the European style. He filled it with modern, expensive furniture, paintings and busts of his favourite European poets and dramatists which he had brought back from Europe.

Had he stopped there, things might still have worked out. But Madhu went a step further. Instead of having his chamber in the same house, he rented some rooms in no. 7, Old Post Office Road. Several other barristers had their chambers in the same area. Perhaps that was what prompted Madhu to join them. Or it could be that neither he nor Henrietta wanted a lot of people thronging his house. Whatever the reason, the fact remained that any money they might have saved by leaving Spence's Hotel was promptly spent on maintaining two different establishments.

Their years in Europe had taught Madhu and Henrietta something else. They now decided to go on holiday. At the time, the concept of going to a different town on holiday—unless it was to visit a relative—did not exist among Bengalis. But Madhu and his family went to Chandan Nagore soon after moving to Laudon Street. Perhaps they chose the place because it still had a strong French presence. Every member of Madhu's family spoke French fluently.

It may be safely assumed that the Dutts enjoyed their holiday very much, and Madhu's health improved. However, two things worked to his disadvantage. The first was a disruption in his work which was slowly building up. The second was related, once again, to his financial resources. On 30 July 1869, he wrote to Gour: '...I stop in Town because living out of Town is a luxury which I can't afford as a new beginner.'

In addition, during his long absence he lost some of his clients. Some time in 1870, less than a year later, a belief grew steadily among his clients that he was unreliable as a lawyer. Madhu's business dwindled, and once again his health began to fail. Years of drinking and neglecting his health now began to take its toll. It became clear at this time that his liver had been affected. Lack of work in Calcutta forced Madhu to take cases from mofussil towns; but going there meant further strain, and longer spells of ill health.

He tried once more to get a job and give up independent practice, or find an extra job with a regular income which he might handle in addition to his practice. In June 1870, he was appointed as the examiner of the records of the privy council. According to the comments made in the *Englishman* on 13 June 1870, his duties involved supervising the English translations of documents originally written in Bengali. The paper further commented (13 June 1870) that there would not have been a better candidate for this job. However, there was no fixed salary; nor was it full-time. Madhu could not have earned more than a thousand rupees a month. About a year later, he seems to have given it up although, considering his difficult financial situation, it is doubtful that he did so voluntarily.

As his income was sadly reduced, in the second half of 1871, Madhu had to give up his chamber in Old Post Office Road. But he did not leave his house in Laudon Street. It is likely that even at this stage, there was some hope left in his heart that one day things would improve. Why Henrietta did not put pressure on him to move to a cheaper area is a mystery. Had they done so, their debts would not have piled up even higher; nor would Madhu have been obliged to travel outside Calcutta just to earn a few pennies. It was in these circumstances that he went to Dhaka in September 1871, and came down with malaria. The attack was so severe that it nearly killed him.

It is likely that Madhu's visit to Dhaka was related not only to a case, but also to exploring the possibility of moving there permanently. There was no barrister there at the time and he must have hoped that that would offer him an advantage over other lawyers. He expressed his optimism in a sonnet that he wrote in Dhaka. *Thacker's Directory* records that he opened a practice in Dhaka, but even so, his plans went no further. It may be that the legal world in Dhaka—small though it was—showed no great pleasure at his arrival. Or perhaps it was his failing health that forced him to return to Calcutta.

The only positive thing that did happen in Dhaka was a reception given in his honour, not by the lawyers in the city, but by writers and others who recognized Madhu as a *mahakabi* (a great poet). In reply, Madhu produced a sonnet written exclusively for the city of Dhaka. In it, he described it as a place where Lakshmi (the goddess of wealth) lived in every household, and Saraswati (the goddess of learning) was a regular visitor. The poem ended with 'Do not hate me, O fortunate woman!' Clearly, Madhu wished to be accepted by the people of Dhaka, and was prepared to seek their help in making a new beginning. But that was not to be.

※※

After his return from Europe, his struggle for survival had stopped Madhu from doing much creative writing. However, *Hektor-badh*, the only thing he did write, was published in September 1871, possibly just before Madhu went to Dhaka.

Hektor was different from all his other works. Madhu's interest in Greek classical literature had made him read the *Iliad*, which had inspired him a great deal. *Hektor* was a prose translation of the *Iliad*. What gave him the idea of doing such a translation?

Madhu had reread the *Iliad* during the time he was housebound after an accident in December 1867, and then again when he was unwell in August 1868. During these two long spells of ill health, as he was going through the *Iliad*, it occurred to him that a Bengali translation might provide a taste of the original to those readers who could not read English. The translation he eventually produced did not follow the original text word for word. What it did retain was the basic concept and spirit of the *Iliad*. Madhu dedicated this book to his friend from college, Bhudeb Mukhopadhyay.

In his introduction, he admitted that there were times when he deleted a few events described in the original, or made some other changes. The reason for doing this, according to him, was that unless he took these liberties, the translation would not sound Bengali enough and he could not have finished the book in the limited time he had. Besides, his health was no longer good enough to allow him to work the long hours he used to. As a result, even when a few pages were found to be missing, Madhu was unable to rewrite them. He pointed this out in his introduction, and added, 'Perhaps, after all this time, I am going to be ridiculed by my readers.'

The truth was that, by this time, Madhu had started to question his own creative prowess. As things turned out, his misgivings proved to be quite unfounded. *Hektor*, as well as some sonnets and other poems he wrote afterwards, bore clear evidence of the strength and vigour that were the hallmark of Madhu's writing. But his perennial battle against poverty, endless stress, and anxiety gave him no chance to rejoice, or to write some more.

Upon his return from Dhaka, Madhu had to go back to looking for work. He had no savings to speak of. Soon, he had to get rid of his domestic staff—his servants, clerks, groom, and driver—without even being able to pay them the money he owed them. The fashionable furniture that he had acquired had not all been paid for, either. His creditors hounded him, and insulted him openly. Eventually, Madhu had to leave his luxurious house in Laudon Street and move to 22 Beniapukur Road, in a poor suburb of Calcutta. There were only small huts and cottages in that area, a far cry indeed from where he was before. But now he had no choice.

There was no one to stand by Madhu. Both he and Henrietta had lost touch with their families. He had also alienated some of his best friends, including Vidyasagar. Now, both he and Henrietta were suffering from poor health. Madhu found it difficult to talk, and suffered from periodic bouts of fever. Obesity made it difficult even to drag himself from one place to another. He developed various symptoms indicating liver damage, caused by his alcoholism. He also had hypertension. His mother had died in her mid-forties, and his father in his early fifties. He probably guessed that his days were numbered. Henrietta was ill, too. They had fought poverty before, but in the past they had a future to dream of. Now, a dark abyss was all they could stare at.

Madhu's biggest anxiety must have been regarding his three small children. Sermista was now twelve. Who was going to take care of her, and have her married? Anxiety drove Madhu to drink more and more. One day, Manomohan Ghosh visited him, and found him sitting in a dark room, drinking his whisky neat. All the doors and windows of the room were shut. Alarmed, Manomohan exclaimed, 'What are you doing? You might kill yourself if you keep drinking like this!' Madhu replied, 'This is a slow but sure way of committing suicide, though not as painful as slitting one's throat!'

In early 1872, he was hired by the petitioner in a case in Purulia, a tiny new town, situated some hundred and fifty miles to the north-west of Calcutta. It was not easy to go there, as it was not yet connected by rail. But Madhu went, nevertheless, possibly in a *palki*, covering a distance of more than forty miles from the nearest railway station.

Like Dhaka, Purulia greeted him warmly, not so much for his legal knowledge, but for his poetry. But another surprise was waiting for him. The local Christian community in Purulia gave a reception for him, and one of their leaders—Kangalicharan Sinha—asked Madhu to be godfather to his son. Madhu accepted gladly, and even wrote a poem to mark the occasion. In one sense this poem was similar to the hymn he had written at the time of his own conversion to Christianity. What is remarkable about this poem is that he expressed his sincere belief that Christianity was superior to Hinduism as a religion.

> O Son, you have achieved a purer birth today;
> By bathing in Jordan's water
> You have joyously built a beautiful temple.
> A purer soul lives in your body now,
> Like fragrance in a flower, when Spring returns
> At the end of winter. What a treasure you have found,
> What a priceless treasure, my child, you will understand soon:
> You have, believe me, become strong with divine strength!

> Great is your fortune. Holding the shield of righteousness,
> Destroy your enemy, sin, in this mortal life:
> With his banner of victory raised on his chariot,
> Victorious is the youth whom people call Khrishtadas:
> Take your name, with my blessing
> And in the love and joy of your father and mother.

It is not known how long he remained in Purulia on that occasion. It seems that his health improved a little before he returned to Calcutta.

It was while he was in Purulia that Nilmoni Singh Deo, the Raja of Panchakot (a neighbouring princely state) learnt of his arrival. He sent a messenger immediately to meet Madhu, but the messenger could meet Madhu only after he went back to Calcutta. Panchakot was a small state with an area of less than three thousand square miles. Nilmoni owned the whole area and was known as its Raja. He wanted to appoint Madhu as the manager of his estate. Madhu would have somewhere to stay, and would be paid a monthly salary, though the amount suggested was less than a thousand rupees. Madhu, who had once expected to earn six thousand rupees a month as a barrister, was now forced to accept this offer, which he would certainly have scoffed at before. He left his family in Calcutta, and went to Panchakot, placing himself under self-exile.

Was he happy? That is naturally difficult to say, but the prospect of having a regular income, however small, must have brought some relief. Once he reached Panchakot, he took on his duties with ample enthusiasm, and began making plans for developing the area by building new roads and providing safe drinking water.

Things might have worked out, but more misfortunes were in store for Madhu. It turned out that, at the time of his appointment, Nilmoni Singh Deo was involved in a court case. One of his lease-holders, Sharadaprasad Mukhopadhyay, had complained that Nilmoni had extorted seven thousand five hundred rupees from him. Around September 1871 (when Madhu was in Dhaka), Nilmoni lost the case and was ordered by the court to return the money with interest. Nilmoni appealed against this verdict, and a few months later, appointed Madhu as his manager. It is clear that Nilmoni wanted to kill two birds with one stone. If his manager was a barrister, his case would be in safe hands and, in any case, it would be useful to have a legal expert on his staff, for it was not unusual for a landlord to be involved in legal battles.

Madhu's chief responsibilities as the manager was to oversee the arrangements made to fight the case. He knew he could not fight it himself in his present state of health; so he appointed one of the best known attorneys, R. T. Allen.[13] Every possible effort was made not only by Madhu, but also by Allen and his colleagues, but Nilmoni's case was weak, and the High Court upheld the previous verdict.

Nilmoni began to look for a scapegoat on whom he could vent his anger. Ailing and infirm as he was, Madhu appeared an easy target. Fortunately, Nilmoni had a few enemies. Before Madhu could come to any harm, one of them informed him. Madhu ran away the same night, to save his life. He did not even wait to collect the sixteen hundred rupees that Nilmoni owed him in terms of unpaid salary.

Strangely enough, after his return to Calcutta, Nilmoni tried to contact Madhu. It might have been because he knew that Madhu was a famous writer, and Nilmoni did not want it known that he had been badly treated in Panchakot. Madhu sent one of his ex-employees, Kailashchandra Basu, to meet Nilmoni. What was said during the meeting is not known, but it seems likely that Nilmoni paid Madhu the money that was owed to him.

With Madhu's arrival in Calcutta, all his problems returned. The biggest of these was overdue rent for his house. Kailashchandra Basu felt moved to write for help to the only person who could—Ishwarchandra Vidyasagar. Pleading Madhu's case on his behalf, Basu enclosed a statement giving details of Madhu's debts. The total amount was a staggering forty-two thousand rupees! Madhu realized that a letter from Basu would not be enough. Despite his somewhat strained relationship with Vidyasagar, Madhu felt obliged once more to write to him himself.

In his letter (undated), he begged for only two thousand rupees

---

[13] R. T. Allen was one of the most successful barristers in Calcutta. He started to practise there in February 1855. His father had also been a lawyer in Calcutta in the 1840s. For details see *Thacker's Directory for Bengal*, 1872. Allen's chamber was close to Madhu's and they knew each other very well. Madhu also appointed two other well-known native lawyers—Upendranath Basu and Bhabanicharan Dutta—to help Allen. The only lawyer on the other side was Srinath Das.

to take care of his immediate needs. He ended by saying, 'I must have this money by tomorrow evening, or mine will be the lot of the fugitive or something still more horrible! I pray God, that this may sound on your gentle ears like a lay of anguish from a breaking heart!'

Sadly, on this occasion Vidyasagar could not help him. At that time, he was himself in some financial difficulties, in addition to being unwell. He wrote to Madhu, expressing his inability to do anything for him, and then declared—quite frankly—that he thought Madhu's problem was so complex that no one would be able to come to his rescue. Needless to say, Madhu was immensely hurt by this reply, although Vidyasagar merely stated a known fact without any deliberate intent to hurt him. After this, Madhu did not write to Vidyasagar ever again, even when he had to starve.

Madhu lived for nine months after his return from Panchakot. It is not known what he did in those months, how his family survived, or whether his few friends gave him any support. The only thing one learns from various remarks made by those who knew him is that there was an ulcer in his throat that bled from time to time. Bouts of fever continued. Perhaps he had tuberculosis or cancer; nothing is known for certain. His earlier problems with high blood pressure and his heart and liver became worse. His stomach and feet began swelling. All his rosy dreams lay in shambles.

Madhu did not require a doctor to tell him that the end was near. He knew it himself. But what must have worried him much more than his own health would have been thoughts of his children, since Henrietta also was seriously ill. Sermista, at the time, was thirteen; Meghnad was eleven; and Napoleon was a little more than five.

At this hour of darkness, a proposal came from the Bengal Theatre Company. They wanted Madhu to write a play. The money offered was not much, but Madhu clutched at this straw eagerly enough. He was no longer strong enough to sit up and write himself. So he had to dictate the whole thing to someone else. He had done this before, even at the height of his success. But now the reason was different. The words spoken came from a dying man, too weak even to hold a pen.

The title of the play was *Maya-kanan* (*The Garden of Illusion*). This title seems to bear a special relevance. From *Tilottama* to *Meghnad* and in all his other writings, Madhu had spoken of the helplessness of mankind before pre-ordained fate. *Maya-kanan* was no exception. It is the story of Ajay (the King of Sindh) and Indumati (the Princess of Gandhar), two star-crossed lovers, who could not be united. Like Romeo and Juliet, they chose death, rather than give in to the unjust demands made on them.

A decade had passed since Madhu had written his last play, *Krishnakumari*. In that time, he had seen life much more closely. Surprisingly, *Maya-kanan* does not reflect the maturity he must have acquired. The play drags on, quite unnecessarily, even after the death of the protagonists. The restraint of a creative artist, which Madhu had not failed to exercise before, is absent in this play. One reason for this is obviously his illness and mental anxiety. But there may be another reason. It has been said that the theatre company, which had commissioned the work, got someone else to add extra lines, which they thought the audience would like.

About the same time when he wrote *Maya-kanan*, Madhu wrote something else. These were a few poems for children. He had written similar poems in Versailles, in the same style as La Fontaine. Why he suddenly decided to write such poems at this late stage is not known. It could be that some publisher had asked him to do so, and paid him in cash. Or it could be that he felt encouraged by the success of some other writers (including Vidyasagar) who had made a lot of money by writing textbooks for children.

Whatever the reason, it was clear by March 1873 that Madhu would no longer be able to write at all. His condition, as well as Henrietta's, worsened. Both were naturally extremely concerned about the future of their children. Sermista was not yet fourteen. Even so, out of sheer desperation, Madhu agreed to have her married. It is easy enough to imagine how difficult this decision must have been for Madhu, especially so soon after writing a play like *Maya-kanan* in which he upheld an individual's right to choose his or her own partner. And in his own life he had been an ardent supporter of love marriage. It was partly in order to uphold this right that he had converted to Christianity.

On 7 may 1873, Sermista was married to William Walter Evans Floyd, an Anglo-Indian.† On that day, Sermista was thirteen years seven months and twenty-two days old. Her husband was much older than her (almost twice her age), and had little education. He earned his living partly by working as a translator in a court, and by selling pictures that he painted. It is likely that Madhu had met him when he, Madhu, could still go to court. At his daughter's wedding, Madhu spent his last penny and offered 'cake and wine' on the printed invitations. Years ago, he had not hesitated to leave not just his home, but his entire community, in order to avoid an arranged marriage to a young girl. Sermista's marriage may be seen as Madhu's ultimate defeat at the hands of his destiny.

Soon after the wedding, Madhu and his family went to Uttarpara, where they had a few friends who were now prepared to look after them, at least for a few weeks. It was Rashbihari Mukhopadhyay, a well-known aristocrat in Uttarpara, who had particularly invited him. But instead of going there, perhaps Madhu and Henrietta should have gone straight to a hospital. Gourdas, at this time, was posted in Howrah as a deputy magistrate. He went to visit Madhu more than once. In his own reminiscences (quoted by Jogindranath Basu), he described his last meeting with Madhu in Uttarpara thus:

I shall never be able to forget the heartbreaking sight that met my eyes when I saw Madhu.... He was lying in bed, gasping. Blood was oozing out of his mouth. His wife was lying on the floor, running a very high temperature. Madhu saw me enter the room and raised himself. Then he started crying. What was upsetting him most was that he could not take care of his wife. He was not concerned with his own pain and discomfort. What he told me was this: 'afflictions in battalions'. I bent over his wife and felt her forehead and pulse. She pointed at her husband, sighed and broke into sobs. She said, 'Don't worry about me, look after him. I am not afraid of death.'

There was really not a lot that Gour could do for his friend. But he was naturally worried and wanted to have him removed to Calcutta. The following day (20–21 June 1873), Madhu and his family left for Calcutta by boat.

Henrietta was taken to her son-in-law's house at 11 Lindsay Street, which was an area where most of the inhabitants were either English or Anglo-Indian. Madhu went straight to Alipore General Hospital. At that time, Hindus in Bengal viewed going to a hospital as fate worse than death. It was conceptually wholly unacceptable, even against their religion. The General Hospital in Alipore, therefore, was used more or less exclusively by foreigners or Anglo-Indians. Madhu was admitted partly because he was a Christian, and partly because Manomohan Ghosh and some other friends pulled a few strings. Madhu's one-time physician, Dr Palmer, who worked at this hospital, must have played a part in this matter.

After his arrival in the hospital, Madhu seemed to improve for a while, but his condition soon grew worse. Apart from a damaged liver and heart, he had diseases related to his spleen and throat. By the time he was removed to the hospital, cirrhosis of the liver had also caused dropsy. The news spread, and now, when the end was so near, many of his friends, and even some of his cousins with whom he had not had any communication for many years, came to visit him. Madhu knew he was dying, but even so, he found it difficult to accept the inevitable—not because he was afraid, but because his old habits and tendencies refused to leave him. Even in these last few days, he could not stop spending money—money that he had to borrow. One day, one of his old employees, called Maniruddin, came to see him. Madhu already owed him about four hundred rupees. Nevertheless, he asked Maniruddin how much money he had in his pocket that day. Maniruddin could produce only a rupee and some smaller coins. Madhu took that money, and gave it to the nurse who was taking care of him.† This action—borrowing money to give it away as a tip—was quite consistent with his earlier behaviour.

Madhu remained in hospital for seven or eight days. On 26 June 1873, he heard about Henrietta's death. She was only thirty-seven. The news could not have come as a surprise, but naturally Madhu was devastated. More than anything else, he was concerned about arrangements for her funeral. Who would take the responsibility and pay for everything?

Manomohan Ghosh came to visit him that day, and assured him that the funeral was over, and all was as it should have been. Madhu wanted to know if Vidyasagar and Jotindramohan Tagore had attended the service. Manomohan consoled him by saying that there had not been sufficient time to inform those men. He had known Henrietta for ten years. When he was in Europe, Henrietta had treated him with great affection. It was for this reason that he took it upon himself to make the arrangements for her funeral. There was something else that Manomohan did. He promised to look after Madhu's sons. It was a promise he did not fail to keep.

Among the visitors Madhu received, were Rev. Krishnamohan Bandyopadhyay, and Rev. Chandranath Bandyopadhyay of the London Missionary Society. They appeared far more concerned than Madhu about his spiritual welfare. On 28 June, when Madhu was lying in his deathbed, all hope gone, Krishnamohan arrived to get his final confession. It is not known what Madhu confessed. What *is* known is Madhu's reply when both Krishnamohan and Chandranath pointed out to him that there might be problems regarding his funeral and burial. According to Rev. Joseph Prannath Biswas, Pastor of Trinity Church, Calcutta, Madhu said: 'I care not for man-made churches nor for anybody's help. I am going to sleep in my Lord and He will hide me in His best resting place. Bury me wherever you like—at your door or under a tree; let none disturb my bones. Let green turf grow over my resting place on earth.'

The end came on 29 June 1873.[†] His well-wishers and his two sons came to see him in the morning; so did several others, who had not bothered to offer him any support when he had needed it the most. But now, Madhu's condition evoked great pity and compassion. Michael Madhusudan breathed his last at two o'clock in the afternoon.

It was then that it became clear how right Krishnamohan had been in anticipating problems over Madhu's burial. Thirty years before his death, the Christian community in Calcutta had made a great deal of fuss over his conversion. But now, they seemed reluctant to give up just six feet of earth for Madhu. Even the local English press did not publish proper obituaries. If anything was said at all, as in the *Friend of India* (3 July 1873), a daily run by the missionaries, it was simply to highlight Madhu's 'irregular lifestyle'. It also mentioned that he squandered his money and left his three children unprovided for. Nothing was said about his success as a writer. It was only a native English paper—the *Mirror*—that paid tribute to him, also on 3 July, saying that he was one of the brightest intellectuals of his time.

The attitude displayed by the Christians at this time was truly extraordinary in its indifference—or anger—towards someone who had just died a most tragic death.

Despite the heat of June, Madhu's body could not be removed the same day. It lay overnight in a dirty, stinking morgue, only because no church would permit his burial. Krishnamohan, a senior priest in Calcutta, went himself to speak to the Lord Bishop, Robert Millman. Millman had arrived in Calcutta six years ago, and was known to have cordial relations with the locals. Moreover, he was a literary person. He had written a biography of Madhu's favourite poet, Tasso. But he was not in favour of priests getting involved in any controversial matter. So he refused to grant the necessary permission.

Since Madhu had become a Christian, his Hindu friends could not arrange a Hindu funeral, either. His body continued to lie in the morgue. The following day, a Baptist priest came forward to help. About the same time, a senior chaplain of the Anglican Church, Rev. Peter John Jarbo, also offered to make arrangements for the funeral. He was the head priest of St James' Church in Lower Circular Road. By risking the Lord Bishop's displeasure, Jarbo displayed amazing courage; he clearly knew where his duty lay.

In the afternoon of 30 June—more than twenty-four hours after his death—Madhu's body was finally taken out and prepared for its final journey. Nearly a thousand people joined the procession that made its way to the cemetery in Lower Circular Road. It is believed that people came from outside Calcutta to pay their last respects. They were from various castes and religions. Sadly, though, not one of the people he made famous by dedicating his works to them—including Vidyasagar, Digambar Mitra, and Jotindramohan Tagore—attended the funeral. Madhu's contemporary during his years in France, Charles Baudelaire, suffered similar neglect. None of the well-known littérateurs of Paris attended Baudelaire's funeral.

Four days prior to that day, Henrietta had been buried in the same cemetery. Madhu's grave was dug next to hers. As the final proceedings were about to begin, the Lord Bishop's permission arrived. But no priest from the Anglican Church, or any other noted religious figure, seems to have come to the funeral; not even Krishnamohan, who had once helped him to become a Christian and who had also attended him at the hospital for his confession. In fact, several priests are said to have expressed their disapproval. It was Rev. Jarbo who performed the last rites. Madhu's name was entered in the register of the cemetery, but not in the burial register of the Anglican Church.

In the Christian community in Calcutta—consisting chiefly of British and Anglo-Indian people—there was no dearth of people whose conduct or lifestyle might have been seen as un-Christian. There were cheats, libertines, murderers, and rapists. Yet, when they died, not once did the church raise any objection to their burial. Even when Henrietta died, only four days before Madhu, no questions were asked, no appeals had to be made. Why, then, was there such violent opposition in the case of Michael Madhusudan Dutt, a well-known man from a distinguished background? In their reminiscences, Christians like Prannath Biswas and Krishnamohan Bandyopadhyay said nothing that might answer this question. On the contrary, they tried to prove that Madhu had died with his faith in Christ unshaken. If that was the case, then the church's reaction is even more puzzling.

It is true that Madhu's behaviour in public was sometimes affected by his drinking, and on occasions he was openly rude and arrogant. But those could not have been the only reasons for the church's reaction. What is most likely is that, whatever his other faults, the one thing that the white British community had always regarded as wholly unpardonable was Madhu's choice of a partner. He—a dark native—first married a white woman in Madras, then left her and 'lived in sin' with another. That was far worse than a white man marrying, or having a liaison with, an Indian woman.

Madhu's friend, Bhudeb Mukhopadhyay, mentions a similar case in his diary. His son had a Muslim friend who married an English woman. According to this friend, every British person who learnt about their marriage reacted as if a close female relative had been robbed of her virtue.

Madhu had had to deal with racism and colour prejudice, both as a student in Bishop's College, and later in England. Even in Madras he faced a great deal of hostility from whites. But the extent to which Madhu had alienated and antagonized fellow Christians became clear only when he died. It was as if the figures of authority and power in the church wanted to settle scores with an inert, dead body, just because, when alive, Madhu had flouted their authority.

Madhu was unquestionably far more talented than anyone in the circles in which he moved. In addition, he acquired several skills that made him stand out in a crowd. It was due to his efforts that literature in Bengal could move forward so swiftly. No other writer—with the exception of Rabindranath Tagore—was able to do as much. But that was not all. Madhu's colourful personality, and some of his extraordinary actions, had turned him into a legend during his lifetime. The blows of misfortune that he suffered in the last two years of his life, and the final fiasco over his funeral, went further to prove how lonely he was, how isolated. As long as he was wealthy, in a position to throw parties, offer food and drink to his friends, or fight their cases without charging a fee, society in Calcutta was prepared to hail his greatness. However, when he lost his money and his health, and could only wait abjectly for death, those 'friends' slowly vanished. Had Madhu left large savings and valuable assets, perhaps the question of his funeral would not have created so many ripples.

Even today, more than a hundred years after his death, Madhu's position in Bengali literature remains unchallenged. Nevertheless, prior to and soon after his death, literary critics in Bengal showed a marked reluctance to shower unmitigated praise on him.

Three noted critics of those times—Ramgati Nyayratna, Rajnarayan Basu, and Bankimchandra Chattopadhyay—divided contemporary society into two sections: those who viewed Madhu's works with disfavour, and those who did not. Madhu's supporters, according to them, were all young and exposed to Western education. The others came from a more conventional and orthodox class. The three critics claimed individually that *they* did not fall into either group, they were followers of the middle-path.

However, a closer look at their comments would show that the 'middleness' of their views is eminently questionable. They, too, were prepared to attack Madhu, not only for his 'desertion' of his people and religion, but also for his straying from accepted literary norms. Madhu's experiments with a new verse form and new interpretations of the Hindu mythology were both frowned on.

Ramgati Nyayratna commented on *Meghnad* while Madhu was still alive. He began by praising it, but ended by saying, 'No matter how proud the poet is of himself, and how much support he gets from other knowledgeable people,... we have to say candidly that no one in this country has been able to like his blank verse, apart from a handful of people like ourselves.'

It is true that it took everyone—including the pundits—a while to understand and appreciate the beauty and significance of blank verse. However, ordinary readers grasped immediately that Madhu was both a rebel and an extraordinary poet. The many reprints of *Meghnad* were evidence of that. By 1869 the fifth edition of *Meghnadhbadh kabya* was published.†

Rajnarayan Basu, on the other hand, found Madhu's views and attitudes to be quite 'alien'. At any rate, they were not nationalistic enough for Basu. 'No other poet shows so few traces of a nationalistic spirit as Michael Madhusudan,' he said. In the early 1860s, he had been openly supportive of Madhu's writing. However, later on, in a lecture on Bengali literature, he withdrew his remarks by saying: 'When Madhu's poetry was first published,...I was extremely partial to it. But now the enchantment of a new love has gone, and I am able to assess all its faults.'

Clearly, Basu was not bothered by Madhu's literary experiments. It was his abandonment of his own people and, in Basu's view, his country, that upset him. It was for a similar reason that the Bengali journals of the time were all hesitant to extend their wholehearted support to Madhu. No one could look kindly upon a man who had turned his back on his own religion.

Bankimchandra Chattopadhyay wrote an article in the *Calcutta Review* two years before Madhu's death.† It was entitled *Bengali Literature*. In it, he both praised and criticized Madhu. He did not consider Madhu to be a 'great poet', but was prepared to call him the 'best' among the poets in Bengal. Bankim found a lot in *Meghnad* that was worthy of his praise, but could see nothing so great in Madhu's sonnets, or his plays. Two months after Madhu's death, Bankim wrote an evaluation of his works in the *Bangadarshan* magazine. Although it was suitably respectful in tone, Bankim's assessment can only be described as lukewarm. It was not as if he had failed to appreciate the literary merits of Madhu's works. What, then, could be the reason behind this lack of warmth? Was it just professional jealousy? Or was it, once again, to do with Madhusudan turning into Michael and becoming a 'sahib'?

The truth is that, at the time, a man was judged by the class and religion he came from, his social background, and his relationship with others in society. Freedom of the individual was a concept virtually unknown. It was for this reason that what overrode Madhu's creative powers was simply the fact that he had broken established norms. In the eyes of his critics, he was a heretic. Madhu was the product of a time when society in Bengal was being rocked by major upheavals. He did what others had never done before, by turning away from age-old customs. His father was also quite unorthodox in his own way. This new 'awakening', seen amongst the educated elite in Calcutta, came to be known as the Renaissance in Bengal, although it bore little resemblance to the Renaissance in Europe. Madhu was arguably one of the best examples of a Renaissance man; a true humanist. Admittedly, he did not study the scriptures and interpret them anew, with a view to making social reforms. Rammohan Roy and Vidyasagar had done that. But in his own way, Madhu studied ancient classical literature and Hindu mythology just as thoroughly, and based his own creations on a new interpretation of those ancient myths, in which Western and Indian epic traditions were blended. Everything he wrote was devoid of the traditional eulogies meant for gods and goddesses. What he spoke of was the struggle of man, pitched against divine powers. Even when the battle was lost, the poet's sympathies lay unquestionably with the vanquished man; even then his voice did not rise to praise the gods.

The biggest tragedy in Madhu's life was that he was far ahead of his time. That, and the beautiful dreams of a better future that blinded him to the realities of the present, worked together to bring about his destruction. His meteoric rise—and then his dramatic fall—might well have been the story of a tragic hero from one of his own works.

There was only one sphere in which Michael Madhusudan was fortunate. Misunderstood and misjudged during his lifetime, posterity granted this uncompromising rebel the honour that he so richly deserved. The passage of time could not dim the brilliance of the tremendous comet. It was Madhu's vision, and his perceptions, that transformed Bengali literature, both in his time, and for all ages to come.

Notes

CHAPTER ONE

p. 4 '...pamphlet....': it was called *Datta-bangshamala* (1876). There is a copy in the India Office Library.

'...suspect that they had never married.': Rajnarayan Basu to Gourdas Basak, 24 November 1889. 'The Madras secret, I believe, is Modhu eloped with the lady with whom he lived as wife [sic] but this myself and my son knew before I corresponded with you about Modhu's life. You did not tell me anything about it.'

'...French.': Rashbihari Mukhopadhyay's memoirs, quoted in Nagendranath Som's *Madhu-smriti* (Calcutta: 1st Bidyoday edition, 1989; 1st ed., 1921). p. 29. Mukhopadhyay, a well-known zamindar of Uttarpara, invited Madhu and family to stay at his place and it was here that he heard Henrietta speak in French to her two children. Of these two children the older had lived in France since his early childhood, and the other one was born in France. Therefore French must have been their first language, and it was natural for them to speak it with their mother. Mukhopadhyay was mistaken in thinking that Henrietta was French.

p. 5 '...Nagendranath Som (1921).': Jogindranath Basu's biography—*Michael Madhusudan Datter Jibancharit*—was first published in 1893. Nagendranath Som's biography of Michael was first serialized in *Bharatbarsha* in 1914–17 and then published as a book in 1921.

NOTES

p. 10   'I have heard it....': Shibnath Shastri, *Ramtanu Lahiri O Tatkalin Banga-samaj* (Ramtanu Lahiri and Contemporary Society in Bengal), Calcutta: New Age, 4 ed., 1983, p. 43.

p. 12   'Rajnarayan Dutt's son does not....': An oft-quoted line, attributed to Madhu. See Pramathanath Bishi's book, *Maikel Madhusudan* (Calcutta: Mitralay, 1941).

p. 19   'Derozio's followers developed....': James Kerr, *A Review of Public Instruction in the Bengal Presidency, from 1835 to 1851*, pt II. (London: W. H. Allen and Co., 1853), p. 23.

p. 21   'Captain sahib....': Rajnarayan Basu, *Atmacharit* [Autobiography], 6th ed., Calcutta: Orient Book Co., 1985; pp. 14–15.
'Even Macaulay said....': Ibid. p. 14. Shibnath Shastri also made a similar comment in his *Ramtanu Lahiri o Tatkalin Banga-samaj* [Ramtanu Lahiri and Contemporary Society in Bengal], Calcutta: New Age, 4 ed. 1983, p. 157.
'...Hunt's papers....': European MSS, India Office Library, British Library, nos 38109, 38110, 106113, 38524, and 38111.

p. 22   '...Dhirendranath Ghosh.':*Maikel-Jibanir Adiparba* [The Early Years of Michael's Life], Calcutta: Modern Book Agency, 1962. However, it was nothing new. Even James Kerr made a similar comment in the early 1850s.

p. 24   'In short, they appear....': *Annual Report of Hindu College 1843–7* (Calcutta: Military Orphan Press, 1848).

p. 29   '...drinking in later years.': From one of Madhu's letters written in October 1841, it seems he wanted, for the first time, to know what wine tasted like.

p. 30   'At that time....': Rajnarayan Basu, *Atmacharit* [Autobiography] 6th ed., Calcutta, Orient Book Co., 1985, p. 26.

CHAPTER TWO

p. 49   '...hymn....': Quote from report in *Hurkaru*, 11 February 1843 (*Conversion and Baptism of a Hindu Youth*).

p. 57   '...George Withers....': The letters from George Withers and A. W. Street quoted here are from the SPG papers (Bishop's College), Rhodes House, Oxford.

p. 58   '...Madhu's pocket money.': According to letters from A. W. Street to G. Fagan, dated 23 July 1847 and 22 November 1847.

p. 61   '...Sanskrit and Bengali.': At that time there were native teachers at Bishop's College, one each for Bengali and Sanskrit. They were Bishweshwar Pundit and Ramchandra Pundit.

'...syllabus....': The syllabus is preserved among the SPG papers.

CHAPTER THREE

p. 70   '...Charles Egbert Kennet....': A letter from A. W. Street to G. Fagan (23 July 1847), preserved in the SPG papers, says that Kennet was going to Madras to appear for an exam before the Diocesan Committee. In another letter dated 22 November 1847, Street wrote that Kennet 'left the other day'.

p. 71   '...arrived in Madras....': His passage is recorded in 'Shipping Intelligence' in the *Athenaeum*, Madras, 18 January 1848.

p. 72   '...M. M. Dutt....': The *Madras Intelligencer* (20 January 1848) also recorded his passage, though it misprinted his name as N. N. Dutt. It also printed the words 'of Bishop's College'. However *Spectator* (19 January 1848) recorded his name as 'Mr Dutt' only.

p. 73   '...more than forty.': *A letter to Robert Lowe, Joint Secretary of the Board of Control, from John Bruce Norton on the Conditions and Requirements of the Presidency of Madras* (Madras: Pharaoh & Co., 1854).

p. 75   '...examiners' report....': *Report of the Male and Female Orphan Asylum and Free Day School, 1850* (Madras: C. M. Pereyra, Current Press, 1850).

p. 76   '...Posnett.': Posnett used to pay regular subscription to the Asylum. See *Report of the Male and Female Orphan Asylum and Free Day School, 1848* (Madras: C. M. Pereyra, Current Press, 1848). Among other subscribers were George Norton, and the Headmaster of Madras High School, E. B. Powell. Both became Madhu's patrons in later years.

'The wedding of Madhu....': Details of Madhu's wedding and Rebecca's parentage are recorded in India Office Record N/2/27 and N/2/13, Oriental Section, British Library, p. 436 and p. 196 respectively.

p. 77   '...attorneys....': *The Bengal Calendar*, 1848.

p. 81   '...cost of printing....': The 24-page Report of the Orphan Asylum for 1848–9 cost thirty-five rupees and four annas.

p. 83   '...*Athenaeum*....': 'Correspondence', *Athenaeum*, 17 April 1849.

p. 87   '...Kashiprasad Ghosh....': Quoted by Swapan Basu in a letter on *Ashar Chhalane Bhuli* in *Desh*, 8 April 1995.

p. 89	'Bethune's reply....': Quoted in Jogindranath Basu's biography of Michael Madhusudan Dutt.
	'...Krishnanagar College....': Quoted in the *Athenaeum* in 1849.
p. 91	'...Bertha.': Her birth and baptism are recorded in India Office Record N/2/28, Oriental Section, British Library, p. 557. In the church document her first name was wrongly spelt as 'Britha'. Madhu has been mentioned as 'school master, Male Orphan Asylum'. According to this document, he was still living in Black Town.
p. 93	'...nine scenes from the play were published.': This is according to Sureshchandra Maitra, in his biography of Madhusudan Dutt, p. 86. He must have found the old files of the *Eurasian* in Madras.
p. 96	'...Eliza White's death....': Recorded in India Office Record N/2/29 Oriental Section, British Library, p. 436.
	'...Letter in the *Eurasian*....': Quoted in the *Athenaeum*, 2 May 1850.
	'Krishnamohan Bandyopadhyay....': This anecdote is mentioned by both Jogindranath Basu and Nagendranath Som. In the Bishop's College Papers, however, there is no reference to this incident, or any incident related to Madhu's drinking habits, or any trouble that he might have been in because of his drinking excesses. However, what might be seen as racist was the college's classification of its students into three distinct categories—Europeans, Eurasians, and Indians. It is also striking that Madhu is never referred to as 'Michael' either in the college documents or in the letters written by his teachers, even when Madhu identified himself as such. But whether this was a deliberate slur, or not, it is difficult to say.
p. 97	'...favourable impression.': *Athenaeum*, 5 October 1850.
	'Comment on the *Hindu Chronicle*': *Athenaeum*, 9 March 1852.
p. 98	'...Rev. Jodunath Ghosh.': His letter was quoted by Nagendranath Som in *Madhu-smriti*, pp. 47-8.
p. 99	...Phoebe.': Baptism recorded in India Office Record N/2/30, Oriental Section, British Library, p. 330.
p. 100	Mr H. Bowers....': See A. J. Arbuthnot's (The Secretary of the Board of Governors) letter to H. Bowers, dated 21 January 1852, in *The Eleventh Annual Report from the Governors of the Madras University for 1851-2* (Madras: Christian Knowledge

Society's Press, 1852), p. 13. Bowers was apparently a good teacher and the governors expressed regret at his loss— '...the Board have directed me to express to you their regret at losing your services in the institution under their charge, which they cannot permit you to quit without placing on record the high sense they entertain of your qualifications as a teacher, and the zeal and regularity with which you have conducted the duties assigned to you during the nine years that you have been connected to the School. Your qualifications as a teacher the Board consider of a superior order, and to have been attended with the most successful result.'

'This gentleman's attainments....': See Resolution of the Board of Governors of the Madras University, dated 26 March 1852, *The Eleventh Annual Report from the Governors of the Madras University for 1851-2*, p. 14. The governors also mentioned that Madhu was educated first at Hindu College, and subsequently at Bishop's College.

'...Rev. Tailor....': See *Report of the Madras Male and Female Orphan Asylum and Free Day School, 1852*.

p. 102 'George Dutt's baptism': India Office Record, N/2/31, Oriental Section, British Library, p. 260.

'...George White....': He was at one time the headmaster of the Asylum school, before he joined Madras School. He continued to take an active interest in the Asylum school and used to pay regular contributions to the school fund. See *Report of the Madras Male and Female Orphan Asylum and Free Day School, 1848* and 'A Letter on the Annual General Meeting of Asylum,' in *Athenaeum*, 2 September 1848.

'Henrietta's birth': India Office Record, N/2/16, Oriental Section, British Library, p. 169.

'White's wedding': India Office Record, N/2/32, Oriental Section, British Library, p. 44.

p. 103 '...number of students....': See *The Twelfth Annual Report from the Governors of the Madras University, 1853*.

p. 105 '...John Henry Kenrick....': Kenrick was a close friend of Madhu's in Madras. He was a well-known figure there. A number of his articles on different scientific topics were published in various periodicals. He was also closely associated with different social welfare organizations, and the establishment of the telegraph in Madras. He was apparently of Eurasian parentage. Kenrick was born in 1815, and married in 1840. In his dedication, Madhu praised his patriotic spirit in particular, and his contribution to the native Christian community.

'...list of teachers....': See *The Report of the Madras University for 1855*. This report contains a useful list of all teachers, including their salaries.

'...Michael James': India Office Record, N/2/36, Oriental Section, British Library, p. 167.

'Letter from Gourdas': Apparently, Gourdas lost all contact with Madhu and did not know his address. He therefore sent the letter (dated 1 December 1855) through Krishnamohan Bandyopadhyay, who was going to Madras. He started from Calcutta on 7 December by a ship called *The Nile*, and reached Madras on 17 December. See 'Shipping Intelligence' the *Athenaeum*, 18 December 1855.

p. 108 'Michael James Dutt's death': India Office Record, N/2/36, Oriental Section, British Library, p. 217.

p. 109 '...Rebecca Thomson Dutt': India Office Record, N/2/74, Oriental Section, British Library, p. 65.

'Holt in the list of passengers': 'Arrivals', Passengers List from Madras, *New Calcutta Directory for 1857* (Calcutta: P. M. Cravenburgh, 1857), pt. XI.

CHAPTER FOUR

p. 112 'Police Court salaries': Names of all staff including their salaries were mentioned in the *New Calcutta Directory for 1858* (Calcutta: P. M. Cravenburgh, 1858), Legal Section.

p. 113 '...told Gourdas about Madhu's death.': According to a letter from Gour to Madhu, dated 1 January 1856, quoted by Nagendranath Som, in *Madhu-smriti*.

p. 114 '...Mr Dirt.': Quoted in the *Athenaeum*. 1 July 1851.

p. 115 '...social issues including Kulin polygamy...': Polygamy was prevalent among a class of Bengali Brahmins known as Kulins. Their ancestors were supposedly given an order of honour by a twelfth-century king of Bengal called Ballal Sen. Some men from these Kulin families compromised their high status by marrying for money into other Brahmin families of an inferior status. The non-Kulin Brahmins sought to go up the social ladder by marrying their daughters to Kulins.

NOTES

The Census Report of 1901 mentions one such Kulin who married as many as 108 wives. The custom became discredited with the spread of education in the second half of the nineteenth century. The movement for banning Kulin polygamy during this period also helped eradicate it as a social vice. For details, see *Anti-polygamy Tracts, No. 1* (Calcutta, 1856), reprinted in *Nineteenth Century Studies*, No. 10 (Calcutta, 1975); K. M. Bannerjea, 'The Kulin Brahmins of Bengal', *Calcutta Review*, Vol. XI, No. 93 (1868), G. Murshid, *Samaj Samskar Andolan O Bangla Natak (Social Reform Movement and Bengali Dramatic Writings)*, Dhaka: Bangla Academy, 1985, pp. 90–117.

p. 116   'I did not know....': Quoted by Jogindranath Basu.

p. 117   'The Sinha brothers....': Gour's recollection, as recorded by Jogindranath Basu.

'I am very anxious....': Jotindramohan Tagore's letter to Gourdas, quoted by Nagendranath Som.

p. 125   'I am thinking....': Raja Ishwarchandra Sinha to Madhu, dated 8 May 1859, quoted by Nagendranath Som.

p. 128   'If I can prove....': This conversation—based on Jotindramohan's reflections—is quoted by Jogindranath Basu.

p. 132   'Sermista's birth': Recorded in India Office Record, N/1/97, Oriental Section, British Library, p. 231.

p. 133   'Letter from Rajnarayan Basu': Quoted in B. N. Bandyopadhyay's *Madhusudan Datta* (4th ed., Calcutta: Bangiya Sahitya Parishad, 1955, 1st ed. 1943).

p. 138   'Story of Krishnakumari': Tod, *The Annals and Antiquities of Rajasthan*, 1 vol. (London: Smith Elder & Co., 1829), pp. 463–4, 465.

p. 145   'Milton Dutt's birth': Recorded in India Office Record, N/1/101, Oriental Section, British Library, p. 38.

p. 146   '...Henry James....': See L. Edel, *Writing Lives: Principia Biographica* (London: W. W. Norton and Co., 1987), p. 140.

p. 147   '...the two women in his life were both half-English.': Rebecca's father, Robert Thompson, was a gunner in the East India Company's artillery. His birth details could not be traced. He might have been English. However, the woman he married, called Catherine Dyson, was undoubtedly an Anglo-Indian. She was identified in Rebecca's baptism document as an Anglo-Briton (India Office Record N/2/13, p. 196). Rebecca was, therefore, not entirely English despite Madhu's claims to that effect in two of his letters to Gourdas Basak. Henrietta, on the other hand, might have been of English parentage. Her father, George Giles White was born in Fulham in London and came to Madras in 1820. On 12 December 1825 he married Eliza Grey. It was not recorded in the marriage document (IOR N/2/11, p. 286) whether she was an Anglo-Indian or fully English. Henrietta might well have been English.

p. 155 '...not paid regularly.': According to a letter from Jotindramohan Tagore to Madhu, dated 27 March 1862, quoted by Nagendranath Som.

CHAPTER FIVE

p. 157 '...*Candia*....': See 'Arrivals and Departures' in *Madras Almanac, 1863* (Madras: Asylum Press, 1863).

p. 158 'Gibraltar and Southampton': *Lloyd's List* (London), 17 July and 19 July 1862.

p. 159 '...Manomohan Ghosh and Satyendranath Tagore....': There is no clear written evidence to this effect. However, Madhu's father, Rajnarayan Dutt, was a close friend of Manomohan's father and Madhu had known Manomohan for a long time as a family friend.

'...Gray's Inn.': Madhu was admitted to Gray's Inn on 19 August 1862. See *Register of Admission to Gray's Inn, 1522–1889* (London: The Hansard Publishing Union, 1889), p. 479.

'Spelling of Madhu's name': Madhu's application for admission to Gray's Inn is preserved in the Gray's Inn Library.

p. 160 'payment to Henrietta': This and many of the other financial details that follow are recorded in Madhu's letters to Vidyasagar.

p. 162 'Tagore in England': Rabindranath Tagore gave a detailed account of his stay at the Scott residence in a collection of his letters *Europe Prabasir Patra* (Calcutta: S. Gangopadhyay, 1881), and also in his autobiography, *Jibansmriti* ('My Reminiscences', Shelaidah: N. Gangopadhyay, 1912).

p. 163 'Deposit at Gray's Inn': Gray's Inn Records, extract from the Pension Minutes, 22 December 1863, quoted in a letter to William Radice by the Librarian of Gray's Inn Library, and printed in Sureshchandra Maitra's biography of Madhusudan Dutt.

p. 164 '...government charity funds....': Documents on Charity, 1863–5, Archives Departementales des Yvelines, Versailles.

p. 165 'Application to Gray's Inn Pension Committee': See 'deposit at Gray's Inn' above.

p. 178 'Sonnet to Dante': Although the Bengali translation was published by the poet along with others in his collected volume of sonnets, *Chaturdashpadi Kabitabali* (Calcutta: Ishwarchandra Basu & Co., 1866), the original transcript of the sonnet was unearthed by Professor Rabindra Kumar Das Gupta in Italy.

p. 181 'Kshetramohan's marriage': Document no. 339, dated 29 June 1866, General Register Office (Catherine House), District of Pancras, Middlesex.

CHAPTER SIX

p. 187 'Justice A. G. McPherson and Justice J. B. Phear': Their remarks dated 25 March 1867 were quoted by Nagendranath Som.

p. 188 '...Madhu's admission to the High Court....': The full text of the court resolution was given by Nagendranath Som.

p. 189 'Letter from Anukulchandra Mukhopadhyay': Quoted by Girindranath Mukhopadhyay, 'Michael O Vidyasagar', *Bharatbarsha*, May 1931.

p. 191 'Letter from Vidyasagar': quoted by Brajendranath Bandyopadhyay in his book, *Madhusudan Datta*, pp. 85–6.

'...sell his property': Sureshchandra Maitra gives the full text of the deed in *Maikel Madhusudan Datta: Jiban O Sahitya* (Calcutta: Puthipatra, 2nd ed., 1985), between pp. 200–1.

p. 192 '...Gopikrishna Gossain....': See *Bengal Law Report*, 1868.

'...Tagore vs Tagore.': See *Bengal Law Report*, vol. IV, ed. By H. Cowell and L. A. Goodeve (Calcutta: Thacker, Spink and Co., 1870), pp. 103–28.

p. 194 'Albert Napoleon Datta's birth': Ecclesiastical Document no. 677, dated 24 April 1867, Versailles Municipal Archives.

p. 203 'Sermista's marriage certificate': Recorded in India Office Record, N/1/144, Oriental Section, British Library, p. 69.

p. 205 'Tip for the nurse': This and other details relating to Madhu's final decline are recorded by Nagendranath Som and Jogindranath Basu.

p. 206 'The end came....': Surprisingly, the Ecclesiastical Records of Calcutta have no mention of Madhu's death, even though he was at the time the most famous poet in Bengal. However, his conversion to Christianity was duly recorded in 1843 when he was just a student of Hindu College.

p. 210 '...fifth edition of *Meghnad*....': It was officially published on 16 March 1869. The third edition of *Birangana Kabya* came out on 15 January, the second edition of *Chaturdashpadi Kabitabali* (the collection of his sonnets) on 17 March, the third edition of *Padmabati* in September and the same of *Sermista* in November that year.

'...Bankimchandra....': *Calcutta Review*, vol. 52, no. 104, 1871.

Works of Michael Madhusudan Dutt

1. *The Captive Ladie* (An Indian Tale) in two cantos. Madras: The Advertiser, 1849.
2. *Rizia: The Empress of Inde* (An unfinished play) published in the weekly Eurasian (Madras), from November to March 1850.
3. *The Anglo-Saxon and the Hindus*, Lecture 1. Madras: Pharoah & Co., 1854.
4. *Ratnavali: A drama in four Acts translated from the Bengali.* Calcutta: Calcutta Printing and Publishing Co., 1858.
5. *Sharmishtha Natak* [A play]. Calcutta: Ishwarchandra Basu Co., 1265 Beng [January 1859].
6. *Sermista: A drama in five Acts.* Translated from the Bengali. Calcutta: Ishwarchandra Basu Co., 1859.
7. *Ekei Ke Bale Sabhyata?* (Prahasan) [Is this Civilization? A Farce]. Calcutta: Ishwarchandra Basu Co., 1860.
8. *Buro Saliker Ghare Ron* (Prahasan) [New Hair on the Old Bird's Neck, A Farce]. Calcutta: Ishwarchandra Basu Co., 1860.
9. *Padmabati Natak* [A play]. Calcutta: Ishwarchandra Basu Co., 1860 (April/May).
10. *Tilottamasambhab Kabya* [A poem]. Calcutta: Baptist Mission Press, 1860 (May).
11. *Meghnadbadh Kabya*, pt. 1 [A poem]. Calcutta: Ishwarchandra Basu Co., 1861 (January).

12. *Krishnakumari Natak* [A play]. Calcutta: Ishwarchandra Basu Co., 1861.
13. *Brajangana Kabya* [A poem]. Calcutta: Ishwarchandra Basu Co., 1861 (July).
14. *Meghnadbadh Kabya*, pt. 2 [A poem]. Calcutta: Ishwarchandra Basu Co., 1861 (July/August).
15. *Birangana Kabya* [A poem]. Calcutta: Ishwarchandra Basu Co., 1862 (February).
16. *Chaturdashpadi Kabitabali* [A collection of 101 sonnets]. Calcutta: Ishwarchandra Basu Co., 1866 (August).
17. *Hector-badh* [A prose adaptation of the Iliad]. Calcutta: Ishwarchandra Basu Co., 1871.
18. *Mayakanan* [A play]. Calcutta: Nutan Bangala Jantra, 1874 (March).

Apart from these books Madhu published many short lyrics, including sonnets and many long narrative poems, mostly in English. His 'Atma-vilap' or Self-lament published in September 1861 in the *Tattvabodhini Patrika* was one of these poems.

Select Bibliography

UNPUBLISHED SOURCES

Birmingham University
James Long Papers, CMS, CI 1/01/185/1-154.

Edinburgh
Public Records Office, Ecclesiastical Records, 1856-70.

Gray's Inn
Gray's Inn Records, Extract form the Pension Minutes, 22.12.1863.
Staff List, Gray's Inn, 1862, Gray's Inn Library.

India Office Records
Ecclesiastical Records
    Calcutta Diocese. N/1 Series, 1843, 1859-63, 1873-1930.
    Madras Diocese, N/2 Series, 1825-56, 1880-1912.
    Madras, N/11 Series (Civil Marriage Register).
Bengal Law Report, V/22/532, vol. 1.
Police Report on Europeans not in the Employ of E. I. Co. Living in Madras, dated 31 December 1827, I. O. R. O/5/30, vol. 4, pt. 3.
Proceedings Civil and Judicial, 1847-8.
Recommendations by the Committee for Sudder Examination to the Bengal Government, January 1859.

Resolutions of the Education Council of Bengal, 1843.

London

Catherine House, Ecclesiastical Records, Pancras, Middlesex, 1866, General Register Office.

Oxford University

Rhodes House. Society for the Propagation of Gospels, Bishop's College Papers, C. Ind. I/1, 6, 11, 12 and 13 Series.
Unpublished D. Phil. Dissertation.
William Radice, 'Tremendous Literary Rebel: the Life and Works of Michael Madhusudan Datta' (a thesis submitted for the degree of D. Phil. in the Faculty of Oriental Studies, University of Oxford, 1986).

Versailles

Ecclesiastical Records, Versailles Municipal Archives, 1864 and 1867.
Aux Archives Departmentales des Yvelines, Document on Charity, 1863–5.

NEWSPAPERS AND PERIODICALS

Athenoeum, 1848–56.
Bengal Hurkaru, 1843, 1847–8.
Englishman, 1861, 1867, 1870, 1873.
Friend of India, 1847, 1873.
Indian Field, 1858–62 (Only the available issues at the British Museum Library).
Lloyd's List (London Museum), 1862, 1863.
Madras Spectator, 1848, 1855.
Awakening in Bengal in Early Nineteenth Century, vol. 1, ed. Goutam Chattopadhyay. Calcutta: Progressive Publishers, 1965.

Bengali

B. N. Bandyopadhyay, ed., *Sangbadpatre Sekaler Katha* [Extracts from Bengali newspapers of the early 19th Century], 2 volumes. vol. 1. 4th ed.; Calcutta: Bangiya Sahitya Parishat, 1971.
———— vol. 2. 5th ed.; Calcutta: Bangiya Sahitya Parishat, 1994.

B. Ghosh, ed., *Samayikpatre Sekaler Samajchitra* [Extracts from 19th century Bengali Periodicals]. Calcutta: Bikshan, 1964.
———— vol. 4. Calcutta: Grantha Bhavan, 1966.

Official and Institutional Publications

Bengal

The Bengal and Agra Directory and Annual Annual Register for 1848, Calcutta: Samuel Smith & Co., 1848.
Bengal Library Quarterly Catalogue, 1869, 1872 and 1873.
New Calcutta Directory for 1857-61, Calcutta: P. M. Cravenburgh, 1857-61.
Thacker's Directory for Bengal, 1862-71. Calcutta: Thacker, Spink and Co., 1862-73.

Education

General Report on Public Instruction in the Bengal Presidency, 1842-43. Calcutta: Military Orphan Asylum Press, 1843.
Annual Report of the Hindu College et., 1843, Calcutta: Military Orphan Asylum Press, 1843.
Annual Report of the Hindu College et., 1846-47. Calcutta: Military Orphan Asylum Press, 1848.
Kerr, J., *A Review of Public Instruction in the Bengal Presidency, from 1835 to 1851, pt. I.* Calcutta: Baptist Mission Press, 1852.
———— *A Review of Public Instruction in the Bengal Presidency, from 1835 to 1851, pt. II.* London: Wm. H. Allen & Co., 1853.
Long, J. *Handbook of Bengal Missions.* London: J. Farquhar, 1848.
Bengal Library Catalogue (The Quarterly List of Publications), October-December 1871; January-March 1874.
Coupland, H., *Bengal District Gazetteer, vol. XXVIII.* Calcutta: Bengal Secretariat Book Depot, 1911.
Cowell, H. and L. A. Goodeve, eds, *Bengal Law Report, 1869-70.* Calcutta: Thacker, Spink & Co., 1870.
The Bengal Law Reports, vol. IX, 1872. Calcutta: Thacker, Spink & Co., 1873.

London

Census Report, 1861.

London Postal Directory, 1861, 1866–7.
British Museum Library.
Index of Manuscripts in the British Museum Library, vol. VIII. Cambridge: Chadwyck Healy, 1985.

Gray's Inn

Register of Admissions to Gray's Inn 152–1889, J. Forster, ed. London: The Hansard Publishing Union, 1889.
The Story of Gray's Inn. London: Chiswick Press, 1950.

Lincoln's Inn

Register of Admission to Lincoln's Inn, J. Forster, ed. London: The Hansard Publishing Union, 1988.

Madras

A Letter to Robert Lowe, Joint Secretary of the Board of Control, From John Bruce Norton on the Condition and Requirements of the Presidency of Madras. Madras: Pharoah & Co., 1854.
Madras Almanac, 1845–59. Madras: Male Orphan Asylum Press, 1863

Madras Asylum School and University

The Opening of the Madras Univesity, 1841. Madras: Vepery Mission Press, 1841.
Annual Report of the Madras University, 1843–50. Madras: Pharoah & Co., 1843–50.
Madras University Calendar, 1866–71. Madras: Male and Female Orphan Asylum, 1866–71.
Reports of the Madras Male and Female Orphan Asylum and Free Day School or Boys, 1848–1852. Madras: C. M. Pereyra, Current Press, 1848–52.
Report of the Madras University, 1851–52. Madras: Christain Knowledge Press, 1852.
The Madras Tercentenary Commemoration Volume, H. Milford, ed. Madras: Oxford University Press, 1939.
The Annual Report of the Madras University, 1853. Madras: Pharoah & Co., 1853
The Eleventh Annual Report from the Governors of the Madras University, 1851–52. Madras: Pharoah & Co., 1852.

Versailles
New Guide, 1858.
Index of Manuscripts in the British Library, vol. VIII. Cambridge.

WORKS OF MICHAEL MADHUSUDAN DUTT

For a complete list of the works see p. 221.

Letters of Dutt. There is no standard edition of his letters. Many letters were first published in Jogindranath Basu's biography of Dutt. More were published later in Nagendranath Som's biography. Almost all the letters were compiled and published in a single volume by Ksetra Gupta under the title *Kabi Madhusudan O Tar Patrabali* [Poet Madhusudan and his Letters], Calcutta: Granthanilay, 1963. This volume is by no means complete and it has many omissions and commissions. I have recently compiled a volume of all his extant letters under the title of *Heart of a Rebel Poet: Letters of Michael Madhusudan Dutt*. The book is forthcoming with Oxford University Press.

BOOKS/ARTICLES ON MICHAEL MADHUSUDAN DUTT

In English

Bose, A., *Michael Madhusudan Dutt*. Delhi: Sahitya Akademi, 1981.
'Life of Michael Madhusudan Dutt in Bengali', *Calcutta Review*, vol. 98, January 1894.
Moreno, H. H. B., 'M. S. S. Dutt and his Anglo-Indian Wives', Bengal Past and Present, vol. 26, pp. 191–4.
Radice, W., 'Milton and Madhusudan' in *Literature East and West, Essays Presented to R. K. DasGupta*, G. R. Taneja and Vinod Sena (eds). Delhi: Allied Publishers Ltd., 1995.
——— 'Xenophilia and Xenophobia: Michael Madhusudan Datta's Meghnad-badh Kabya' in *Classics of Modern South Asian Literature*, R. Snell and I. M. P. Raeside (eds). Harrassowitz: Wiesbaden, 1998.
Seely, C., 'Michaeler Ramadi Charitra', *Jadavpur Journal of Comparative Literature*, vol. 29, 1990–1.
——— 'Homeric Similes, Occidental and Oriental: Tasso, Milton, and Bengal's Michael Madhusudan Dutt', *Comparative Literature Studies*, vol. 25, no. 1, 1988.

———— 'Raja's New Clothes: Redressing Ravana in Meghanadavadh Kavya' in *Many Ramayanas*, P. Richman (ed.). Berkeley: University of California, 1991.

———— 'Rama in the Nether World: Indian Sources of Inspiration', *Journal of the Americal Oriental Society*, vol. 102, no. 3, 1982.

In Bengali

Bandyopadhyay, B. N., *Madhusudan Datta*. 4th ed. Calcutta: Bangiya Sahitya Parishat, 1955.

Basu, J. N., *Michael Madhusudan Datter Jibancharit*. 1st De's ed., Calcutta: 1983. 1st ed., 1893.

Bishi, Pramathanath, *Michael Madhusudan: Jibanbhashya*. Calcutta: Ranjan Publishing House, 1941.

DasGupta, R. K., 'Michael O Vidyasagar', in *Aitihya O Parampara: Unish Shataker Bangla*. Calcutta: Papyrus, 1999.

———— 'Michael O Neeldarpan', ibid.

———— 'Gray's Inne Michael', ibid.

———— 'Meghnadbadh Kabyer Prasange', ibid.

———— 'Michael Madhusudaner Sonnet', ibid.

———— 'Michaeler Ekkhani Bismrita Grantha', ibid.

Datta, B., *Madhusudan-smriti*. Calcutta: Sahityam, 1989.

Ghosh, Dhirendranath, *Michael-Jibanir Adiparba*. Caclutta: Modern Book Agency, 1962.

Maitra, S. C., *Madhusudan Datta: Jiban O Sahitya*. 2nd ed. Calcutta: Puthipatra, 1985.

Majumdar, M., *Kabi Sri Madhusudan*. Howrah: Bangabharati, 1947.

Mukhopadhyay, G., 'Michael O Vidyasagar', *Bharatbarsha*, May–June, 1931.

Nath, Dwijendralal, *Madhusudan: Sahitya-Pratibha O Shilpi-byaktitva*. Calcutta: Puthipatra, 1986.

Sen, S. M., *Madhusudan (Antarjiban)*. Calcutta, 1921.

Som, Nagendranath, *Madhu-smriti*. Calcutta: Vidyodaya ed., 1989. First published in 1921.

AUTOBIOGRAPHIES AND BIOGRAPHIES

Bagal, J. C., *Rajnarayan Basu*. 2nd ed. Calcutta: Bangiya Sahitya Parishat, 1955.

Bandyopadhyaya, B. N., *Bhudeb Mukhopadhyay*. 3rd ed. Calcutta: Bangiya Sahitya Parishat, 1957.

———— *Ishwarchandra Vidyasagar*. 5th ed. Calcutta: Bangiya Sahitya Parishat, 1955.
———— *Ramkamal Sen, Krishnamohan Badyopadhyay*. 2nd ed. Calcutta: Bangiya Sahitya Parishat, 1957.
———— *Ramnarayan Tarkaratna*. 5th ed. Calcutta: Bangiya Sahitya Parishat, 1959.
———— *Rangalal Bandyopadhyay*. 4th ed. Calcutta: Bangiya Sahitya Parishat, 1956.
———— *Satyendranath Thakur*. 2nd ed. Calcutta: Bangiya Sahitya Parishat, 1960.
Chattopadhyay, B. K., *Jyotirindranather Jiban-smriti*. Calcutta: Shishir Publishing, 1920.
Chattopadhyay, N. N., *Mahatma Raja Rammohaner Jibancharit*. 3rd ed. Calcutta: Sadharan Brahmo Samaj, 1987.
Ghosh, B., *Vidyasagar O Bangali Samaj*. Reprint. Calcutta: Orient Longman, 1993.
Ghosh, M., *Karmabir Kishorichand Mitra*. Calcutta: Adi Brahmo Samaj Press, 1926.
(Mitra) Kailasbasini Debi, *Atmakatha*. Calcutta: Hirak Ray, 1982.
Pal, P., *Rabijibani*, vol. 1. Calcutta: Bhurjapatra, 1982.
———— *Rabijibani*, vol. 2. Calcutta: Bhurjapatra, 1984.
Ray, Kartikeyachandra. 'Atma-jiban Charit', *Sahitya*, Phalgoon 1303 [February 1897].
Sarkar, B. L., *Vidyasagar*. 2nd Orient ed. Calcutta: Orient, 1991. 1st ed., 1895.
Shastri, P. N., ed., *Maharshi Devendranath Thakurer Patravali*. Calcutta: Adi Brahmo Samaj, 1909.
Shastri, S. N., *Ramtanu Lahiri O Tatkalin Bangasamaj*. 4th ed. Calcutta: New Age, 1983.
Vidyasagar, I. C., *Vidyasagarcharit, Vidyasagar Rachana Sangraha*, 3rd vol. Calcutta: Niraksharata Durikaran Samiti, 1972.

In English

Bell, Q., *Virginia Woolf*. Triad/Paladin, ed. London: Triad/Paladin, 1987.
Edwards, T., *Henry Derozio* with an Introduction by R. K. DasGupta. Calcutta: Riddhi-India, 1980. (First published in 1884).
Holmes, R., *Shelly the Pursuit*. London: Penguin Books, 1987.
Levinson, M., *Keats's Life of Allegory*. London: B. Blackwell, 1988.
MacCarthy, F., *Byron: Life and Legend*. London: J. Murray, 2002.

Moore, T., *Life, Letters and Journals of Lord Byron*. London: John Murray, Albemarle St, 1838.
Pichois, C., *Baudlaire*. London: Hamish Hamilton, 1989.

Books on 19th Century Bengal

In Bengali

Bandyopadhyay, B. N., *Bangiya Natyashalar Itihas*. 4th ed. Calcutta: Bangiya Sahitya Parishat, 1968.
Basu, Rajnarayan, *Bangala Bhasha O Sahitya Bishayak Baktrita*. Calcutta: Nutan Bangala Jantra; 1935 Sangbat [1878].
Ghosh, B., *Banglar Samajik Itihaser Dhara*. Calcutta: Pathbhaban, 1968.
Mitra, R., *Kalikata-Darpan*. Calcutta: Subarnarekha, 1988.
Murshid, G., *Samaj Samskar Andolan O Bangla Natak, 1854–76*. Dhaka: Bangla Academy, 1985.
——— *Naripragati: Adhunikatar Abhighate Banga Ramani*. 2nd ed. Calcutta: Naya Udyog, 2000.
Nayaratna, R., *Bangala Bhasha O Sahitya Bishayak Prastab*. ed. by A. Bandyopadhyay. Calcutta: Supreme Book Distributors, 1991. 1st ed. 1872.
Sen, S., *Bangala Sahityer Itihas*, vol. 3. 7th ed. Calcutta: Ananda Publishers, 1994.

In English

Ahmed, A. F. S., *Social Ideas and Social Change in Bengal 1818–1835*. Leiden: E. J. Brill, 1965.
(Chatterji, Bankim Chandra) 'Bengali Literature', *Calcutta Review*, vol. 52, no. 104.
DasGupta, R. K., 'Dante in Bengali Literature', in *East–West Literary Relations*. Calcutta: Papyrus, 1995.
——— 'Shakespeare in Bengali Literature', ibid.
——— 'Indian Response to *Paradise Lost*', ibid.
——— 'Indian Response to Western Literature', ibid.
Kopf, D., *British Orientalism and the Bengal Renaissance*. Berkeley: University of California Press, 1968.
——— *Brahmo Samaj and the Shaping of the Modern Indian Mind*. Princeton: Princeton University Press, 1979.
Mayhew H., *London Labour and the London Poor*. L. Griffin, Bohn & Co., 1861.

Murshid, G. *Reluctant Debutante: Response of Bengali Women to Modernization.* Rajshahi University: Sahitya Samsad, 1983.

Odie, G. A., *Social Protest in India.* Delhi, Manohar, 1979.

Raychaudhuri, T. *Europe Reconsidered.* 2nd Impression. Delhi: Oxford University Press, 1989.

Richardson, D. L., *Selections from the British Poets from the Times of Chaucer to the Present Day with Biographical and Critical Notes.* Calcutta: Baptist Mission Press, 1840.

Salter, J., *The Asiatics in England.* London: Seely, Jackson & Halliday, 1873.

Sinha, P., *Nineteenth Century Bengal.* Calcutta: Firma K. L. Mukhopadhyaya, 1965

Tod, J., *Annals and Antiquities of Rajasthan, or the Central and Western Rajpoot States of India,* 2 vols. London: Smith, Elder & Co., 1829-32.

Trial of the Rev. James Long for the Publication of the 'Nil Durpan'. London: James Ridgway, 1861.

Index

Anglo-Saxon and the Hindu, The 104–5, 114, 147
Asiatic Society 111, 117, 129
Asylum, Male and Female Orphan 72, 73–4, 75, 89, 92, 96, 99, 100, 102; history of 73; syllabus 74
Athenaeum 83–4, 92, 97, 99, 101
Atma-vilap 149–50, 152

Bahadur, Kalikrishna 188
Bandyopadhyay, Brajendranath 9
Bandyopadhyay, Chandramohan 205
Bandyopadhyay, Ganesh 11
Bandyopadhyay, Harimohan 154
Bandyopadhyay, Hemchandra 155–6
Bandyopadhyay, Krishnamohan 19, 45, 46, 47, 48, 57, 96, 106, 142, 205, 206, 207, 208
Bandyopadhyay, Rajkrishna 188
Bandyopadhyay, Rangalal 11, 131, 135, 154
Bandyopadhyay, Swarup 82
Banerji (See Bandyopadhyay)
Bangabhasha, 149, 178
Bangabhumir Prati 156
Basak, Gourdas 26, 27, 29, 30, 33, 34, 35, 36, 38, 42, 44, 47, 49, 50, 52, 54, 55, 58, 60, 62, 66, 69, 71, 72, 75, 79, 80, 81, 82, 83, 85, 87, 88, 89, 91, 94, 95, 98–9, 105, 106, 107, 108, 109, 110, 111, 113, 116, 117, 118, 120, 121, 122, 123, 124, 125, 131, 133, 144, 157, 162, 165, 168, 172, 173, 174, 179, 180, 183, 193, 204
Basu, Ishwar C. 168
Basu Jogindranath 5, 6, 8, 67, 192, 204
Basu, Mankumari 5
Basu, Rajnarayan 21, 27, 29, 30–1, 42, 45, 62, 112, 113–14, 127, 129, 130, 131, 132, 133, 135, 136, 140, 141, 142, 143, 144, 146, 147, 148, 149, 150, 152, 153, 155, 209, 210
Baudelaire, C. 207
Bell, Q. 5, 6
Bengal Hurkaru 22, 85–6, 87, 90
Bengal Renaissance 134
Bengali language, contemporary attitude towards, 24
Bengali society (early nineteenth century) 15, attitude to English

language 17, attitude towards forbidden food 30-1, attitude to drinking 29-30, 31, attitude towards prostitution 10, 177
Bengali theatre 115-16
Bentinck, Lord 20
Bentley's Miscellany 36
Bethune, J. E. D. 82, 89, 90, 91
Bibidhartha Sangraha 129, 130, 131
Bidyotsahini Sabha 142
Birangana Kabya 132, 151-2; autobiographical element 151-2, 153
Bird, W. 47
Bishop (of Madras) 64, 65, 72
Bishop's College 11, 52, 57, 58, 59, 60-1, 62, 63, 65, 67, 68, 70, 72, 74, 82, 90, 96, 110, 110, 111, 114, 208; establishment of 59
Biswas, Prananath 206, 208
Blackwood's Magazine 35-6
Blank verse 86, 125, 128, 129, 130, 131, 142, 152, 209
Brahmo 29, 30, 135, 143
Brajangana 134-5
Burns, R. 19
Buro Saliker Ghare Ron (New Feathers on Old Bird) 115, 125, 126, 127
Byron, Lord 19, 22, 28, 32, 35, 42, 84, 86, 114

Calcutta High Court 186, 187, 188, 201
Calcutta Police Court 111, 112
Calcutta Review 56, 87
Campbell, T. 19, 32
Captive Ladie, The 79-88, 89, 90, 91, 92, 117, 118, 120, 121, 128, 129, 148; disappointment with 87-8, high hopes concerning 81; plot 80-1; review 83-4, 85-6, 87
Carew, P. 59

Chandra, Bholanath 27, 29
Chattopadhyay, Bankim C. 193, 210
Chattopadhyay, Mahadeb 154, 160, 161, 165, 166, 167, 170, 191, 192
Chaucer, G. 22
Coleridge, S. T. 131

Dante 23, 174, 178-9
Dealtry, T. 46-7, 49, 50, 53, 54, 72
Deb, Radhakanta 10
Deo, Nilmani S. 200, 201
Derozio, H. V. L. 18, 19, 20, 21-2, 45, 54, 58, 111
Dey, Ramdulal 9
Dique, A. 5
Dique, L. 5
Dow, A. 93
Duff, A. 47, 56
Dutt, Albert N. 3, 4, 194, 202
Dutt, Banku B. 26, 27, 82
Dutt, Bertha, B. 91, 107
Dutt, Frederick M. 3, 4, 145, 202
Dutt, Geroge J. 102, 107
Dutt, Henrietta 95, 96, 102-3, 107-8, 110, 112, 120, 122, 124, 129, 132, 133, 136, 137, 141, 150-1, 160, 161, 162, 168, 172, 178, 181, 183, 189, 194-5, 200, 204, 205, 208; family background 3; mistaken identity 3-5; not French 5
Dutt, Janhabi (See Janhabi Debi)
Dutt, Kedarnath 4
Dutt, Khetramohan 181
Dutt, Michael M. birth 11; marriage 77-8; opposition to 78; breakdown of marriage 108, 115; crisis after breakdown 112-13; illness 196, 198-9, 202, 204; death 206; burial 207; opposition to burial 206-7; family background 2-3, 6-8;

phases of his life 16; education 27–9, 53, 56, 60, 61; at Bishop's College 59–60, 62–3, at Hindu College 27–47; language learning 60, 61, 91, 171, 173; unorthodox upbringing 29; personality traits 1–2, 4, 12–13, 61–2, 210–11; ego-trip 71–2, 90; attitude to British Raj 98, 114; attitude to Christianity 45, 50–2, 56, 64, 66, 104–5, 114, 147, 199–200; conversion 46–47, 48–50, 69; crisis after 55; hostility of Christians to Dutt 207, 208; attitude to Hinduism 51, 68; 104–5; desire to become a missionary 51, 57, 63, 64, 65, 69; attitude to love, marriage and women 2, 31, 32, 33, 41–2, 43–4, 51; attitude to his roots 14–15, 159; ; attitude to Bengali language and literature 90, 157; attitude to western culture 2, 45–6, 104–5, 158, 172, 173; attitude to western dress and food 2, 30, 31, desire to become a lawyer 2, 3, 122–3, 152–3; qualifies as a barrister 183; admission to High Court as a barrister 187–8; income as a barrister 193; failure as a barrister 193–4, 200; desire to become a poet 2, 35; desire to go to England 33, 36, 38, 53, 70, 152; drinking 137, 199 ; smoking 29; conflict and reconciliation with parents 45, 53, 63, 66, 67, 68; goes to Madras; goes to England 158–9; goes to Purulia and Panchakot 199–201; goes to Versailles 162; returns to Calcutta from Madras 106, 110; hardship 147, 158, 178, 179–81, 182, 190–1, 198, 201–2, 203; identity crisis 85, 91–2, 99, 122, 165–71; influence of Bishop's College 61; litigation 113, 150, 152; love for Henrietta 95–6; living beyond means 186, 189, 195–6; love for Rebecca 78, 80, 95; love for Sagardari 13, 14–15, 39; patriotism 34; place in Bengali literature 1, 209, 210–11; place in Bengali society 210–11; patriotism 147; secular attitudes 147–8; sympathy towards Islamic culture 93–4; synthesis of three cultures 94; work at Asylum 74, 75; work at Madras School 100–1

Dutt, Phoebe 99, 107
Dutt, Pyarimohan 49, 113
Dutt, Rajnarayan 2, 7, 12, 13, 29, 30, 32, 39, 40, 41, 42, 44, 45, 48, 52, 53, 54, 57, 63, 66, 68, 76–7, 102, 106, 113, 191; family background 2, 7–8; income 8–9; lawyer 9; personality traits 10–11; second marriage 66–7
Dutt, Rebecca 74, 76; 77–8, 79, 91, 95, 96, 99, 107–8, 109, 110, 115, 120, 124, 133, 150, 152, 157, 177–8
Dutt, Sermista 3, 132, 133, 199, 202, 203–4

East India Co. 49
Eastern Guardian 97
Ekei ki bale sabhyata? (Is This Civilization?) 30, 115, 125, 126, 127
Eurasian 92–3, 94, 96, 97, 101

Floyd, W. W. E. 203–4

Ganguli, Keshab 93, 125, 129, 138, 139, 140

INDEX

Ghosh, Jodunath 98
Ghosh, Kashiprasad 18, 22, 87
Ghosh, Maheshchandra 20, 45, 57
Ghosh, Manomohan 153, 159, 161, 162, 171-2, 180, 186, 199, 204, 205
Ghoshal, S. 48, 49
Goethe 23
Gray 24
Gray's Inn 159, 163, 165, 166, 168, 169, 180, 182, 183

Hare, D. 21, 27
Hector-badh 26, 190, 197-8
Hindu College 14, 15, 17, 18, 19, 20, 21, 23, 24, 25, 26, 29, 30, 36, 46, 47, 48, 49, 53, 54, 56, 58-9, 60-1, 62, 64, 68, 73, 83, 87, 100, 111, 112, 122, 128, 131, 179; syllabus 23-4
Hindu Intelligencer 85, 87
Hindoo Patriot 111, 145, 154
Homer 23, 190
Hugo, V. 174
Hume 18, 24
Hunt, L. 21

Indian Field 123, 124, 132, 142
Indigo Rebellion 145
Inner Temple 154, 159

James, H. 146
Janhabi Debi (Dutt's mother) 11-12, 13, 23, 28, 44, 67, 98
Jarbo, Rev. P. J. 207

Kadambari Debi 6
Kailasbasini Debi (Mrs K. C. Mitra) 112
Kalidas 90, 141, 142, 146, 175
Kant 18
Kapotaksha (river) 175
Keats, J. 22, 84
Kennet, Charles 70, 72, 76, 91, 99

Kennet, Charles E. 59, 63, 70, 72, 105, 163
Kenrick, J. H. 105
Kerr, J. 19, 23, 48, 54, 83
Khan, Mirza Abu Talib 37
King Porus 34, 47, 58
Krishnakumari 138, 139, 140, 203; plot 138; similarities with *Iphigenia in Aulis* 140
Kulin polygamy 115, 126

La Fontaine 173
Lahiri, Ramtanu 24, 27
Law, Shyamacharan 26
Lincoln's Inn 159
Long, Rev. J. 145

Macaulay, Lord 17, 21, 22
Madras 69-70; background 72-3; arrival in 71; passage to 71
Madras Circulator 78, 79, 81, 92
Madras Hindu Chronicle 95, 97, 99, 101, 113
Madras School/University 88-9, 100-1, 102, 103, 104, 105, 114
Madras Spectator 92, 93, 105, 107, 113
Mahabharata 12, 90, 118, 164, 165
Maitra, Sureshchandra 5
Mallik, Ramkrishna 9
Mallik, Rasikkrishna 19-20
Mann, G. 63, 64
McTavish, D. 77, 78, 102
Meghnadbad Kabya 124, 132, 134, 135, 136, 137, 138, 140, 141, 142, 143, 144, 145, 146, 147, 148, 149, 155, 164, 165, 179, 202, 209, 210
Middle Temple 159
Millman, Bishop R. 206, 207
Milton, J. 22, 24, 27, 90, 114, 141, 142, 145, 146
Mitra, Baidyanath 113, 161, 165, 166, 170

Mitra, Digambar 82, 111, 141, 160, 161, 165, 166, 167, 168, 170, 207
Mitra, Dinabandhu 115, 145
Mitra, Goplachandra 57
Mitra, Kishorichand 111, 112, 113, 124, 131, 142
Mitra, Nabinkrishna 45
Mitra, Rajendralal 129, 130, 131, 188
Mitra, Ramchandra 24, 49, 82
Moore, T. 19, 28, 86, 118
Mukhopadhyay, Anukulchandra 170, 182, 189, 190, 191, 192
Mukhopadhyay, Bhudeb 25-6, 30, 42, 47, 62, 82, 88, 95, 112, 198
Mukhopadhyay, Dakshinaranjan 20, 22
Mukhopadhyay, Ramkamal 11, 28
Mukhopadhyay, Rashbihari 4, 204

Nailor, J. S. 72, 73, 76, 79, 84, 88, 91, 103
Newton, I. 28
Nil Darpan 115
Norton, George 83, 88, 89, 99, 103
Norton, J. B. 73
Nyayaratna, Ramgati 209

Old Church 49, 54
Ovid 151

Padmabati 124, 125, 127, 130, 136, 137; plot 124, 128
Paine, T. 18
Pepin, T. B. 5
Pope, A. 24, 38
Posnett, R. 74, 76
Powell, E. B. 89, 100, 101
Powell, W. P. 75

Racism 96, 114, 162-3, 208
Ratnavali 115, 116, 117

Ray, Bharatchandra 132
Ray, Kartikeya C. 177
Ramayana 12, 90, 115, 143, 148, 152
Reid 18
Richardson, D. L. 20-1, 22, 23, 28, 32, 45, 48, 54, 76, 83, 87, 100; affection for Dutt 23, 35
Rizia 93-4, 121, 128, 130, 148; plot 94
Romantic poets 21, 22, 28, 32, 56, 60, 84, 131, 148
Roy, Ramaprasad 9, 10
Roy, Rammohan 9, 15, 30, 37, 134, 211
Runjit Singh 141

Sagardari 13, 14-15, 39
Sambad Prabhakar 9
Sanskrit College 25, 113
Scott, W. 19, 86
Sea voyage. 37-8
Sen, Ramkamal 17, 24
Sepoy Mutiny 114, 115, 145, 147
Sermista 117, 118, 121, 123, 124, 126, 128, 138; plot 118-19, language 122; success 121; review 123-24
Shakespeare, W. 21, 22, 24, 27, 28, 56, 114, 139, 140, 174
Shastri, S. 51
Shelley, P. B. 22, 24, 28, 34, 35, 79, 84
Simkins, A. P. 83, 92, 97
Sinha, Ishwarchandra 10, 15, 116, 118, 120, 121, 122, 124, 125, 126, 127, 128, 129, 131, 138, 139, 140, 144, 146
Sinha, Kaliprasanna 113
Sinha, Pratapchandra 115, 116, 117, 118, 120, 122, 124, 126, 127, 128, 129, 131, 138, 139, 140
Smith, Rev. T. 55-6, 57

Som, Nagendranath 5, 6, 66, 76
Somprakash 130
Sonnets 128, 149, 173–9
Spence's Hotel 186, 187, 188, 195
Street, Alfred W. 52, 59, 60, 62, 64, 65
Stewart 18
Subhadra-haran 165
Swayambar Sabha 164

Tagore, Devendranath 30
Tagore, Dwarakanath 37
Tagore, Jnanendranath (Gyanendranath) 192–3
Tagore, Jotindramohan 117, 118, 120, 122, 125, 128, 129, 130, 132, 139, 142, 153, 188, 192, 205, 207
Tagore, Prasannakumar 9, 10, 192
Tagore, Rabindranath 43–4, 146, 162–3, 164, 208
Tagore, Ramanath 188
Tagore, Satyendranath 153, 159, 171
Tarkaratna, Ramnarayan 115, 117, 121
Tasso 23, 142, 207
Tattvabodhini Patrika 32, 143
Tennyson, Lord 22, 174
Thompson, Catherine 77, 78
Thompson, Robert 77–8

Tilottamasambhab Kabya 124, 128, 129, 130, 131, 132, 133, 134, 136, 137, 139, 141, 142, 152, 174
Tod, J. 138, 139

Versailles 163–4
Vidyabhushan, Dwarakanath 130
Vidyalankar, Shrishchandra 113, 190, 191, 192
Vidyasagar, Ishwarchandra 113, 130, 131, 134, 153, 155, 160, 161, 166, 167, 168, 169, 170, 172, 174, 175, 179, 180, 182, 185, 186, 188, 190, 192, 194, 199, 201–2, 205, 207, 211
vira ras 148
Virgil 23, 141
Visions of the Past 51, 61, 86, 87, 120, 128

Walker, C. 63
White, G. G. 74, 75, 100, 102, 103, 105
Widow Remarriage Movement/Act 98, 113, 114, 115, 126
Withers, Geroge U. 52, 57, 60, 62, 64
Woolf, V. 5, 6
Wordsworth 32, 36, 131

Young Bengal 19, 61, 86, 111